the complete

A-Z
ICT AND
COMPUTING

h a n d b o o k

the complete

A-Z
ICT AND
COMPUTING
handbook

**Bob Penrose
and
Bill Pollard**

Hodder & Stoughton

A MEMBER OF THE HODDER HEADLINE GROUP

British Library Cataloguing in Publication Data
A catalogue record for this title is available from The British Library

ISBN 0 340 80277 4

First published 2001

Impression number   10 9 8 7 6 5 4 3 2 1
Year 2005 2004 2003 2002 2001

Typeset by GreenGate Publishing Services, Tonbridge, Kent
Printed in Great Britain for Hodder & Stoughton Educational, a division of Hodder Headline Plc, 338 Euston Road, London NW1 3BH by The Bath Press Limited.

HOW TO USE THIS BOOK

The *A–Z of ICT and Computing* provides an alphabetical list of the main concepts and ideas central to an A level course in either subject area. It gives a wide range of definitions of basic terms that are likely to be met by students taking AS or A level ICT or Computing. The entries cover the breadth of terminology that is crucial for an understanding of the subject area together with developments of more important topics where greater understanding is required. The subject area lends itself to the use of lots of jargon and acronyms and care has been taken to try and give clear meaning to these. The extended entries should help to clarify more difficult concepts and enable students to provide more depth to their examination answers.

There is an extensive cross-referencing within the A–Z that is critical to an understanding of the way topics link together. Each entry is developed in line with its importance. Most entries are short, concise definitions with others progressing to more detail and relationships with other aspects of the same topic. This approach has been taken, rather than more lengthy entries covering wide-ranging issues, in order to demonstrate the way in which a large number of concepts are not confined to discrete ideas. Cross-referenced and associated entries are identified by the use of italics.

During your course, the *A–Z of ICT and Computing* will be an essential companion and a book to refer to often, to pick up and put down and to browse through and use to clarify your understanding of new ideas. It should also help to improve and build upon basic ideas. It will prove to be invaluable at the end of the course as a guide to revision when reinforcing basic knowledge.

As an assistance, three appendices have been provided to help with the wide use of acronyms, the multitude of file extensions that you will come across and some useful web sites that will provide additional sources of research.

We hope that the *A–Z of ICT and Computing* proves to be an invaluable resource, effective from the beginning of the course right through to the examination at the end.

Bob Penrose
Bill Pollard

ACKNOWLEDGEMENTS

The production of this book has been an experience for us both. Neither of us anticipated the time and effort required to put together, revise and check the amount of material required to provide what we feel is a worthwhile resource for students of ICT and Computing.

Thanks go from Bob to his wife Janet for her tolerance, patience and support in ensuring that we made it to the finish.

Thanks go from Bill to his wife Anne for all the support provided while the book was being written, and to his parents for giving him the opportunities to be in a position to write the book.

In addition, thanks are also due to Barbara Wilson for the use of some of her ideas in Hints for Exam Success.

Bob Penrose
Bill Pollard

A-to-D converter: see *analogue-to-digital converter.*

abort: to stop the execution of a program function before it has finished naturally. The term abort refers to both requested and unexpected terminations. The execution may be aborted by the program itself, the *operating system* or an operator.

For example, many applications let you abort a search or a print job. On the other hand, programs can abort unexpectedly for any of the following reasons:

- *bugs* in the software
- unexpected input that the program cannot handle
- *hardware* malfunction.

When a program aborts, you are usually returned to the operating system level. Contrast abort with a crash, which makes the entire system, including the operating system, unusable.

absolute address: an absolute address is a fixed address in memory. The term absolute distinguishes it from a *relative address,* which indicates a location by specifying a distance from another location. Absolute addresses are also called 'real addresses' and 'machine addresses'.

absolute code: the code that must reside in a particular area of memory.

absolute path: a *path* that begins with the *root directory.* The absolute path is also known as the 'full pathname'. Contrast with *relative path.* On most PCs the main hard drive is identified as drive C; thus an absolute path could be 'C:\MyWork\Project\Documentation.doc'. This file (Documentation.doc) is stored in the 'Project' folder that is one of the folders in the 'MyWork' folder, which is directly accessible from the root drive (C).

absolute reference: an absolute reference is used in *spreadsheet* applications. An absolute cell reference always points to the same *cell,* no matter where the reference appears. The cell reference in most spreadsheet applications is designated, for example, as A3, i.e. the contents of column A, row 3. In the example below this would be the value 7. An absolute reference is often referred to in the form $A$3. This fixes the reference in a formula to that particular cell and not relative to the cell in the formula. See *relative reference.*

	A	B
1		
2		
3	7	
4	10	=$A$3+2
5		=$A$3+2

	A	B
1		
2		
3	7	
4	10	9
5		9

abuse – computer: computer abuse is generally taken to be the wrongful use of computer systems. This can be anti-social or for illegal purposes such as hacking, *viruses,* fraud or computer pornography. See *hacker.*

acceptable-use policy (AUP): a set of rules enforced by an organisation on what is and is not acceptable when using their computers. A school may, for example, ban the use of their facilities for the finding or downloading of pornography.

acceptance testing: the process of getting the end-user or customer to agree that a *system* works as specified.

access: the term used with computer *systems* meaning to allow a user to log on to a system or *network*, allow a user to read or write data files or *web pages*, or to log onto the *Internet*, etc. It is frequently used in the term 'unauthorised access' meaning the entry into a system by a person who does not have the right to do so.

Access is also the name of the *relational database* from Microsoft.

access controls or levels: the various layers of access to *servers*, *directories* and *files* that can be set within a system. A *network manager* will need to access all the files and areas within a system to add new software or install new users, whereas clerical staff may only need to read and write to certain limited files and not require access to other areas.

access privileges or rights: the permissions or types of operations granted to a user when they log on to a *system*. The highest level of privilege is usually given to the system administrator or *network manager*. Assigning access privileges to other users helps the system administrator to maintain *security* on the system, as well as the privacy of confidential information, the ability to read and write to certain *files* and to allocate system resources.

access time: the time a program device takes to locate a single piece of information and make it available to the computer for processing. This can be from *main store* or a *backing store*. It is also frequently used to describe the speed of disk drives. Access times are measured in milliseconds (thousandths of a second), often abbreviated as ms.

account: 1 A mechanism used by *networks* and multi-user *operating systems* for record keeping and keeping track of authorised *users*. *Network accounts* are created by the *network manager* and are used both to validate users and to allocate permissions.

2 A record-keeping arrangement used by *on-line service providers* to identify a subscriber. This allows a record of customer usage to be maintained for billing purposes.

accumulator: a special storage *register* within the *arithmetic logic unit* (ALU). It is used to hold the data being processed by the central processor. The results of any calculations end up in the accumulator before they are transferred to their own location in memory.

Acrobat: a program from Adobe Systems, Inc. It converts fully formatted documents created on a variety of platforms into portable document format (PDF) files. These files can then be viewed on other platforms. Regardless of the application used to create the originals, Acrobat allows users to send documents that contain colour, graphics, photographs and distinctive text, electronically to recipients. Recipients need the *Acrobat Reader* to view the files.

Acrobat Reader: a free program produced and distributed by Adobe Systems, Inc., for displaying and printing documents that are in portable document format (PDF).

acronym: a term which is derived by taking the letters at the start of other words, e.g. CPU is an acronym for central processing unit.

action bar: the line of titles for *menus*. This can be placed across the top or bottom of the screen. Users can select an item by pointing and clicking or using an appropriate key. Choices are frequently displayed as a drop-down menu.

active cell: the highlighted *cell* in a worksheet in a *spreadsheet* package that is being operated upon. It is also called the 'current cell' or 'selected cell'.

active content is the material on a *web page* that changes on the screen in response to user action or with time. It is implemented through the use of *ActiveX* controls.

active device: a *sensor* that is connected to a computer that requires an external power supply to make it function. When no external power supply is needed the sensor is referred to as a *passive device.*

active matrix LCD: a type of *liquid-crystal display* (LCD) used on *laptop computers.* Active matrix displays are made by sandwiching a film containing tiny transistors between two pieces of glass. They achieve high contrast and brightness by applying voltage across the horizontal and vertical wires between the two glass plates, balanced by using a small transistor inside each *pixel* to amplify the voltage when so instructed. Also known as thin film transistor (TFT) displays.

active program: the *program* that is actually being executed (run) by a computer at that moment in time.

active window: a *window* is a temporary area opened on a screen for displaying information or the activity of a program. At any one time, several windows can be open on a screen. The active window is the one accessible to the user. Other windows may have activities happening but are not accessible until they are selected by the user.

ActiveX was developed by Microsoft in the mid-1990s. It is a set of technologies that enables *software* components to interact with one another, regardless of the language in which the components were created. ActiveX is used primarily to develop interactive content for the *World Wide Web*. ActiveX controls can be embedded in *web pages* to produce animation, interactive objects and other *multimedia* effects.

actuator: a physical device that can be connected to a computer to allow it to communicate some required action to a machine. Actuators can control valves, pumps, heaters, lights, etc.

adder: the logic circuits that perform the function of addition in the *arithmetic logic unit* (ALU) of the central processor unit (CPU) are called adders. A circuit that adds two *binary digits* (BITs) to produce a sum and carry bit is called a *half adder*, and one that adds together two bits and the carry from the previous bit addition is called a *full adder.*

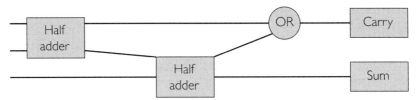

Parallel addition of the contents of two *registers* is achieved by combining several full adders together, with the carry from one position becoming an input to the next full adder.

Serial addition of the contents of two registers is achieved by using one full adder and linking the carry back (after a suitable delay) to become an input when the next pair of bits are added together.

add-on: a small *program* written to extend the features of a larger one. An example is an add-on to allow original US versions of Lotus 123 to print £ signs.

address: an address can take a variety of forms (see below). The basic concept is that of a number used to locate the position in memory of a piece of data or a program instruction.

- An *absolute address* is one which is the real address used by the internal electronics of the computer. This type of address does not need to be modified. Sometimes this is referred to as a real or *machine address*.
- A **base address** is an address that serves as a reference point for other addresses.
  Real addresses are worked out from this starting address number by adding another number to it called the offset or *relative address*.
- A **relative address** is an address specified by indicating its distance from another address, called the base address. For example, a relative address might be B+12, B being the base address and 12 the distance (called the offset).

address book: a reference section in an e-mail program, listing individuals' names, *e-mail addresses* and other related information.

address bus: a collection of wires connecting the central processor with main memory that is used to identify particular locations (*addresses*) in main memory. The width of the address *bus* (that is, the number of wires) determines how many unique memory locations can be addressed. In practice, a bus is a common pathway shared by signals to and from components of a computer. The bus is made up of two parts: the address bus carries identification about where data is being sent, and the data bus carries the actual information.

address generation: a cycle during execution of an *instruction* in which an effective *address* is calculated by means of indexing or *indirect addressing*.

Adobe Type Manager: software from Adobe Systems, Inc. that manages *PostScript* fonts on a system.

ADSR: an acronym for attack, decay, sustain and release, used in describing a *volume envelope* when referring to sound.

advanced disk filing system (ADFS): the name given to the disk *operating system* used in BBC Master, Acorn and Archimedes computers.

Advanced RISC Machine (ARM): a *microprocessor* developed by Acorn for use in the Archimedes computer. The ARM is the microprocessor in Apple's *Newton*.

advanced technology attachment packet interface (ATAPI): an enhancement to *integrated drive electronics* (IDE) that allows easier installation and support of *CD-ROM drives* and other devices.

adventure game: a computer game in which the player becomes a character in a story or adventure (role-playing) exploring a computer-generated environment. To make progress and complete the game, the player must solve problems and avoid or overcome attacks from other characters in the game. Early adventure games were purely text-based. The latest games require accelerated graphics cards, large amounts of memory, are multi-player and can be played across *networks* and the *Internet*. Because of the problem-solving within the games and their imaginative nature, adventure games pitched at appropriate levels have been widely used in education with great success.

after-image is a copy of a record after it has been updated (see *before-image*). It is saved as part of the *transaction* logging procedure used in certain *backup* strategies.

alert box: in a *graphical user interface* (GUI), an on-screen box that is used to deliver a message or warning.

ALGOL: an early (1958–68) compiled high-level programming language (ALGOrithmic Language) using numeric data. It is a language from which other languages such as *Pascal* and FORTRAN were derived.

algorithm: a sequence of steps, *instructions* or *procedures* designed to solve a problem or perform a particular task. Algorithms can be written in any suitable form, such as a programming language, *pseudo-code*, prose or diagrams. Algorithms include precise details about the operations to be performed.

For example, the following algorithm is for testing various sensors and switching security lights or alarms on as appropriate.

```
Repeat
      Test active
      If active = true then
            Test external motion sensor
            If external motion sensor = true then
                  security light:= on
            else
                  security light:= off
            endif

            Test internal motion sensor
            Test window contact
            Test door contact
            If ((internal motion sensor = true) or (window contact = false) or
            (door contact = false)) then
                  Alarm:=on
            else
                  Alarm:= off
            endif
      endif
until set = false
```

Many standard algorithms have been developed to do common tasks such as *sorting*. These are frequently published and available for general use.

algorithmic language: a programming language, such as *ALGOL*, Basic, C or *Pascal*, that uses algorithms for problem solving.

alias: used with e-mail to provide a more memorable name, which gets converted into a real *e-mail address*. For example, 'MD' could be an alias for 'managing_director@hodder.co.uk'. Aliases can be used in many other contexts in the IT world.

aliasing: a term used to describe the jagged edges that are found on bitmapped *graphics*.

align: used in an application such as a *word processor*, to position lines of text, graphics, drawing objects or tables relative to some point, such as the page margin or a set distance from other objects. The most common types of alignment for text are left, right aligned and centred. There are several ways to align drawing objects. You can align them with other drawing objects, such as when you align their top or bottom edges. You can align them in relation to the entire page, for example, at the top or left edge of a page. You can also align objects by using a grid to align them as you draw or move them. You can align drawing objects so they are equal distances from each other, either vertically or horizontally.

alignment: the arrangement of objects in fixed or predetermined positions, rows, or columns. See *align*.

alpha testing: the testing of a new version of software using a restricted number of users within the development company. After this testing has been carried out, appropriate changes are made and a *beta test* version released to a selected number of clients and their comments sought. This beta version is close to the final product.

alphanumeric: consisting of letters or digits, or both, and sometimes including *control characters*, space characters, and other special characters.

alphanumeric data is the term for data that includes letters, digits and sometimes punctuation. It can include both *character* and *string* data types.

AltaVista: a search engine for the *World Wide Web* (WWW). It is a majority-owned operating company of CMGI, Inc. It can be found at http://www.altavista.com.

AM: an abbreviation for amplitude modulation.

America Online (AOL): an online information service that provides *e-mail*, news, educational and entertainment services, and *Internet* access. America Online is one of the largest American ISPs (*Internet service providers*). It recently merged with Time Warner to form the largest media company in the world.

American Standard Code for Information Interchange (ASCII): an agreed set of codes for each character for use in transmitting data.

ASCII is a binary code for representing English characters, with each character assigned a binary pattern between 0000000 and 1111111. For example, the ASCII code for uppercase A is 0100001. The original ASCII character set uses just seven bits for each character, allowing the use of digits (0–9), uppercase letters (A–Z), lower case letter (a–z), etc. Subsequently an eighth bit was added, with the 128 additional characters used to represent non-English characters such as: Ç, ç, è, ü.

Most computers use ASCII codes to represent text, which makes it possible to transfer data from one computer to another.

Text files stored in ASCII format are sometimes called ASCII files. *Text editors* and *word processors* are usually capable of storing data in ASCII format.

analogue signal: a continuously variable signal. Examples are temperature and pressure. Computers cannot deal with analogue signals and these have to be converted using an *analogue-to-digital converter.*

analogue-to-digital converter: this converts analogue (continuously varying) signals into digital (discrete) signals for processing. This process can be referred to as digitising. Analogue sound input has to be converted to digital before it can be processed by a computer.

analysis: an important part of the development of a computer system. The analysis of an existing *system* or the objectives of a proposed system leads to the specification of the users' requirements. The requirements specification is then approved by the initiating organisation before the *design* stage is undertaken. It is important that as many mistakes as possible are identified at this stage to reduce the likelihood of producing a final system that does not meet the expectations of the intended user.

anchor: an HTML tag that turns ordinary text into a *hyperlink.* Anchors are used to allow easy navigation within a single large document or to link different documents.

AND is a logical operation which, when used with Boolean values, produces a true result only when the two inputs are both true. As a *logic gate* it produces a 1 output only if all inputs are 1. It may be written as O = A AND B, or in *Boolean algebra* notation as O = A.B

The symbol used for an AND gate is:

and its associated *truth table* is:

Input A	Input B	Output O
0	0	0
0	1	0
1	0	0
1	1	1

animation: an illusion of movement using the capabilities of a computer, obtained by replicating the same image in slightly altered positions and displaying the resulting series in quick succession. The images can all be drawn separately, or starting and ending points can be drawn, with the intervening images provided by software. There are many animation software packages.

annotation: notes or comments added to computer programs or flowcharts, usually by the programmer or software developer, to provide additional guidance. These notes can be read by other developers at a later stage to help them understand the original intent and logic. In addition, annotation can be a note or comment attached to some part of any document to provide related information. Frequently, it is a requirement of examination coursework, to assist in moderation. Some applications support voice annotations.

ANSI character set: an internationally agreed *character set* that provides access to various lines and shapes as additional characters. These can be used, for instance, to produce screen displays.

anti-aliasing: a software technique which reduces *aliasing* (steplike lines where they should be smooth) in computer *graphics*.

antivirus program/software: a computer program designed to identify, isolate, and eliminate *viruses*. It can examine incoming files for viruses as the computer receives them and also scan a computer's memory and mass storage.

APL is a high-level programming language used in science and engineering. APL stands for A Programming Language. It is an interpreted language with a functional structure and uses numeric and character data. It requires a lot of memory, is difficult to read and uses symbols not always found on normal keyboards.

append is a term used in *file operations* to add a new item to the end of an existing *file*.

Apple Macintosh: see *Macintosh*.

applet: a small, self-contained, application that can be downloaded over the *Internet* and executed on the receiver's machine. Applets are typically used to customise or add interactive elements to a *web page*. Applets are often written in the *Java* programming language and run within *browser* software.

application generator: a code generator that produces programs based on a description of the desired functionality in a particular application area, for example, a payroll generator.

They are generally limited in scope and are included with some database programs. They use built-in instruction sets to generate the program code. Modern application generators are capable of producing fast and efficient code.

applications program or package: a *program*, or set of programs together, designed to carry out a specific task or tasks. They can be generic (i.e. general purpose, such as word processing and database management) or specialised, such as those for accounting, or inventory management. They enable users to employ the computer to perform a variety of specific functions and tasks. Applications have been designed for diverse industries with examples that range from engineering design and airline reservations to project management and banking. Applications programs are developed for both *mainframe* and *personal computers*.

applications programmer: the person who writes the code to produce *applications packages*.

architecture: the design or physical construction of a computer *system* and its components.

archive: to copy *files* onto a disk or tape for long-term storage purposes where the files will not be changed again. This is distinct from backing up a file, where the *backup* is done so that the file can be recovered to replace a damaged version of the file if necessary in the future.

archive file: a *file* containing data stored for long-term purposes, which, for legal or organisational reasons, must be kept and not deleted. It is frequently historical or seldom used data. The file is generally stored away from the main computer system in a secure location. Archive files are accessed very infrequently and often the data is stored in 'read-only' form.

argument: see *parameter*.

arithmetic logic unit (ALU): the part of the central processing unit (CPU) where all arithmetic calculations and logic operations are carried out.

arithmetic shift: the bits in a *register* are moved left or right, but the sign bit is preserved. The effect of left arithmetic shifting a register is to multiply the contents of the register by two, whereas right arithmetic shifting divides by two. In the examples below the numbers are held in *two's complement* form.

The register below holds the decimal number +42

0	0	I	0	I	0	I	0

Left arithmetic shifting the above register one position yields:

which is the *binary* for the decimal number 84.

Arithmetic shifting this register left again will result in arithmetic overflow.

Arithmetic shifting the original register one position right yields:

Sign bit is preserved

0	0	0	I	0	I	0	I

which is the binary for the decimal number 21.

The register below holds the decimal number –4 (two's complement representation).

I	I	I	I	I	I	0	0

Left arithmetic shifting the above register one position yields:

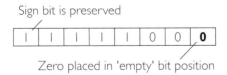

Zero placed in 'empty' bit position

which is the binary for the decimal number – 8.

Arithmetic shifting the original register one position right yields:

which is the binary for the decimal number – 2.

ARPAnet: the US Advanced Research Project Agency network, which was the first large multi-site computer *network*. The ARPAnet is generally regarded as the start of the *Internet*.

array: a *data structure* that provides a way of organising data in a computer in which the sequence of the data is significant (as opposed to a set, which is a collection of data in which order is not significant). An array variable in a program stores a finite number of data items of the same data type, each of which is accessible using a subscript; e.g. the fifth element of the array Names would be accessed using the variable Names[5] in a program. Arrays are referred to by the number of dimensions available: one, two, etc. The most commonly used arrays are *one-dimensional* and *two-dimensional*.

arrow key: any of the four keys labelled with arrows pointing up, down, left, and right on a computer keyboard. These move the *cursor* in the corresponding directions on the display screen. In some programs, such as *word processors* or *spreadsheets*, with the aid of additional keys pressed simultaneously, they can move the cursor a word or paragraph at a time, or extend a highlighted section.

artificial intelligence (AI) is the branch of computer science concerned with making computers think and reason like humans. This is often done by learning and improving a computer's performance through the use of repetitive experience. Artificial intelligence includes developments in *expert systems*, *fuzzy logic*, games playing, *natural language*, *neural networks* and *robotics*.

Currently, no computers exhibit full artificial intelligence (that is, are able to simulate human behaviour). Artificial intelligence technologies are developing but have not lived up to expectations. There is still no HAL-9000 talking to you, as in 2001: A SPACE ODYSSEY. AI is making progress in small steps, often invisible to the ordinary observer. *Voice recognition* systems are now entering the mainstream. There are even home and entertainment robots on the market today. Advances in artificial intelligence will continue to affect our everyday lives.

There are several programming languages that are known as AI languages because they are used almost exclusively for AI applications. The two most common are LISP and Prolog.

ascenders: the parts of lower-case characters that rise above the main area of the character.

assembler: a *program* that translates a program written in *assembly language* into *machine code*.

assembler directives: instructions to the *assembler*, which do not have a *machine language* equivalent. Directives are recognised by the assembler and action taken at the translation stage. They perform such functions as reserving blocks of memory for the program or assigning values to *identifiers*.

assembly language is a programming language that is once removed from a computer's *machine language*. Machine languages consist entirely of numbers and are almost impossible for humans to read and write. Assembly languages have the same structure and set of commands as machine languages, but they enable a programmer to use *mnemonics* instead of numbers.

Each type of CPU has its own machine language and assembly language, so an assembly language program written for one type of CPU will not generally run on another. In the early days of programming, all programs were written in assembly language. Now, most programs are written in a *high-level language*. Programmers still use assembly language when speed is essential or when they need to perform an operation that is not possible in a high-level language.

The program written in the assembly language of the computer is translated (assembled) into the machine code of that computer by an *assembler*.

assignment operator: in programming the result of the calculation or operation to the right of an assignment operator is placed in the variable to the left of the assignment operator. The assignment operator is usually denoted by ': =' or '=', depending on the language being used. It is not the equivalent of 'equals' in arithmetic.

associative law: a law that states that the order in which three items of data are added or multiplied together is irrelevant.

$$A + (B + C) = (A + B) + C$$
$$A * (B * C) = (A * B) * C$$

associative storage is the same as content-addressable storage.

asynchronous transmission is a method of transmitting data where the receiving and transmitting ends are not synchronised. *Start bits* and *stop bits* are added: a start bit marks the beginning of a character and one or two stop bits mark the end of the character. A character is sent as soon as it becomes available rather than waiting for a synchronisation signal. See also *synchronous transmission*.

@ (at) sign: the separator between account names and domain names in *Internet e-mail addresses*. When spoken, @ is read as 'at', e.g. xyz@msn.com is read as 'xyz at msn dot com'.

ATM stands for *automatic teller machine*. It can also stand for asynchronous transfer mode and for *Adobe Type Manager*.

attachment: a *file* that accompanies an *e-mail* message. An attachment is an exact copy of the original file located on the sender's computer. The file can be a document, an executable program, or a compressed file. The file is not part of the actual e-mail message. It is generally encoded automatically for transmission with the message. The receiver of the message must have an e-mail program capable of decoding the attached document.

attack refers to a concept within a sound envelope. It is the rate at which the envelope rises to its initial peak before starting to decay.

attribute: the information held about an *entity* in a *relational database*. A database entity is an item about which data is to be held. Examples of attributes associated with an entity Car could be: licence number, colour, engine size. An entity usually forms a table within a relational database. These are the *fields* that make up each Car *record*.

The size of a field or the type of information it contains (alphanumeric, date, integer, etc.) are attributes of a database record.

audio controller: an audio controller can generate MIDI (*musical instrument digital interface*) control signals from audio sounds.

audit is a term used to describe the task of checking a company's accounts to ensure that no financial mistakes have been made and that no fraud has taken place. This applies equally to computer-based applications, where it can involve checking data files, data collection and processing. Audit is a much more complicated operation with a computer-based system than a paper-based system, as only a sample of all transactions can be checked. Audits can also be provided for other types of non-financial systems, such as the records of notes from doctors in a medical centre.

Audit Commission: a body which appoints *auditors* to all local authorities and NHS bodies in England and Wales. In 1982, the Government brought local authority auditing in England and Wales under the control of a single, independent body that was given the task of examining the overall management of local government. That body is the Audit Commission; it began work in April 1983. In 1990, its role was extended further to include National Health Service authorities, trusts and other bodies. Under the Local Government Act 1992 the Audit Commission was given additional responsibilities including a duty to direct local authorities to publish annually comparative indicators of performance.

audit controls track all the activity on a *network*, including the number of times a *server* is accessed, which *users* have logged on and for how long, how many unsuccessful attempts have been made to log on from any terminal, which programs are used, which data files are accessed and how many read and write operations have been executed. It is possible to use monitoring software to produce profiles of users, providing information on data files and programs that have been used. An auditing log can be generated to record all of this data.

audit package: a software application that allows an *auditor* to check computer *files*. This can include verification that all data is present in records, comparison of files to show up any differences, analysis of file contents and a selection of files for checking.

audit requirements: it is a legal requirement that a company's accounts are audited. An *auditor* is the person responsible for undertaking this task and he or she must have access to all the relevant records within an organisation.

audit software: the same as *audit package.*

audit trail: an automatic record of the transactions carried out on a computer system. The ability to do this is generally required for legal reasons with financial and educational institutions. It enables a transaction to be traced through its stages of processing. This allows any errors to be traced and the causes determined. An *auditor* would often be involved in these types of systems development and the systems designer would be required to build special audit trails into the software.

auditor: the person responsible for undertaking the task of auditing a *system.*

authentication: in computer *security*, this is verification of the identity of a *user* or the user's eligibility to access an object.

authoring software: software packages that allow the user to develop interactive *multimedia* training software.

authorisation: in computer security, this is the process of granting a user either complete or restricted *access* to an object, resource, or function.

AutoCorrect: a function in Microsoft Word for Windows that automatically corrects errors as soon as a user types text. It can also make other substitutions such as © for (c) when indicating copyright. AutoCorrect can be set up to fix misspellings, such as 'adn' for 'and', or to change 'straight' quotation marks to 'smart' quotation marks (' ' to ' '). The user can select which AutoCorrect features to enable.

autoexec.bat: a *file* that is part of the start-up sequence for MS-DOS and similar *operating systems*. The other main file is called *config.sys*. The autoexec.bat file comprises a list of commands that the computer executes when it starts up. The commands can come from the operating system, from the user, or from loading software.

For example, 'SET BLASTER=A220 I5 D1 H7 P330 T6' is a command line generated by the installation of software for a sound card.

automatic answering: a machine feature that permits a station to respond without *operator* action to a call it receives over a *switched line*. When this happens, the receiving data terminal equipment (DTE) automatically responds to the calling signal. The call can be established whether or not the DTE called is attended. See also *automatic calling*.

automatic calling: a feature that permits a station to initiate a connection with another station over a switched line without *operator* action. When this happens, elements of the selection signal are entered into the data network contiguously at the full data signalling rate. The selection signal is generated by the data terminal equipment. A limit may be imposed by the design criteria of the *network* to prevent more than a permitted number of unsuccessful call attempts to the same *address* within a specified period. See also *automatic answering*.

automatic data capture is the collection of *data* in such a way that it is automatically entered into a computer. This is generally through the use of sensors which can, for example, monitor temperature, wind speed, traffic counts and other data requiring collection on a regular basis.

automatic fallback: a feature allowing *modems* to drop to a slower speed if conditions such as *noise* make it necessary.

automatic logoff: the process that a *server* uses to disconnect a connection when no data has been transmitted for a given period of time.

automatic repeat request (ARQ): when data is being transmitted from one device to another using *modems*, the receiving device asks the sending device to retransmit the data whenever it detects an error.

automatic teller machine (ATM) is a dispenser enabling people to withdraw cash or check their bank statement. The principle is that a bank or credit card is inserted in the ATM. The machine reads and verifies the card; the user then enters a PIN number plus a request to show, for example, a balance, or to withdraw money. The machine initiates the transfer of the money from the customer's account.

automation is the use of a computer, a system or a machine such as a *robot*, to undertake repetitive or intricate tasks normally done by or controlled by people. This can, for example, be large scale processing of data or the painting of a car.

autonomous peripheral transfer: the transfer of data between computer and peripheral carried out independently of the processor. This type of data transfer allows the processor to carry out another task whilst the transfer is taking place.

autosave: a feature incorporated into a number of programs whereby data or *files* are periodically saved without user intervention. For example, a user might enable the feature to save automatically a document being worked on at ten minute intervals.

auxiliary storage device: a data storage device which is not part of the computer, e.g. *disk drive, magnetic tape* unit, *CD-ROM drive*, etc.

AZERTY keyboard: a European version of the keyboard. The letters are arranged differently from the UK/USA QWERTY keyboard. It is commonly used in France.

B

backbone: a high speed *data* link which is used to create a *network* by linking together several smaller networks. *Fibre-optic cable* is normally used for this high speed link.

background processing: a method of processing which allows certain jobs to continue being processed (background jobs) whenever the processor is not occupied with more important jobs (foreground jobs). A user on a microcomputer using a word processor can continue typing in characters (foreground job) while another document is being printed (background job).

backing store: a permanent area where large amounts of *data* and *programs* are stored. From here they can be recalled by the computer. The contents of backing storage are not lost when a computer is switched off. Such a store is referred to as non-volatile. A wide range of different backing storage media is available. Examples are *magnetic disk* (*hard* or *floppy disk*), *magnetic tape*, *optical disks* (*CD-ROMs* and *DVDs*) and *magneto-optical disks.*

backslash: the character \ , used to separate *directory* names in *path* specifications, e.g. C:\data\personal. When the path specification begins from the topmost level, it is used as a leading character, e.g. \data.

backspace key: a key on a *keyboard*, sometimes referred to as 'backspace delete', that moves the cursor to the left, one character at a time, usually erasing each character as it moves.

backtracking: the processing of *records* in reverse order. This technique can be used when locating the cause of a fault. Each record is processed in reverse order until the one that caused the fault is found. Remedial action can then be carried out to overcome the problem.

backup: copying *files, programs,* etc. to a separate source and keeping them in a safe place so that if anything happens to the originals (*corruption* or loss), they are available again and the system can be restored. Backups should be made periodically and the copies stored in a secure location with, if necessary, a second copy off-site.

- **Full or global backup** is when a copy is taken of every file on disk. This can take a long time to complete but does ensure that a copy of every data file and program is available and can be restored. The computer cannot be used for anything else whilst this is in progress.
- **Backup hardware** is the equipment required to undertake the process. Possibilities are *Zip* drives, removable *hard disks* and re-writable *CD-ROMs* and optical disks for relatively small volumes of data (say up to 650 Mb). For larger storage, DAT drives, DVD-RAM, *Jaz drives* and *magnetic tape* drives can be used.
- **Incremental backup** is a type of backup where only those files that have been changed or created since the last backup are copied. Copies are labelled according to when they are made. This is usually combined with a full backup once a week. Incremental backup is less time consuming than

a full backup but it is much more difficult to restore all the data as back-ups have to be entered in the correct sequence.

- **On-line backup** is when data is written simultaneously to a number (two or three generally) of different disks. For organisations (airlines, banks, hospitals) that cannot lose even a few moments of data this ensures that in the event of one drive failing, a switch can be made automatically to the second drive. In some instances, it may be that a third drive is at a remote location in case of a major catastrophe.

- **Backup strategy** is a plan to ensure that, whatever the circumstances, valuable programs and data are never lost. The strategy depends upon the size of the organisation. Small organisations can back up everything once a day. Larger organisations may need an incremental or on-line strategy. Decisions would be made as to how often backups should be made, and when and where they should be stored. Factors to consider would be how often does the data change, its value and the amount of data. Can the backups be restored easily? Is this checked frequently? Is storage required off-site? Is it necessary to have a service agreement with a company able to provide engineers quickly?

- **Backup tapes** are large volume storage used by a *tape streamer* in the backup process.

Backus–Naur form: a method developed by Backus and Naur to describe the *syntax* of a *programming language*. The method involves defining the basic components of the language and then using these definitions to build more complex components. For example, a digit could be expressed in BNF as:

<digit> ::= 0 | 1 | 2 | 3 | 4 | 5 | 6 | 7 | 8 | 9.

This reads 'digit is defined as 0 or 1 or 2 or 3, etc.'

An *unsigned integer* could then be defined as:

<unsigned integer> ::= <digit> | <unsigned integer> <digit>

An unsigned integer is either a digit or an unsigned integer followed by a digit.

backward compatible: software is said to be backward compatible when files created by a previous version are still usable by the new version.

badging is when components of a computer system are made by a small number of manufacturers and built into other systems. These are then sold by the company that builds the system under its own name.

bandwidth: the range of frequencies that can be transmitted over a data communications channel.

bank switching: a method of accessing large amounts of *random-access memory* (RAM) when the processor is only capable of accessing small amounts. The RAM is organised in 'banks', only one of which can be active at any moment in time and the software selects the appropriate bank.

banner: a section of a *web page*, usually spanning the width of the page that contains it. Banners are used for advertisements and frequently contain a link to the advertiser's *web site*.

banner page: 1 An initial screen in a program or application, used to identify a product and credit its producers.

2 A title page that may be added to printouts by most *print spoolers*. Such a page is used primarily to separate one print job from another but typically incorporates account ID information and job length.

bar chart: (sometimes referred to as a bar graph) a *graphic* representation of *data* using rectangular bars displayed vertically or horizontally, distinguished from one another by colour or shading, to show relationships between different values. There are various types of bar chart, such as clustered and stacked. These can also be represented in a 3-D format for a different effect.

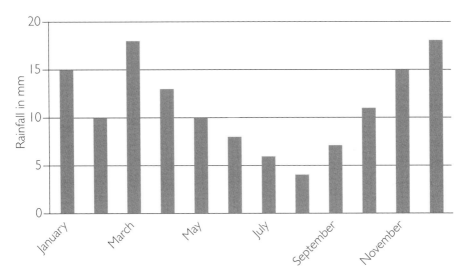

bar code: a pattern of black and white lines. Bar codes are used to store a variety of *data* or a code number that can be read automatically. The data from the bar code can be used to identify a product and look up its description and price.

bar code reader or scanner: the input device that reads *bar codes*. It shines laser light onto the bar code and interprets the reflected patterns. These are frequently built into supermarket checkouts. The hand-held version is sometimes referred to as a wand. It operates in the same fashion by reading the light reflected from the bar code.

basic input output system (BIOS): the part of a computer that manages the peripheral hardware units, e.g. *disk drives, printers, keyboards,* etc.

batch-control slip: see *batch total.*

batch file: a *file* holding a series of commands for the *operating system* of a computer system. When executed, the instructions in the batch file are executed sequentially.

batch processing: a method of processing data to update *master files* where the transaction data is all collected together over a period of time and used to update the master files in a single run of the programs. Batch processing is commonly used in applications like payroll, where information of hours worked is collected over a week or month and then used to update the master files and produce the necessary pay details.

batch total: when *transactions* are collected together ready for *batch processing* they are placed in small batches. Each of these batches has a batch control slip attached, which is subsequently used to identify the batch and check that none of the transactions has been mislaid. A batch total, which could be a count of the number of transactions in the batch or the contents of a field on each transaction totalled, is placed on each batch control slip. This batch control total is checked before the processing of the transactions in the batch begins.

baud: the unit used to measure transfer rate when data is transmitted serially over a *communications link*. It is the number of times a signal representing digital data can change per second. Because each piece of data has additional bits added (start/stop bits, etc.) the baud rate is different from the bit rate.

before-image: a copy of a *record* before it has been updated (see *after-image*). It is saved as part of the *transaction* logging procedure used in certain *backup* strategies.

benchmark or benchmark tests: a standard set of computer tasks designed to measure the performance of software or computer systems. They are tasks such as multiple printing, reformatting large documents, saving large numbers of records, multiple repetitions, etc. These tests provide data that can assist users and customers in the evaluation of software and hardware.

benchmark program: a *program* used in the comparison of the processing power of different *processors*.

bespoke software is *software* that is specifically written for a particular user or organisation. It can be written especially for them by an outside agency or by in-house programmers. It is sometimes referred to as *tailor-made* software.

beta testing is the testing of an application or *software package* after it has been tested by the developers and checked by the person or organisation that commissioned the software (see *alpha testing*). Beta-testing is carried out off-site by a number of potential users who have expressed an interest or who have an earlier version of the software. They agree to use the application in real situations and report back on any errors found. This means that the application is tested on a number of different platforms and with a variety of data. Only when both types of testing are complete and any errors fixed, will the software or application be released to the general public.

binary: having two components, alternatives, or outcomes. The binary number system has 2 as its base, so values are expressed as combinations of two digits, 0 and 1, i.e. 38 in binary = 100110. Computers use a binary system based on 0 and 1. The two digits can represent the logical values true and false as well as numerals. In electronic devices, they can represent the two states on and off, recognised as two voltage levels. Computers are programmed with machine code instructions that use a combination of these two digits. Binary numbers are difficult for people to interpret because they are repetitive strings of 1s and 0s. Programmers and others who work with a computer's internal processing frequently use *hexadecimal* (base-16) or *octal* (base-8) numbers.

binary coded decimal: each digit is coded as four *binary* digits (bits) with 0000 representing the digit 0, 0001 representing the digit 1, etc. Since there are 16 possible combinations but only ten are used to represent the digits 0–9, six combinations are not used.

0 0 0 0	0
0 0 0 1	1
0 0 1 0	2
0 0 1 1	3
0 1 0 0	4
0 1 0 1	5
0 1 1 0	6
0 1 1 1	7
1 0 0 0	8
1 0 0 1	9
1 0 1 0	Not used
1 0 1 1	Not used
1 1 0 0	Not used
1 1 0 1	Not used
1 1 1 0	Not used
1 1 1 1	Not used

Using this notation the binary pattern 0010 1001 represents the decimal number 29.

When adding numbers together in this notation it is important to compensate for the six unused patterns. Example adding 16 to 17:

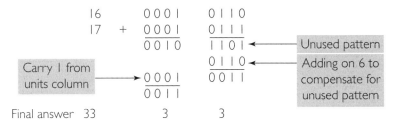

```
        16        0 0 0 1     0 1 1 0
        17   +    0 0 0 1     0 1 1 1
                  0 0 1 0     1 1 0 1  ←──── Unused pattern
                              0 1 1 0  ←──── Adding on 6 to
  Carry 1 from                                compensate for
  units column ────────→ 0 0 0 1     0 0 1 1     unused pattern
                         0 0 1 1
  Final answer  33          3          3
```

binary device: any device that processes information as a series of on/off or high/low electrical states.

binary digit (BIT): either of the two digits 0 or 1 in the *binary* number system.

binary operator: an *operator* that acts on two items of data, e.g. *AND*, +, *OR*.

binary search: the data to be searched must be held in memory (normally in an *array*) and be sorted into order on the *field* to be searched. Three *pointers* are established: one pointing to the top, one pointing to the bottom and a third pointing to the mid-point of the data list. The item of data held at the mid-point is compared with the search item. If the two items match the search is complete, otherwise one half of the data can be discarded (the half not holding the search item). This search method continues until either the item is located or all three pointers are pointing at the same item of data which is not the required item in which case the item being searched for does not exist.

In the algorithm below the array Data is searched to find 'Searchitem'.

TP indicates the pointer identifying the top of the data.
BP indicates the pointer identifying the bottom of the data.

MP indicates the pointer identifying the middle of the data.

```
TP := 1
BP := 9
found := False
While NOT (found or (TP>BP)) Do
        MP := (TP + BP) Div 2
        If Data[MP] = Searchitem Then
                found := true
        Else
                If Data[MP] > Searchitem Then
                        BP := MP - 1
                Else
                        TP := MP + 1
                Endif
        Endif
Endwhile
If found Then
                Display 'Item found in location ' MP ' of array'
Else
                Display 'Item not found'
Endif
```

The diagram below shows the stages involved in searching for 13 in the array.

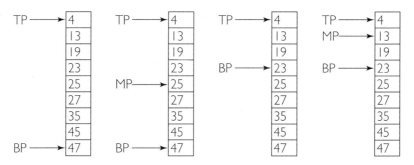

binary tree: a *tree* structure in which there are never more than two branches coming out of any *node*. The binary tree provides a hierarchical method of structuring data for use in applications.

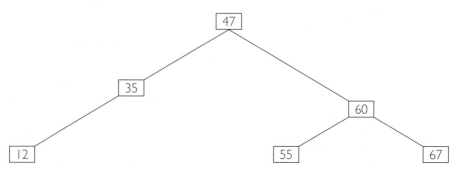

One use of the binary tree is to sort data into order. The first item of data is placed in the root node with the position of subsequent pieces of data being determined by whether they are less than (move left) or greater than (move right) the data at a node. In the above diagram '40' would be added by the following method:

- compare with contents of root node; 40 is less than 47 – move left
- compare with 35; 40 is greater than 35 – move right
- place 40 in node to the right of 35.

A binary tree is held in memory using either two arrays – one for the data and one for the pointers – or a single array of records. The above tree would be stored in two arrays as:

	Data	Left pointer	Right pointer
Row 1	47	2	3
Row 2	35	5	0
Row 3	60	4	6
Row 4	55	0	0
Row 5	12	0	0
Row 6	67	0	0

where 0 is used as the *null pointer.*

bitmap: a method of storing an image in a file ready for subsequent display on a monitor and for printing. For an image that is black and white, with no shades of grey, each bit in the file stores the necessary information to indicate if a particular *pixel* is to be on or off. If the number of bits per pixel is increased, then shades of grey can be reproduced. For example, using 4 bits for each pixel allows 16 greyscales to be stored in the image; 8 bits per pixel will allow 256 greyscales to be reproduced. For a colour image that is to be reproduced on a monitor, channels are needed for red, green and blue colours. Here, eight bits per pixel for each of the three colours will allow the image to store $256 \times 256 \times 256$ colours (i.e. more than 16 million different colours). Since details of every pixel have to be stored, images that are held on file in bitmap format often require very large files. Bitmap images are frequently stored in compressed form in the JPEG format. See also *colour monitor, lossless compression, joint photographic expert group.*

bits per cm: a measure of the number of bits stored in a centimetre of magnetic tape.

bits per second (bps): is a measure of the speed with which data moves between different parts of a computer system. It is sometimes referred to as the bit-rate.

black-box testing: testing of a computer system independent of the code. The test data is specified by someone looking at the system specification but with no knowledge of the program code that has been written. This style of testing ensures that the system does what was intended when the system was specified and designed.

block: often referred to as the physical *record* in file storage. A block can contain several data records but is transferred as a whole between the computer's memory and the physical device. The block size is often determined by the size of the *buffer* between the physical device and the computer. When records are being written to a device the records are placed in the buffer until it is full, when its contents are transferred to the physical device. This unit of transfer is referred to as a block.

block diagram: a diagram made up of rectangles (sometimes standard symbols are used) where each rectangle represents part of the system. The rectangles are connected by lines to indicate the relationship between the parts of the system.

block structured language: a *language* which identifies sections of code (blocks) to be regarded as single units. *Pascal* is an example of such a language, using the command BEGIN to identify the start and END to identify the end of each block.

blocking factor: the number of *records* held in a *block*. A block holds complete records, hence the blocking factor is always an integer.

BNC connector: short for British Naval Connector or bayonet nut connector or Bayonet Neill Concelman, it is a type of connector used with *coaxial cables*. A coaxial cable normally has a plug-type BNC connector at each end. The plug-type connector has a centre pin connected to the single cable conductor and a metal tube connected to the outer cable shield. A rotating ring outside the tube locks the cable to any socket connector.

A BNC barrel connector allows two cables to be connected together and a T-connector is used to join a network card in a computer to the network cable.

Some monitors provide four BNC connectors (one for the red signal, one for the green signal, one for the blue signal and the fourth for synchronisation purposes) and this allows a more accurate signal to be sent from the video adapter.

boilerplate: sentences and paragraphs used repeatedly in different documents, such as standard letters and reports.

bold: a type style that when applied to text makes it appear darker and heavier than the surrounding text. **These words are in bold.** Some applications allow the user to select text and apply a 'bold' command; others require special control codes before and after the text selected.

bookmark: a location or selection of text that you name for reference purposes. It is usually somewhere you wish to return to later. It can also be applied to *web pages*.

Boolean algebra: an algebra developed by George Boole based on the *binary* system, on which circuit design in computers is based.

Boolean variable: a data type which can take only one of two values – True or False. This type of variable is used to represent *flags* in programming to indicate whether a flag is set or unset. The flag could be being used to indicate if data that has been entered is valid. The use of a Boolean variable here makes the program more readable.

```
Repeat
     Writeln('Enter Name');
     Readln(Name);
     Validate (Name);
Until Valid_name_entered;
```

In the above segment of a *Pascal* program 'Valid_name_entered' is a Boolean variable whose state (True or False) is set by the procedure Validate. See *data types*.

boot: starting up a computer; specifically, the process of loading the *operating system* into memory. A cold boot is when the computer is first turned on. A warm boot is when the computer is restarted using the *reset* button.

boot disk: a disk (floppy or CD) that contains key *system* files that can *boot* (start) a PC. Computers normally boot from their hard disks. A boot disk is used when there is some problem with starting the PC from the hard disk.

bootstrap: a small program capable of loading the *operating system* into the computer's memory from disk. This program is used whenever the computer is booted. It is sometimes called a bootstrap loader.

bottom-up programming: where a series of small units of a *program* are written first. These units are then used to create other units until the whole program is created. This method of programming is used in languages like LOGO.

bottom-up testing: a method of testing a *program* by starting with the lower level units and working up until the complete program is tested. For a system made up of several programs the initial testing would start with the *modules* (*procedures, functions, subroutines*, etc.), move on to testing each program and finally test the whole system.

Each module of a program should be tested with:

- typical data – data the module is designed to process
- extreme data – data that ensures that the module works at the upper and lower bounds of acceptable data
- erroneous data – data that should be rejected by the module, which should be done without the module crashing.

Once the modules for a program are combined the program should be tested to ensure:

- that every possible route through the system functions and produces the expected results
- that every program instruction has been executed at least once
- that the results produced are as expected from the original specification.

box: see *dialogue box, list box, operation box, process box* and *text box.*

branch instruction: a programming *instruction* that transfers control to a different part of a program. See *conditional jump/branch* and *unconditional jump/branch.*

breakpoint: a breakpoint is placed in a computer program so that execution will stop when it is reached. Once execution stops the contents of variables can be inspected. A breakpoint helps a programmer to find faults in a program. After inspection of the variable contents at the breakpoint, the execution of the program can be resumed.

bridge: a hardware device that allows two *networks* using the same *communication protocols* to be linked together. See *gateway.*

British Computer Society: a chartered professional institution for the field of information systems engineering. It exists to provide service and support to the information systems community, including individual practitioners, employers of information systems staff and the general public.

It was formed in 1957, and now operates under a Royal Charter granted in 1984 which requires it, amongst other things, to promote the study and practice of computing and to advance knowledge therein for the benefit of the public. The web site address is www.bsc.org.uk.

brown-out: a reduction in the voltage from a power supply caused by heavy demands on the supply.

browse: to look for information, for a particular item or for anything that seems to be of interest on the *Internet*. It can also refer to looking for information stored in a database, or the contents of documents in a word processing program. Browsing implies looking for information, rather than changing it.

browser: see *web browser*.

B-tree: see *binary tree*.

bubble sort: a method of sorting data where items of data are compared in pairs and swapped if they are not in the correct order. The sorting continues, making several passes through the data, if necessary, until no more changes are made during a pass through the data when the data will be in the required order. The number of items to be compared in a pass can be reduced by one after each complete pass, as at least one item is placed in its final position during each pass.

bubble-jet printer: another name for an *inkjet printer*. It is a printer that uses quick drying ink from a cartridge in a fine spray of dots to produce the characters. They are quiet, the quality is good and they can print in colour. The colour version uses four colour cartridges, cyan, magenta, yellow and black. The print head on the printer travels backwards and forwards across the page.

buffer: a temporary storage area used to hold data when it is passing between a hardware device and computer. The buffer is needed to compensate for the differences in speed of the two devices.

bug: a fault in either the *hardware* or *software* of a computer system.

bulletin board: the electronic equivalent of a notice board. Bulletin boards are sited on a computer system and the users access the computer via a *network* or by electronic mail. They can carry news, information or be a place for reading and posting messages for others to read. They can also have reviews and items of software to download. Usually they are based on special interest groups such as games, films, etc. Some also allow users to chat online with other users. Many software and hardware companies run bulletin boards for customers that include sales information, technical support, and software *upgrades* and *patches*.

bundled software: software included with a computer system when it is purchased. Some of this software is essential (e.g. the *operating system*) but other packages (e.g. games) are added to make the whole purchased system more attractive.

bureau: see *computer bureau*.

bus: a connection between various parts of the central processor which allows the passage of data, *address* or control signals to be sent.

Business Software Alliance (BSA): formed in 1988, the Business Software Alliance has been the voice of the world's leading software developers to governments and consumers in the international marketplace. Its members represent the fastest growing industry in the world. The BSA educates computer users on software *copyrights*; advocates public policy that fosters innovation, expands trade opportunities and fights software *piracy*. The web site address is www.bsa.org.

button: 1 On a *mouse*, a finger-operated switch that is pressed to pass a signal to the computer; pressing the button causes a clicking sound. Most models of mouse have two or more buttons. What happens when a mouse button is pressed depends upon the software and the place on the screen that is being pointed to by the mouse.

2 *Screen button* – a graphic element on the screen or in a dialogue box that is used to select an action. The user activates the screen button by clicking on it with a mouse or, if the button is already highlighted, by pressing the Return or Enter key.

byte: the name given to eight consecutive bits (*binary digits*) of data. A byte is the smallest addressable unit of store within a computer system.

cable: 1 A collection of wires used to connect the components of a computer system, for example, to connect a printer to a personal computer. The wires are shielded within a protective covering. Examples of devices usually connected to a computer with cables are a mouse, a keyboard and a printer. Printer cables typically implement a serial or a parallel *path* for data to travel along.

2 Shorthand for the cable television (CATV) distribution system. Cable TV is a broadband service and it can carry data (such as an Internet connection) at very high speed.

Common types of cable are *coaxial* and *fibre-optic*.

cache memory: part of the *main store*, between the central processor and the remainder of the main store. It is a special memory subsystem in which frequently used data values are duplicated for extremely fast access. A *memory cache* stores the contents of frequently accessed *RAM* locations and the *addresses* where these data items are stored, to take advantage of its short fetch cycle. When the processor references an address in memory, the cache checks to see whether it holds that address. If it does hold the address, the data is returned to the processor; if it does not, a regular memory access occurs. Cache memory can greatly reduce processing time because it is always faster than main RAM.

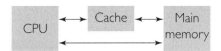

call centre: a place where people work for an organisation answering calls and questions from customers. One use of call centres is for technical support, where the person who answers the call takes specific information from the caller concerning the query and uses this information to search a computer database to see if the answer is there, either from a previous enquiry or amongst standard answers provided by the company. This technical support is generally provided by computer or software companies but can be for other types of organisations. Call centres are frequently located in out-of-the-way areas and Freefone, local or national telephone numbers given to customers are re-routed to this location.

candidate key: a possible *field* in a *database* table that could be used as a *primary key*, chosen to identify a *record*. If there is only one candidate key in a table, it automatically becomes the primary key. If there are multiple candidate keys, the database designer must designate one (or a combination) as the primary key. Any candidate key that is not the designated as the primary key is an alternate key.

card: a printed circuit board placed in an expansion slot inside a personal computer that provides added *functionality* or new capability not built into the computer such as communications or graphics. Cards are sometimes referred to as 'boards', 'expansion cards' or '*interface cards*'.

caret (^): the symbol on the top row of a keyboard typically found on the '6' key. The caret is sometimes used to represent the Control key (Ctrl) on the keyboard, e.g. ^Z means press the Control key and Z key together. In some programming languages, the caret is used as an exponentiation *operator*, e.g. the expression $5 \wedge 2$ represents five to the power of two, i.e. 25.

cartridge: a unit that can be inserted into a slot in small computers and games computers to perform special functions. Many of the software programs available for early personal computers were stored on cartridges. A cartridge may contain a storage medium, such as a tape, or it may contain software stored in ROM. *Laser printers* also make use of cartridges, on which additional fonts are stored. See also *ink cartridge, tape cartridge.*

cash dispenser: see *automated teller machine.*

cashless society: the notion that society can exist without cash, especially small change. Cash would be replaced by some form of *smart card* enabling users to purchase milk, newspapers, tickets, pay for parking meters, all without the need to carry lots of coins. However, the concept has been tried in various places as far apart as Swindon, New York and Hong Kong, so far without much success. The expense to small traders of installing the machinery has been a sticking point and also the reluctance of people who generally prefer cash. However, the amount of money being spent by large companies in trials around the world would seem to indicate that it will ultimately come to fruition.

CD: an abbreviation for compact disk.

CD-R: an acronym for compact disk-recordable. This is a type of *CD-ROM* that can be written on once using a CD recorder, never overwritten and then *read* on a CD-ROM drive.

CD-ROM: an acronym for compact disk read-only memory. A form of storage, similar to audio CDs, characterised by high capacity (approximately 650 Mb) and the use of laser optics rather than magnetic means for reading data. Data is recorded by a laser burning tiny holes in the surface of the disk. The disk consists of a single spiral track divided into sectors. It is read by a laser, which reflects off the surface of the disk detecting the presence or absence of holes. These in turn then represent binary digits 1 or 0. The term 'read-only' refers to the ability to read data from the disk, and not to write data to the disk. CD-ROMs are extremely good for multimedia applications, where they are used for storing not only programs but also text, sound and full-colour video.

CD-ROM drive: a device, attached to a computer, for retrieving data from CD-ROM disks. Many CD-ROM drives have a SCSI (*small computer systems interface*) connection, although some are connected to a PC via a controller for a *disk drive.*

CD-RW: an acronym for compact disc-rewritable. Special *CDs* used with a CD-RW drive can be written and read, deleted and overwritten with new information.

Ceefax: the BBC teletext system that uses the television to deliver a variety of information. It is a one-way service than can be accessed by a viewer pressing buttons on a remote control handset to replace the television picture with pages of text.

cell: the intersection of a row and a column in a *spreadsheet*. Each cell is displayed as a rectangular space. A cell can hold text, a value or a formula. Each row and column in a spreadsheet is labelled, so a particular cell can be uniquely identified, e.g. cell A3 is at the intersection of column A and row 3.

	A	B	C	D
1				
2				
3				
4				

cellular phone: a portable radio-telephone that uses microwaves to transmit conversations. The country is divided into overlapping circles (cells), each with a low powered transmitter/receiver. Each transmitter/receiver handles the calls made within its area. If the caller moves out of range of the transmitter/receiver, it is automatically switched to an adjacent cell.

central processing unit (CPU): an older term for processor and microprocessor, this is the central unit in a computer containing the logic circuitry that performs the instructions of a computer's programs.

centring: alignment of text around a central point located in the middle of a line, a page, or another defined area. This has the same effect as placing the text an equal distance from each margin or border.

CGA: see *colour graphics adapter*.

change file: a *file* in a database management software program that records all retrievals of, and changes to, the contents of the database. This can provide a basis for updating a master file or as part of establishing an *audit trail*. It is also call a transaction log.

changeover: when an organisation moves from an old system to the installation of a new system. There are several methods of changeover from one to the other. *Direct changeover* is where an existing system is totally replaced by the new system at a certain point in time. The old system is then no longer used at all. Direct changeover is cheap as only one system is in operation at any time. However, it has risks in that there is no backup if the new system does not function as expected or it goes wrong. Staff need more training to feel confident in moving from a system that they are familiar with to a new system. Other methods are *parallel changeover* or *parallel running, phased conversion* or *pilot conversion*.

changes file: another name for a transaction file. This is a file that contains a collection of records of events taken over a period of time, daily, weekly or monthly, that are used to update a *master file* when using *batch processing*.

channels of communication: the flow of information and data within an organisation. Well-defined procedures ensure that information is received quickly by the people who need it and in the most appropriate format for them with no redundant or superfluous information. This can be presented in the form of memos, formal reports, e-mails, *electronic data interchange, intranets* or meeting and talking to colleagues face-to-face or through the use of *video conferencing*.

character: a letter, number, punctuation mark, space or other symbol or control code that can be stored in a computer. A character requires one *byte* of storage. All characters are not necessarily visible, either on the screen or on paper when printed. Computers must also manage the formatting of text and the transfer of electronically stored information. A character can be a control code (or *control character*) and can indicate a carriage return, a signal to sound a beep, to begin a new page, or mark the end of a file.

character code: a code stored as a *binary* integer that represents a particular character in a specific set, such as the ASCII character set; e.g. lower case 'a' is 97. The character code for a given key depends on whether another key, such as Shift, is pressed at the same time. This can change lower case to upper case or numbers to symbols. depending on the nature of the keyboard.

character printer: a *printer* that operates by printing one character at a time. Examples are *daisywheel printers* and a golf-ball printers. These printers can print graphic characters when the daisywheel or golf ball contain such characters, but cannot print graphics.

character recognition: see *optical character recognition* or *magnetic ink character recognition.*

character set: a grouping of alphabetic, numeric, and other characters that have some relationship in common, e.g. ASCII character set. Computers used in Japan, for example, understand a different character set than those used in the UK.

characters per second: 1 A measure of the speed of printers (other than laser printers).

2 A measure of the speed of transfer of data between devices.

check digit: an extra digit added to the end of a code number such as customer number, product number, *bar code* or account number. These numbers are lengthy and prone to transcription and *transposition errors.* The check digit is calculated from the original digits (the most common being a modulo-11 system) and then recomputed when the number is read. If the calculation does not match the check digit, this process determines that an error has occurred.

checksum: the assignment of numeric values to computer operations, used to test data for the presence of errors that can occur when data is transmitted or when it is written to disk. These numeric values can then be summarised and compared with each other, by a computer program, as a means of error detection. The checksum is calculated for given data by sequentially combining all the bytes of data with a series of arithmetic or logical operations. If the sums of the transmitted and received messages are not equal, an error has occurred. Checksums cannot detect all errors nor can they be used to correct erroneous data.

chip: the general name for an *integrated circuit.* Chips are made of silicon, on which large numbers of components such as transistors and resistors can be stored. These are formed into connected circuit elements.

clicking: pressing the *button* on a *mouse,* which usually produces a 'click' sound. When the screen pointer, controlled by the mouse, rests on a button, icon or menu item, clicking the mouse button produces a particular action, such as selecting an item or activating a program. Another action is to 'double-click' (press the mouse button twice in quick succession) which can produce a different action. It is also possible to click the left or right mouse button, producing additional different actions. See *double-clicking*.

client/server architecture: an arrangement used on *local area networks* that treats different devices as either *clients* or *servers*. The client devices can be a number of stand-alone personal computers. These send requests for particular services from the specific server devices. These services can be requests, for example, for the retrieval of data or printing. The server components can be a *personal computer*, a *minicomputer*, or a *mainframe* that acts as the *file server* and controls other devices such as printers.

The client portion of the *network* is typically optimised for user interaction and performs some of the processing tasks; others are performed by the file server. The server portion provides the centralised functionality, distributes programs and data as requested, and controls communications through the network. If the server machine goes down then the whole network is affected. Usually *security* through *passwords*, *user IDs*, etc. are controlled centrally, as are *backups*.

client/server database: an arrangement in a *database management system* whereby the *server* machine manages the (generally large) database. Client stations can access the data and request searches, sorts and reports from the server software. Client stations may also be allowed to update the database. This means that the database is stored in only one place and not copied to individual stations. It is more consistent as only one copy of the data is held. The database processing is normally carried out by the server which minimises communication time between the server and client machines.

clip art: a collection of pictures, cartoons, diagrams, maps, drawings, and other such *graphics* that can be cut and pasted and incorporated into other documents. These are usually supplied on a disk or CD or as part of a suite of programs. They are used to add graphics without having to actually draw the item from scratch.

clipboard: a special area of *memory* used for storing text, pictures or information that is in the process of being moved from one location to another. The clipboard stores the last information that was copied. A paste operation can then pass the information from the clipboard to a new location or program. A clipboard allows information to be transferred from one program to another, provided the second program can *read* the data generated by the first.

clock: 1 The system clock is an internal device, electronic unit or circuit, in a computer that generates a steady stream of pulses at a constant rate. The pulses are used to synchronise every operation and keep components in step. The system clock signal is set precisely by a quartz crystal. The clock rate of a computer is one of the prime factors governing how fast a computer can work. It can only go as high as the slowest component will allow.

2 The battery-backed circuit that maintains the computer's current date and time. It is available to the software in use.

clock rate or speed: the frequency at which the system *clock* generates pulses.

CMYK: a colour definition based on the four colours cyan, magenta, yellow and black. It is used in *desktop publishing* (DTP) software when creating separate colour films to use for printing.

coaxial cable: a cable, often used in *local area networks*, which allows data to be transmitted at high speed. It is the same type of wiring as that used for cable television. It comprises a two-conductor cable consisting of a central copper wire, a layer of insulation and then a second wire (or sheath) of many strands braided together around the insulation. The two wires are covered with an outer layer of PVC or fire-resistant material.

COBOL (common business oriented language) was the first widely-used high-level *programming language* for business applications. Many payroll, accounting, and other business application programs written in COBOL over the past 35 years are still in use and it is possible that there are more existing lines of programming code in COBOL than in any other programming language. COBOL was an effort to make a programming language that was similar to natural English, and both easy to write and had code that was easy to read. Many COBOL programs required change to overcome the problem at the change of the century (the *Y2K* problem).

codes of conduct: a set of guidelines produced by an employer to ensure that their employees are aware of legal requirements when working with computer systems, as well as their responsibilities and the standards of behaviour expected. The intention should be to make employees aware of the company's policies on *security*, copying or introduction of software, introduction of *viruses*, use of *e-mail* and the *Internet*, *data protection*, etc. Breaches of the code can result in verbal or written warnings, or even dismissal if the breach is of a serious nature. The *British Computer Society* produces a professional code of conduct for its members that sets out the social, moral and ethical standards of behaviour expected.

codes of practice: a set of guidelines about the standards and quality of work intended to ensure that a high level of professionalism is maintained in working with computer systems and software. The *British Computer Society* produces a code of practice for its members.

coding form/sheet: a special sheet of paper ruled with horizontal and vertical lines to aid in handwriting program instructions for older *languages* that have position-dependent *syntax*. The code is then typed into the system at a later time. The use of coding forms has declined in favour of typing programs directly into the computer using a *text editor*.

coding information: the use of codes to convert information into data for processing. Examples are M and F for male and female, or a branch sort code such as 40-02-39, to replace a name and address. The advantages are that coding is generally short and easier to enter, it takes up less storage space and makes validation easier. The disadvantage is that it can lessen the precision of the information.

colour graphics adapter (CGA): a *video adapter* board introduced by IBM in 1981; the earliest graphics systems for IBM personal computers. CGA was capable of several character and graphics modes. CGA had a relatively poor resolution and a minimal number of colours (16), and has since been replaced by other, more sophisticated systems such as enhanced graphics array (EGA), *video graphics array* (VGA) and super video graphics array (SVGA).

colour monitor: a video display device, connected to a personal computer, designed to work with a video card or adapter to produce text or graphics images in colour. A colour monitor has a screen coated internally with patterns of red, green, and blue phosphors that glow when struck by an electron beam. To create other colours, the three are lit together in varying proportions.

column: 1 In a *spreadsheet*, a vertical group of *cells* each given a column label, usually A, B, C, etc.

2 In a *word processing* document, it is a narrow block of text similar to that used in a newspaper.

.com: 1 The top-level domain in the *Internet's domain name system*, that identifies *addresses* operated by commercial organisations. The domain name '.com' appears as a suffix at the end of the address.

2 The *file extension* that identifies a command file in MS-DOS.

COM: 1 A name reserved by the MS-DOS *operating system* for serial communications ports. If there are two *serial ports*, these are identified as COM1 and COM2 by the operating system.

2 An acronym for computer output on microfilm. It is a technique that can produce output from a computer directly onto *microfilm*.

command-line system: a *user interface* to a software package in which the user responds to a visual prompt by typing in a command on a specified line, receives a response back from the system, and then enters another command, etc. The MS-DOS prompt application in a *Windows* operating system is an example of a command-line interface. Typically, most of today's *Unix*-based systems offer both a command-line interface and a *graphical user interface*.

communications channel: the physical means by which communications occur between two computer devices. Information (data, sound, and/or video) can be carried by a communications channel, depending on its type, in either analogue or digital form. A communications channel can be a physical link, such as a wire or *fibre-optic cable*, or it can consist of some electromagnetic transmission such as in radio, microwave or infra-red.

communications devices: devices such as *modems* and ISDN adapters that allow computers to be linked to other computers and to the *Internet*.

communications link: the connection between computers that enables data transfer to take place. Telephone lines can be public, in which case the length of time taken determines cost, or they can be private or leased lines, where the line can be used as often as required for a fixed annual fee.

communications protocol: a set of rules or standards for data communications between two or more computers designed to enable computers to connect with one another and to exchange information with as little error as possible. It requires that the format of data be specified along with the signals to start, control and end transfer. The *protocol* generally accepted for standardising overall computer communications is a seven-layer set of hardware and software guidelines known as the OSI (*open systems interconnection*) model. Without these rules or standards, data would be lost and errors in transmission would go undetected.

communications security: the use of *encryption* or callback procedures to prevent data being intercepted or read during transmission.

communications software: software programs that are designed to handle the communication function. Communications software can control a *modem* in response to user commands, such as dialling other computers, and monitors the process of making the connection together with the speed and method of transmission.

communications technology: the principles involved in how computer systems communicate with each other and the standards, *protocols* and conventions that determine how such systems communicate. This generally involves data transfer from one computer to another through a telephone, physical cable, microwave relay or satellite link. Connection of computers is generally through the linking of workstations by cables in a *network*, through the public telephone service or the use of *leased lines*.

compact disk read-only memory: see *CD-ROM*.

compatibility: the degree to which a computer, an attached device, or a program can work with or understand the same commands, formats, or language as another device. Compatibility is becoming increasingly important as computer communications, *networks*, and program-to-program *file transfers* become essential aspects of modern communications and working practices.

- **Hardware:** the extent to which a piece of hardware conforms to an accepted standard. This means that the hardware operates in all respects like the standard on which it is based. In a looser sense, it can also indicate that machines support the same software.
- **Software:** the extent to which a software package can work and share data from a previous version or can incorporate images or files created using another package.

compiler: a translation program that converts statements written in a *programming language* into the machine language (*machine code*) that a computer's processor uses. Typically, a programmer writes language statements in a language such as *Pascal* or C, one line at a time, using an editor to produce a file containing the *source code*. The programmer then runs the appropriate language compiler, specifying the name of the file that contains the source statements. The file produced is known as the object file (this is nothing to do with object oriented programming) and contains the object code, i.e. the executable code.

The object oriented *Java* programming language has introduced the possibility of compiling output (called bytecode) that can run on any computer platform for which a Java bytecode *interpreter* is provided.

composite key: a key that consists of two or more *fields* in a *file*, *columns* in a *table*, or *attributes* in a *relationship*. This enables a file or table to be accessed and sorted in a more complex order.

compression: a technique for reducing the size of a *file* with the intention of saving disk space or transmission time.

CompuServe: an *Internet service provider*. CompuServe provides information and communications capabilities, including *Internet* access.

computer abuse is generally taken to be the wrongful use of computer systems. This can be anti-social or for illegal purposes such as hacking, *viruses*, *fraud* or computer pornography.

computer-aided design (CAD): a computer-based system involving specialised software programs and *workstations* used in designing anything from equipment to buildings, aircraft and integrated circuits. Engineering, civil engineering, architectural, and scientific models can be developed using a combination of previously drawn shapes together with accurate freehand drawing. CAD generally incorporates state-of-the-art graphics capabilities. CAD applications can create objects in two or three dimensions, presenting the results as solid objects, as substantial models with shaded surfaces or as wire-frame skeletons. Drawings can also be multi-layered so that only a certain aspect is displayed when required. Some CAD programs can rotate or resize models, show interior views, generate lists of materials required for construction, and perform other allied functions. CAD programs rely on mathematics, often requiring the computing power of a high-performance workstation. CAD essentially automates a lot of the functions performed by the designer and draftsman. Advantages are consistency, no need to re-draw when changes are made and the ability to store copies for future reference. CAD is sometimes known as computer-aided drafting.

computer-aided design/computer-aided manufacturing (CAD/CAM): the use of computers throughout the design and production process in a factory, from initial design through to the final stages of manufacturing. With CAD/CAM, a product is designed with a CAD program. The finished design is then translated into a set of instructions that can be transmitted to, and used by, the machines dedicated to the manufacture of the item. See also *computer-aided manufacturing*.

computer-aided learning (CAL): the use of a computer running educational programs to serve as a teaching tool. The computer supplements material presented in the classroom with tutorials, exercises, and question-and-answer sessions. It can present a topic and test the student's comprehension. Students may then be directed to complete additional exercises or *simulations* on the computer to provide additional practice.

CAL programs are excellent aids for presenting factual material and for allowing students to pace their own learning. Subjects can range from simple to complex and cover a range of educational and specialised topics.

computer-aided manufacturing (CAM): the use of computers in automating and controlling aspects of manufacturing and assembly. The computer with the CAM program is interfaced to the machine making the parts and provides the necessary instructions to perform the various tasks involved. CAM can be used in the manufacture of products ranging from small-scale items to the use of *robotics* in full-scale car assembly lines.

computer animation: an illusion of movement, using the capabilities of the computer, obtained by replicating the same image in slightly altered positions and displaying the resulting series in quick succession. The images can all be drawn separately, or the start and end points can be drawn, with the intervening images provided by software. There are many animation software packages.

computer-assisted learning: see *computer-aided learning*.

computer-assisted manufacturing: see *computer-aided manufacturing*.

computer-based music system: computers and electronic music devices, such as musical keyboards, microphones, amplifiers and loudspeakers, linked together so that music, speech and singing can be recorded, stored, manipulated and reproduced. It can also generate original compositions. The sounds can be synthesised to replicate a range of musical instruments. Associated musical software can be used to generate the musical notation from the input or to allow a composer to write the notes to a conventional music stave using a mouse. This can then be played back.

computer-based training (CBT) is very similar to *computer-aided learning* but the scope of the learning is limited to clear training objectives such as learning to use a new software application.

computer bureau: a specialist computer company that offers a range of services to users. These services can cover such things as advice on the purchase of hardware and software, training, assistance in data preparation, consultancy on the Internet and networks and the design and production of web pages.

computer crime: any criminal act where the use of a computer is the main implement. This can take the form of theft of data from files or databases, theft of money through fraudulent transfer of payments or funds, theft of goods by re-routing their destination, and malicious vandalism through hacking and the introduction of *viruses*. Other issues revolve around the illegal use of software by copying or having insufficient licences to cover the number of machines available.

The legal framework protecting users and companies depends on a number of pieces of legislation including the *Computer Misuse Act*, the *Data Protection Act* and the *Copyright, Designs & Patents Act*.

Computers are increasingly being used to assist police forces in the detection of crime. A special police unit in London has been set up to deal with computer crime. Details of known criminals, fingerprints, access to car details, tracing of telephone calls and the linking of crimes in different areas are all available to police forces and capable of providing valuable information that can be searched and sorted.

computer engineering: the field of engineering involving the design and development of computer hardware.

computer generations are ways of distinguishing between major advances in computing technology.

First generation computers used valves and had very limited storage capability. Typically they were very large, occupied one or more rooms and used enormous amounts of power. Examples of first generation machines are EDSAC, EDVAC and ENIAC.

Second generation computers used transistors instead of valves. This meant that they were cheaper, more reliable, and used less power. Examples of second generation machines are UNIVAC and ATLAS.

Third generation computers used integrated circuits instead of transistors. This made computers cheaper still, even more reliable, more powerful, more compact, and power consumption was lowered again. Examples of third generation machines are the IBM 360 series and the ICL 1900 series.

Fourth generation computers use large scale integration (LSI) of circuits onto silicon *chips*. This allowed the development of the *microprocessor*, which in turn led to the development of the microcomputer. This, coupled with the increase in speed of processors, and the fall in cost of internal and external memory, has led to current widespread use of *microcomputers* by individuals.

Fifth generation computers are still not clearly defined. The current developments and advances are in the use of very large scale integration (VLSI), increased use of parallel and distributed processing and the move towards input and output devices using voice recognition and speech. The fifth generation will not be fully defined until a sixth generation comes along.

computer graphics: the creation and display of various images, such as charts and drawings, on a computer screen or output to a printer. Computer graphics can also refer to the creation of *animation* generated and displayed on the screen.

computer language: an artificial language, with its own words and *syntax*, used to write computer programs. The language specifies instructions to be executed on a computer. There is a wide range of languages, from binary-coded machine language (*assembly language*) to *high-level languages*. Computer languages are also known as programming languages. Common examples of high-level languages are BASIC, Pascal, COBOL, FORTRAN, C and C++.

Computer Misuse Act: an Act of Parliament passed in 1990 to make provision for securing computer material against unauthorised access or modification, and for connected purposes. It was designed to combat a variety of activities using computers that had not previously been covered by other laws.

Three categories of criminal offence are specifically identified. These are:

- unauthorised access to computer material
- unauthorised access with intent to commit or facilitate commission of further offences
- unauthorised modification of computer material.

In effect, this comes down to using a particular system without permission or accessing parts of a system without permission. It covers the intent to modify or delete data from systems, hacking, the introduction of *viruses* to cause damage, and using a computer for fraudulent purposes.

computer network: see *network.*

computer output on microfilm (COM): a technique by which *microfilm* can record data directly from a computer. This can be a very economical storage for archive material.

computer personnel: the range of people involved in the operation, support and management of computer systems. This covers many jobs and tasks, examples of which are *programmers*, analysts, designers, operators, support personnel, engineers, data processing and administration staff and *network controllers.*

computer service engineer: see *service engineer.*

computer (service/maintenance) engineer: a specialist in the maintenance of computer hardware. Such an engineer is frequently someone employed specifically by a contract service company.

computer system: the set of all functional components that make up a single computer installation. It includes associated *hardware, power supplies, peripherals* and *communications links.* A basic *microcomputer* system includes a console, or system unit, with one or more disk and *CD-ROM* drives, a monitor, a *mouse* and a *keyboard.* Additional hardware can include such devices as a *printer*, a *modem* and a *scanner.*

Whether software is regarded as part of a computer system is debatable, although the *operating system* that runs the hardware is known as system software. The combination of all of these is known as the *configuration* of the system.

computer types: see *laptop, mainframe, microcomputer, minicomputer, multimedia, notebook, palmtop, personal computer, personal digital assistant* and *supercomputer*.

config.sys: a special text *file* for directing the way in which the *operating system* will be set up on the computer. Commands in the config.sys file enable or disable system features, set limits on resources (for example, the maximum number of open files), and extend the operating system by loading device drivers that control hardware specific to an individual computer system. This is an example of a config.sys file:

```
Device=C:\WINDOWS\himem.sys
Device=C:\WINDOWS\emm386.exe noems
DOS=HIGH
Files=40
REM ******** IDECDROM DEVICE DRIVER ******************
Device=C:\IDECDROM\IDECDROM.SYS /D:MSCD001 /V
Device=C:\WINDOWS\COMMAND\display.sys con=(ega,,1)
Country=044,850,C:\WINDOWS\COMMAND\country.sys
```

configuration: 1 With reference to a single computer, the set up of the internal and external components, including monitor, memory, disk drives, keyboard, video, mouse, modem, and printer that make up the system.

2 With reference to *networks*, the entire interconnected set of hardware, the way in which a network is laid out and the manner in which elements are connected.

3 With reference to software, the user's choices established through configuration files such as the *autoexec.bat* and *config.sys* files on IBM PCs and compatibles. This can specify the amount of storage space available for program files, what types of printers will be employed, etc. Occasionally hardware (switches and jumpers) needs to be changed to assist in configuring the system to work correctly.

Consumer Credit Act: a piece of legislation designed to protect consumers when they pay for shopping using a credit card. The same legislation applies when shopping is done by credit card over the *Internet*.

content-addressable storage: a memory-based storage method in which data items are accessed not on the basis of a fixed *address* or location but by analysis of their content.

contingency plan: a plan for recovery from disastrous or unplanned events. The intention is to have a plan of action that can be followed by all concerned so that the disruption caused is kept to a minimum. Ideas for contingency planning can include fast call out contracts with a maintenance company, bureaux to run identical software with backed up data, spare computer equipment, systems on more than one site and fault tolerant hardware that switches to backup devices. *Uninterruptable power supplies* and, with large organisations, backup generators, can minimise the dangers of power failure. Damage from fire and flood can be minimised by having detectors and sensors linked to fire extinguishers, by placing the main computing facilities on a high floor and using a fire-proof safe for keeping backups of disks and tapes. Computer rooms can be protected by security systems, swipe cards for entry, etc. Organisations should have *codes of conduct* for employees to prevent problems caused by unauthorised software and *viruses*. See *backup*.

continuous stationery: perforated paper, usually on a roll or in folded form, for use with most impact and *ink-jet printers* and some other printing devices. It is designed for an appropriate paper-feed mechanism, with each sheet connected to the sheets before and after it so that sheets can be printed one after another without the need to load the paper into the printer one sheet at a time. The paper usually has holes punched along each side so that it can be pulled by a tractor-feed device. Continuous stationery can include blank sheets for documents, or business forms such as cheques or invoices.

control character: 1 Any of the first 32 characters in the ASCII character set, 0–31, each of which is defined as having a standard control function, such as carriage return, linefeed, or backspace. Word processing programs often make use of *control keys* in conjunction with other keys, e.g. Ctrl-P (Ctrl +P) to start a new page. See *American Standard Code for Information Interchange* (ASCII).

2 Any of the 26 characters, Ctrl-A to Ctrl-Z, that can be typed at the keyboard by holding down the control key and typing the appropriate letter.

control key: a key labelled CTRL or Ctrl on a PC keyboard that, when pressed in combination with another key, causes a specific action to be taken. See *control character*.

control panel: 1 The display or keypad on a device that allows a user to set various options, e.g. on a printer this may change the paper source or access a menu of options.

2 A utility in Windows and Macintosh systems that allows the user to control aspects of the *operating system* or hardware, such as system time and date, display characteristics and *network* parameters.

conversion: see *changeover, direct changeover, parallel running, parallel changeover, phased conversion, pilot conversion*.

cookies: small *files* that recognise repeat users of a *web site*. These store personal information so that it does not have to be re-entered on each visit. They take up space on the hard drive but are intended to save time. In Windows with Internet Explorer, these are stored in the C:\Windows\Temporary Internet Files directory. Each file takes up 1 Kb.

copyright: the legal right of an author to control the reproduction, distribution and sale of literary, artistic, or intellectual material. Copyright protection extends to written work, music, films, paintings, etc., and now computer software and data. See *Copyright, Designs & Patents Act (1988)*.

Copyright, Designs & Patents Act (1988): this is the act that establishes the rights of authors not to have their work copied and sold without their permission. It now applies to computer software as well as books and other publications. The Act makes it illegal to copy or steal software or distribute copies of manuals that come with software, without the permission of the copyright holder, which is usually the company that produces the software. It is an offence to run software at the same time on more than one machine without purchasing individual copies for each machine or a licence for an appropriate number of copies. It is also illegal to transmit software over a telecommunications line to create a copy. In addition, companies cannot encourage or force employees to make copies of software.

corporate information systems: the hardware, software, data, networks, etc. that make up the *system(s)* within an organisation. See *corporate plan*.

corporate plan: a plan for the whole or parts of an organisation on how to implement its objectives. These can be for the organisation as a whole, or just for finance, marketing, ICT, etc. An organisation should have a corporate plan for ICT to ensure that hardware and software purchased for the organisation is compatible and allows the exchange of data to be straightforward. Organisations with an extensive geographical spread need *local area networks* and a *wide area network* that assists data flow within the organisation. Consideration needs to be given to the information requirements of the management of the organisation and ensuring that the information technology system is in place to deliver this.

correspondence quality: see *letter quality*.

corruption: unintentional change to data in memory or on disk, or to programs which alters their meaning, destroys them or stops them working.

CPS: an acronym for *characters per second*.

crash: the sudden failure of a software application or operating system, or of a hardware device such as a hard disk.

CSV file: an acronym for comma separated values. It is an extension assigned to text files containing tabular data of the type stored in database fields. Individual data entries are separated by commas with a carriage return at the end of each record, e.g. handbook.csv could contain the entries:

> Bob Penrose, writer, A–Z Handbook
> Hodder and Stoughton, publishers, A–Z Handbook

This data could be imported into a database or a *spreadsheet*.

cursor: 1 A symbol on a computer screen, such as a blinking vertical line or underline, that marks the place, usually in text-handling situations, where the next keystroke will appear when typed. When a key is pressed, the cursor automatically moves on to the next typing position.

2 In applications and *operating systems* that use a mouse, the arrow or other icon on-screen that moves with movements of the mouse.

cursor movement/control keys: keys that direct the movement of the *cursor*, generally in text-handling situations. These are also referred to as arrow keys, because each is labelled with an arrow ($\uparrow$ up, $\leftarrow$ left, $\downarrow$ down, $\rightarrow$ right). As well as these four keys, certain others keys, such as Backspace, Home, and End and combinations of these with the control key (Ctrl) also move the cursor around the screen.

customising software: modifying or designing software to suit the needs or preferences of the user or for a specific customer. Certain products allow the developer or user to create, select and customise toolbars and icons. Menus can be amended to meet specific needs. Other products, such as Access, Dbase and Lotus 1-2-3, are designed specifically to provide the flexibility and tools required to produce tailor-made applications that are simplified for a particular user, so that the user need not access the interface supplied with the package. See also *bespoke software.*

cut and paste: a technique for cutting a portion of a document, text, graphic or diagram from one part of the document and then reinserting it elsewhere in the same document or in a different document. The portion to be moved is selected, removed to storage in a temporary memory area such as the *clipboard* (or on to disk) and then copied back where required.

cut-sheet feeder: see *sheet feeder.*

cybernetics is concerned with discovering what mechanisms control systems, in particular, how systems regulate themselves, and translating this into the control of processes by a computer system, e.g. *robotics* and industrial processes. Cybernetics was originally the study of biological and artificial control systems but has evolved into many disparate areas of study. The term was first used in 1943 by Norbert Weiner.

cybershopping: shopping directly over the *Internet.* Many businesses are using the Internet to sell their products and services. Customers can now purchase almost anything: food, flowers, clothes, and even cars. Just as with mail and telephone order shopping, it is important for customers to keep in mind that common sense is required when shopping online. If something sounds too good to be true, it probably is. The same laws that protect you when you shop by telephone or mail apply when you shop in *cyberspace.*

cyberspace: describes the impression of space and community created by computer systems, computer *networks*, and their users, the 'virtual world' that *Internet* users inhabit when they are online. Online systems create a cyberspace within which people can communicate with one another (via *e-mail*), go shopping, or do research. Unlike real space, exploring cyberspace requires only a computer system, and pressing keys or moving a mouse.

The term 'cyberspace' was invented by the author William Gibson in his science fiction novel NEUROMANCER (1984).

D-channel: the channel in the *integrated services digital network* (ISDN), that carries control and signalling information. The B-channel ('B' for 'bearer') carries the main data.

D-to-A converter: see *digital to analogue converter*.

daisywheel printer: an out-of-date impact printing technology in which the characters are embossed on a metal wheel similar to typewriter keys. Printing occurs when a hammer strikes the wheel against the ribbon. The print quality with this type of printer was high, but the process was slower than other printers and it has been superseded by laser printers.

data: a collection of raw facts and figures before they are processed. These can be considered as information that is coded and/or structured for later processing. Data is meaningless unless placed into its correct context. For example, '26' is data. If it is in the context of a house number with a street name then it becomes information.

data archiving: see *archive, archive file*.

data bus: a set of hardware lines (wires) used for data transfer between the components of a computer system.

data capture: the process of collecting information for processing by a computer system. There are several alternative methods from basic input through a keyboard to *optical mark readers* (OMR), *optical character recognition* (OCR), *bar code readers*, *magnetic ink character recognition* (MICR), *data logging* devices such as those used by meter readers and various *sensors* for monitoring temperature, light or weather.

data carrier is another name for a *communications channel*.

data channel is another name for a *communications channel*.

data compression: a means of reducing the amount of space needed to store or transmit a large *file* or *block* of data. There are many different data compression methods suited to different types of files.

data consistency: within a *relational database*, the notion that an item of data is stored only once, however many applications use it. This ensures that when an item requires updating, it needs updating only once and is then consistent whatever use is made of it.

data definition or description language (DDL): a *language* that defines specifically all the attributes and properties of a database, especially *data structures*, *record* layouts, *field* definitions, *key fields*, file locations and storage strategy.

data dictionary: a *file* that stores all the various schema and file specifications about data and their locations within a database, i.e. name and description of each data item, its characteristics (numeric, alphanumeric, date, etc.), what *tables* and *fields* are included, and the relationships between tables. It can also contain information about which programs use which data and which users are interested in which reports. It is not generally accessible to the user.

data directory: another name for *data dictionary*.

data encryption: putting data into a secret code so it is unreadable except by authorised users.

data file symbol: (also called an on-line data file symbol) used in *system flowcharts* to indicate any data held in an *on-line* file, for whatever purpose.

See also *data symbol.*

data flow: the movement of data through a *system*, from input through storage and processing to output.

data flow diagram (DFD): a diagrammatic method of representing the operations and processes within a system. Data flow diagrams use only four symbols:

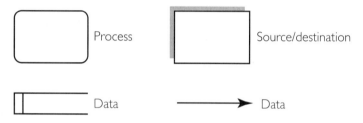

Process is an operation carried out on the data, e.g. sorting it, calculations with it, using it for printing reports.

Source/destination refers to the people or departments providing or receiving the data.

Data stores can be input records, transaction records, files or reports. The symbol can also be used to represent data in a filing cabinet, on a file, on disk or in memory.

Data flow arrows indicate the direction of movement of the data between the above symbols, and should be clearly labelled to indicate the data involved.

It is not always possible to represent the whole of a system within a single diagram. Frequently, several levels of diagram are needed, each one showing more detail than the previous level. A level 0 DFD represents the whole system as one process box. As the system is refined, the diagram can be expanded to show processing of incoming and outgoing data flows. This may then be split into smaller parts of the system to give greater detail. These are referred to as level 1 and level 2 DFDs.

data flowchart: another term for a *data flow diagram.*

data glove: a data *input device* or controller in the form of a glove worn on the hand of a user of a *virtual reality* system. The glove is fitted with sensors that convert movement of the hand and fingers into commands. Data gloves are also known as *wired gloves*.

data importing: to *read* in to an application a data file created by a different application.

data inconsistency: the duplication of data where two or more entries for a data item are different. This generally happens where data is stored in more than one *file* or in a single table with multiple entries.

data independence: the separation of data in a database from the programs that manipulate it. This means that any changes to the data, by the addition of an extra *field* or an extra *table* do not affect the programs that access the data. Data independence makes stored data as accessible as possible.

data input/output symbol: used in *system flowcharts* to indicate any input or output of data, however achieved.

data integrity: the accuracy and correctness of data and its continued correctness, especially after being transmitted or processed. Errors can be caused by incorrect input, by *operators*, program errors, data transmission and in a number of other ways. If data contains errors then it can cause a lack of confidence to users of the data.

data logging: the capture and storage of data for later use.

data-manipulation language (DML): a form of *high-level language* used to access and manipulate data in a *database management system.* The query language is most used is SQL (*structured query language*) and the data can be accessed using a series of statements with this language.

data mining: the process of identifying commercially useful patterns or relationships in very large databases through the use of advanced statistical tools. Data mining is a new technology that looks for things such as trends in data, allowing companies to adjust their marketing strategies. The huge amount of data stored is referred to as a data warehouse.

data model: a diagrammatic representation of a database. It shows the entities (items in the database) and their attributes (the information held about the items). A data model is sometimes referred to as an *entity-relationship diagram* because of this. The relationships between the entities are indicated and successive levels are worked out to give the best working representation of the database before implementation. A simple example is:

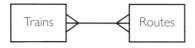

The above diagram shows two entities, Trains and Routes. No attributes are included although these could include, for Trains, the number of carriages, number of passengers, and for Routes the start and finish points and the distance.

Lots of routes can be used by one train and lots of trains can use one route. It is, therefore, a *many-to-many relationship.* This is difficult to implement, so it could be broken down further by adding another entity called Journey. Each train makes lots of journeys but each journey is made by only one train. Similarly each route has many journeys made over it but each journey is only on one route. This would break the diagram down as follows:

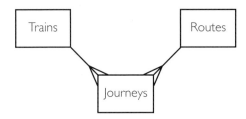

This produces a diagram with two 'one-to-many' relationships, which is much easier to implement.

data-output symbol: see *data input/output symbol.*

data portability: the ability to transfer data from one *package* to another or from one *hardware platform* to another. The notion of portability involves the transfer of data by electronic means thus avoiding errors and the need to re-enter data unnecessarily, which could lead to further errors. Windows programs generally offer easy portability exporting and importing data between packages, and also the facility to use files and data from earlier versions of the software. Documents in different manufacturers' products can also be imported by the use of *filters.*

data preparation: the translation of data into a form that can be read by a computer. *On-line transaction processing* systems do not generally need data preparation.

data-preparation staff: the staff responsible for organising and entering data into a computer system.

data privacy: ensuring that data is kept secret so that it cannot be accessed by unauthorised users.

data processing: the general tasks performed by computers; more specifically, the manipulation of data to transform it into some desired result. Generally this is associated with businesses, banks and government departments, where transactions are carried out on small amounts of data but large numbers of records. Examples are accounting, payroll and stock control.

In addition, it is often the name given to the section of an organisation that carries out the above tasks.

data-processing manager: the person with overall responsibility for the *data processing* department or section.

data-processing symbol: the symbol used in a *flowchart* to indicate where data is being processed. It looks like this:

data protection: the use of various safeguards to ensure the preservation, *integrity*, *privacy* and *reliability* of data.

Data Protection Act 1998: an update to the 1984 Act of Parliament setting out the requirements of the law as applied to the control of personal data stored on computer systems. It also applies to smart cards, document image processors and telephone logging systems. The Act was phased in during 2001. Users of personal data have to register with the *Data Protection Registrar*. Failure to do so can lead to a fine of up to £5000.

The following is a summary from the web site of the Data Protection Commission.

Anyone processing personal data must comply with the eight enforceable principles of good practice. They say that data must be:

- fairly and lawfully processed
- processed for limited purposes
- adequate, relevant and not excessive
- accurate
- not kept longer than necessary
- processed in accordance with the data subject's rights
- secure
- not transferred to countries without adequate protection.

Personal data covers both facts and opinions about the individual. It also includes information regarding the intentions of the data controller towards the individual, although in some limited circumstances exemptions will apply. With processing, the definition is far wider than before. For example, it incorporates the concepts of 'obtaining', holding' and 'disclosing'.

Exemptions to the Act where there is no need to register:

- data for personal, family, household or recreational purposes
- data kept for the purposes of calculating payroll, pension and accounts
- personal data, name and addresses used for mailing lists; individuals have to be asked if they object to their personal data being held by the user
- data that is already required by law to be made public
- data held for the purposes of national security or to fight crime.

The following are useful web site addresses to get more detailed information:

http://www.dataprotection.gov.uk/
http://www.dpr.gov.uk/
http://www.hmso.gov.uk/acts/acts1998/19980029.htm

Individuals are allowed by the Act to gain access to the information held about them and, where appropriate, have the information corrected or deleted. Individuals can make a request to a data user in writing to receive a copy of the personal data held about them. The data user may charge a fee of up to £10 for supplying the information. Individuals can complain to the Data Protection Registrar if they feel that the law has been broken. Individuals can also sue for compensation through the courts if the information held about them has been used in such a way as could damage them.

Data Protection Commissioner: the new name for the Data Protection Registrar to be used when the 1998 *Data Protection Act* is finally in force.

Data Protection Registrar: the role of the registrar is set down in the *Data Protection Act* and the duties include:

- maintaining a register of data users
- making available information about the Act and how it works
- encouraging individuals and organisations to comply with the data protection principles
- encouraging development of codes of practice to assist users in complying with the principles of the Act
- acting as an ombudsman for the consideration of complaints about breaches of the Act
- prosecuting offenders or serving notices on anyone contravening the principles.

data redundancy: unnecessary duplication of data.

data reliability: the degree of confidence that the user can have in data from a particular source.

data representation: converting a character (letter, number or symbol) into a *binary* code. Binary code is a series of 1s and 0s. The most generally used character codes are those of the ASCII system, where a letter 'X' would be represented by 01011000.

data retrieval: extracting meaningful information from stored data, usually from large amounts of data stored in a database. See also *data mining*.

data security: keeping data safe from accidental damage and physical loss. This could be due to fire, floods, theft, hacking, *viruses* or hardware failure such as disk crashes. It should involve systems to restore the data in the event of loss or damage occurring. There should also be procedures in place to prevent the unauthorised changing or deletion of data.

data structure: a method of linking data together to make easier the tasks of interpreting the data or performing operations on it. Data structures include *arrays, linked lists, trees, tables, strings* and *files*.

data symbol: see *data file symbol*.

data terminator: a specified value, frequently −1, 0 or 9999, used to indicate the end of a list of data items. The value has to be one that is not expected to be part of the data. A terminator allows all the items of data to be processed until this value is reached, however many items there are. If data is being entered from a keyboard, then just pressing the Enter or Return key (i.e. a blank input) can be the terminator.

data transmission: the process of using a data link to move data from one data source to another. Data transmission can be:

- serial or parallel
- *duplex, simplex* or *half duplex*
- synchronous or asynchronous (see *synchronous transmission* and *asynchronous transmission*).

Various checks are carried out to ensure the data received is the same as the data sent:

- *parity checks*
- echoing.

data type: a description of the kind of data that a variable in a program is capable of holding. Data types include:

- Boolean – true/false (see *Boolean algebra*)
- *integer* – whole numbers
- real – decimal numbers
- char – a single character
- string – a collection of characters.

In some programming languages programmers are able to define their own data types.

data validation: see *validation.*

data verification: see *verification.*

database: a collection of data that is organised so that its contents can easily be accessed, managed, and updated. The most common type of database is the *relational database*, a tabular database in which data is defined so that it can be reorganised and accessed in a number of different ways. A *distributed database* is one that can be spread to different points in a *network*. An *object oriented programming* database is one that is congruent, with the data defined in *object* classes and subclasses.

database administrator (DBA): the person within an organisation responsible for the supervision, monitoring and control of the database and its functions. These tasks can include some, or all, of the following:

- design and creation of the database
- monitoring the performance of the database
- keeping users informed of changes
- allocating *passwords* and specifying access privileges to individuals
- maintaining the *data dictionary*
- assessing and providing training for users
- determining procedures for *security* and *backups.*

database design: the process of determining the tables, fields, properties, relationships and structures that go into making a database. This process can include the production of *entity-relationship diagrams*, the *normalisation* of the data and the selection of appropriate *primary keys.*

database management system (DBMS): a software *interface* between the database and the user that makes access to the data as straightforward as possible. A database management system allows:

- the definition of the database
- data to be added, deleted and edited
- data to be searched, sorted and reports to be produced
- the structure of the database to be altered
- the user to import and export data
- control of backup, security and data integrity requirements.

Microsoft Access is an example of a DBMS.

database normalisation: see *normalisation.*

database QBE (query by example): see *query by example.*

database security: see *data security.*

database server: a station on a *peer-to-peer network* dedicated to storing and providing access to a shared database. Client stations can access the data and, if authorised, can maintain the database. The server usually carries out the processing of the database. Queries are sent by client stations, the outcomes assembled by the server and returned to the client station.

database SQL (structured query language): see *structured query language*.

database tables: see *table*.

date data: a form of data recognised by a computer as representing a date, e.g. 12/02/01, 12/02/2001, 12-Feb-01.

date stamping: the process of attaching a date to items of data to ensure that they are up-to-date. Date stamping can also apply to data files and reports. This ensures that if there are two versions of a file or report available then the order in which they have been produced is clear.

daughterboard: a small printed circuit board that plugs into a *motherboard* on a personal computer. The motherboard (main circuit board inside a computer) contains the central processing unit, memory sockets, expansion slots, and other components. The additional boards plugged into slots are the daughterboards.

DDE: an acronym for dynamic data exchange.

deadlock: also known as deadly embrace. A situation in which each possible activity is blocked, waiting on some other activity that is also blocked. This can happen for a variety of reasons.

A program example of deadlock would be where process W is waiting for process B to complete at the same time as process B is waiting for process W to complete.

A file example would be user A accessing record 1 and locking it at the same time as User B accesses record 2 and locks it. When user A tries to access record 2 and user B tries to access record 1, before releasing their respective locked records, deadlock is achieved.

debug: to fix problems in hardware or software.

debugger: software that provides a programmer with a variety of tools that can be used to locate *bugs* in programs.

decay (sound): refers to a concept within a sound envelope. It is the rate at which an envelope falls from its initial peak to a steady sustain level.

decision box: a symbol used in *flowcharts* to indicate points where decisions are made in a program.

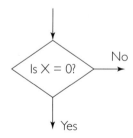

decision support system (DSS): a sophisticated *management information system (MIS)* that comprises a set of programs and related data designed to help with analysis and decision making. A decision support system provides more help in formulating decisions than a *management information system* or an executive information system (EIS), both of which are more passive. It can include a database, a body of knowledge about the subject area, a language used to formulate problems and questions, and a modelling program for testing alternative decisions. Its emphasis is on providing senior management with more information about strategic decisions that have to be made. It does this through the use of sophisticated analysis techniques, extrapolation of figures for forecasting and determining optimum choices from several possibilities.

Decision support systems are usually used in one-off management situations and generally with unstructured data. A simple example would be the use of a *spreadsheet* to provide what-if calculations for various changes in the value of *cells* that could represent prices, profits, etc.

decision table: a table that specifies the actions to be taken when certain conditions occur.

The example below illustrates possible decisions as to whether to allow payment for overtime working. N and Y (no and yes) indicate the value of the conditions. Blank entries indicate that no action is possible or that no action decision is needed.

Condition	Value of condition
Action	Value of action

Weekday	N	Y	Y	Y	Y
Before 5pm		Y	N	N	N
After 5pm			Y	Y	Y
After 6pm			N	N	Y
Permission			N	Y	
Overtime approved	X			X	X

Column 1 indicates that someone working at a weekend always receives overtime. Column 5 indicates that if it is after 6pm then overtime payment is received provided permission has been obtained.

declaration: a statement within a computer program that provides the translator with information on how to treat the objects concerned, rather than specifying actions to carry out. Variables are declared so that the translator knows what kind of data to permit to be stored in them. Arrays are declared so that the required amount of memory can be made available.

declarative language: a language where the program is written as a set of rules and facts rather than as a set of instructions. Prolog is an example of a declarative language.

decoder: hardware or software that translates a coded signal to enable a computer to recognise *instructions* and *addresses*

decollate: to separate the sheets of multi-part *continuous stationery* by tearing along the perforations.

dedicated line: a telephone line that has been leased (rented) for private use. In some contexts, it is called a *leased line*.

de facto standard: a design, program, or language that has become so widely used and successful that it dominates the market, but whose status has not been officially recognised. They are not necessarily technically the best, but have evolved through commercial pressures.

de jure standards: these are standards defined by government or industry groups; i.e. they have not been created by a single company and no-one has the rights to them. They form the basis of connectivity between machines and systems.

default option: a choice made by a program when the user does not specify explicit instructions. Defaults are built into a program when a value or option must be assumed for the program to function. *Files* within a *directory* are listed in alphabetical order unless the user requests them to be listed by size or date. Most defaults are the most commonly used options but can be customised by the user if required.

default value: the most commonly used value in various situations, such as printing one copy. They save the user from having to specify it on each occasion.

defragmentation: *files* that are split and stored on different parts of a disk are said to be *fragmented*. The process of collecting these elements together is called defragmentation. This can improve the access speed of the disk and improve the performance of the system. Most *operating systems* have a defragmentation utility of some sort.

deinstall: the same as *uninstall*.

demodulation: the removal of the modulated carrier wave from a modulated signal to leave the data signal. See *modulation*.

denary notation is the familiar number base 10. It uses hundreds, tens and units, and a numbering system with the digits 0–9.

deque: a double-ended queue; that is a list of elements on which insertions and deletions can be performed at both the front and rear.

DES: see *data encryption standard*.

design: the stage in a *system life cycle* following *analysis*. It is the process of determining how a requirement's specification can be implemented. The designer can consider a range of different approaches to the solution and should look at the user interface, inputs, types and volume of outputs, record layouts, files and file formats, forms and tables required, the processing and procedures required and how data is to be kept secure. Design should also include thorough testing plans and the selection of appropriate hardware to ensure that the system works as required.

Prototyping is a form of design where a working model of part of a system is developed and then amended interactively with a user. This allows for modifications to a design as it proceeds.

design structure diagram: see *structure diagram*.

desktop publishing (DTP): the use of a computer and specialised graphics, charting and page make-up software, to combine text and graphics to create a document that can be printed on either a laser printer or a typesetting machine. The type of software associated with DTP enables the user to layout text and graphics in a sophisticated way on the screen, see what the results will be and make amendments as necessary, before printing or producing files that can be used by a printer for a high-quality final output to produce leaflets, manuals, books, etc.

developmental testing: see *alpha testing* and *beta testing*.

device driver: a piece of software that permits a computer system to communicate with, and control, a device such as a *printer* or *video adapter*. Many devices, especially video adapters on PC-compatible computers, will not work properly without the correct device driver installed on the system. A printer driver, for example, would include features about the printer and its capabilities and the control sequences necessary for the printer to produce various formats and undertake other functions such as paper feed, etc.

diagnostic program: a program that assists a programmer by attempting to detect and locate faults in another program by supervising its operation and listing possible errors.

dial up networking: the use of ordinary telephone lines (with the user paying for the telephone call) to provide *wide area networking* of computers.

dialogue box: in a *graphical user interface*, a special *window* displayed by the system or application to obtain a response from the user. This is usually a choice or a selection from a number of options. It will normally offer the opportunity to cancel the request as well as to continue. For example, a print command can bring up the following dialogue box:

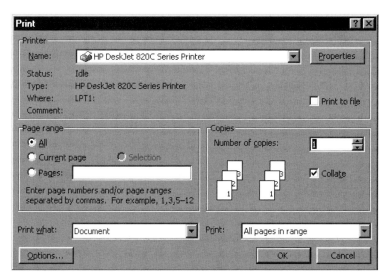

There are options to select the page range, the number of copies, advanced features from the Properties button and also the opportunity to cancel.

dictionary: a list of words used for spell checking in *word processing* and other applications that use text. Sometimes applications can have the facility for a user to add a custom dictionary for unusual, specialist or technical words. Dictionaries can also be provided in a number of languages.

digital camera: a type of camera that captures and stores photographed images electronically instead of on traditional film. The main advantage is that there is no film to develop.

A digital camera uses a charge-coupled device (CCD) element to capture the image through the lens when the operator releases the shutter in the camera; circuitry within the camera then stores the image captured by the CCD in a storage medium such as solid-state memory or a hard disk.

After the image has been captured, it is downloaded by cable to the computer, using software supplied with the camera. Once the image is stored in the computer, special software can be used to manipulate the image, much like the image from a scanner or related input device. Pictures from digital cameras are used in the development of web sites and also in a wide variety of literature.

digital signal: a signal transmitted within or between computers or devices, in which information is represented by discrete bit patterns, for example, high and low voltages, rather than by fluctuating levels in a continuous stream, as in an *analogue signal.*

digital sound generation: the representation of sound waves by numbers and their manipulation to produce music and special effects.

digital-to-analogue converter: a device that translates digital data (e.g. from a CD or CD-ROM) to an *analogue signal* (sound and audio signals). A digital-to-analogue converter takes a succession of discrete digital values as input and creates an analogue signal whose amplitude corresponds, moment by moment, to each digital value.

digital versatile disk (DVD): also known as digital video disk. An optical storage medium which has greater capacity and bandwidth than a *CD.* DVDs can be used for multimedia and data storage. A DVD has the capacity to store a full-length film, including audio track, with up to 133 minutes of high quality video in MPEG-2 format.

digitisation: the process of translating data into digital form (*binary* coded files for use in computers). Examples of digitisation include: scanning images, sampling sound, and converting text on paper into text in computer files.

dimension: a measure of the size of an array in terms of its rows and columns. A one-dimensional array is a simple list, for instance:

Abigail	Debbie	Janet	Lucy	Theresa

A two-dimensional array PEOPLE(3,2) would have three rows and two columns, e.g.:

David	Butcher
Peter	Baker
Tony	Candlestick maker

It is perfectly feasible to have an *n*-dimensional array, but it would have to be visualised in more than the three dimensions that we have.

DIN socket: a multi-pin connector conforming to the specification of the German national standards organisation (Deutsche Industrienorm). DIN connectors are used to link various components in personal computers, the most common of which is a five pin DIN connection for audio systems.

DIP switch: (short for dual inline package switch) one or more small rocker or sliding-type toggle switches mounted together. Each DIP switch can be set to one of two positions, closed or open, to control options on a circuit board.

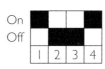

direct access: data is said to be directly accessible if the time taken to access any item of data is roughly the same regardless of its position on the storage medium.

The opposite of direct access is *sequential access*. Disks are direct access media, whereas tapes are sequential access media.

direct addressing: the use without any alteration of the *address* provided in the instruction to access memory. Thus:

> LDA 100

would mean load into the *accumulator* the contents of location 100.

direct changeover is where an existing system is totally replaced by a new system at a certain point in time. The old system is then no longer used at all. Direct changeover is cheap as only one system is in operation at any time. However, it has risks in that there is no backup if the new system does not function as expected or it goes wrong. Staff need higher levels of training to feel confident in moving from a system that they are familiar with to a new system.

direct data entry is the input of data to a key-to-disk unit for *batch processing*. The data might be held in a temporary file and validated before subsequent processing.

direct memory access (DMA): a method of transferring data from one memory area to another without having to go through the central processing unit(CPU). Computers with DMA channels can transfer data to and from devices much more quickly. The use of DMA allows blocks of data to be moved between fast peripherals (*hard disk drives*) and *random access memory* (RAM) very quickly. To transfer a block of data from RAM to disk the CPU provides the DMA controller with the start *address* in memory of the data block to be transferred, and its size.

directive: a statement in a computer program that influences the translation process.

directory: a catalogue for filenames stored on a disk. The topmost directory is called the root directory; the directories within a directory are called *subdirectories*. Filenames in a directory can generally be viewed and ordered in various ways, e.g. alphabetically, by date, by size, or as icons in a *graphical user interface*. In the Macintosh and Windows 9x *operating systems*, directories are called *folders*.

Directories provide a way of grouping *files* for easy organising and access.

disassembler: a program that converts *machine code* back into *assembly language*.

disaster avoidance: measures taken to try to prevent disasters from occurring with computer systems. These measures can take the form of physical measures such as smoke detectors in computer rooms and around the building, uninterruptable and backup power supplies, extra *network* links and technical measures such as strict password management, *virus* scanning software, *firewalls* and regular *backups*.

disaster recovery: see *contingency plan*.

disk access time: the time taken to access a single piece of data on a disk.

disk cache: a temporary storage area for frequently accessed or recently accessed data. Disk cache is a section of *random access memory* (RAM) that provides a cache between the disk and the central processing unit (CPU) of the computer. The use of RAM in this way enables the computer to operate faster by placing recently accessed data in the disk cache. Next time that data is needed it may already be available in the disk cache allowing very fast access to it. Otherwise the hard disk would need accessing, which is relatively much slower.

Disk cache can also be used for writing data to disk. The data is written to disk cache at high speed and transferred to disk during idle machine cycles.

disk cylinder: the set of tracks in a disk pack above each other. Once the *read/write heads* are in position data can be transferred between computer and disk from any of the tracks in a cylinder, without any further movement of the heads.

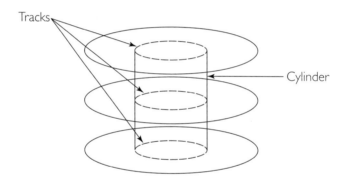

disk drive: the mechanism that rotates the disk and controls the positioning of the *read/write heads* so that data transfer can take place between a magnetic disk and the computer.

disk file symbol: used wherever data is held on disk. The symbol is:

disk formatting: preparing a disk (*floppy disk*, *hard disk*, some forms of *CD*, etc.) so that *data* can be written on it and read back by a computer. Formatting a disk includes creating the physical tracks and sector identification, and creating the indexes specific to the *operating system* that the disk will be used on.

disk pack: a collection of hard disk platters fastened onto a common spindle, allowing large quantities of data to be stored in the same unit. The *disk drive* used has to be capable of handling disk packs since each surface requires its own *read/write head*. These disk drives and disk packs are normally only found on large commercial mainframe computers, although some hard drives in microcomputers use multiple platters.

disk verification: checking to ensure that all sectors on a disk are usable after it has been formatted.

display adapter: see *video adapter*.

distributed database: a database implemented on a *network* where several computers (nodes) share part of the data and co-operate to make it available to the user. Depending on the specific update and retrieval traffic, distributing a database can significantly enhance overall performance.

distributed network: a *network* in which processing, storage, and other functions are handled by the *network operating system* without the user having to take any specific action.

distributed processing: a form of information processing in which work is performed by separate processors on a communications *network*. This type of processing requires a highly structured environment that allows hardware and software to communicate, share resources, and exchange information freely.

DMA: see *direct memory access*.

DML: see *data manipulation language*.

DO loop: a type of loop where the instructions are executed a fixed number of times. See *FOR loop*.

document output symbol: used to indicate that data is to be printed.

document reader: an input device that scans printed text and uses *optical character recognition* to convert it to computer text files. It can also read special forms on which marks or characters are made in pre-determined positions.

documentation: see *maintenance documentation*, *program documentation* and *technical documentation*.

domain name system: a database system that allows the user to convert an *IP address* into a domain name and vice versa. For example, a numeric address like 232.452.120.54 can become something like 'www.abc.com' whereas 'www.mysite.com' returns '123.45.67.89'. Copies of the domain name system are distributed through the *Internet*.

dongle: a piece of hardware that plugs into a standard computer interface and prevents software from running if it is not present. It is used to reduce the possibility of software *piracy*. It is also called a hardware key.

DOS: acronym for disk operating system. See *Microsoft Disk Operating System*.

dot-matrix printer: any printer that produces characters made up of ink dots using a rectangular wire-pin print head. Dot-matrix printers are often categorised by the number of pins in the print head – typically 9, 18, or 24. The quality of the output from a dot-matrix printer depends largely on the number of dots in the matrix, which might be low enough to show individual dots or high enough to approach the look of fully formed characters.

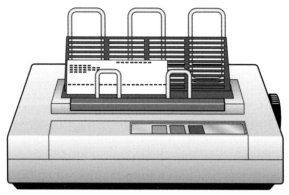

dot pitch: the distance between a dot and the closest dot of the same colour (red, green or blue) on a colour monitor. The smaller the dot pitch, the clearer the image. Monochrome displays do not have dots, and therefore provide a sharper image than the best colour screens.

double buffering: in computer graphics, the process of using two *frame buffers* for smooth animation. The contents of one frame buffer are displayed while updates occur on the other buffer. When the updates are complete, the buffers are switched. Only complete images are displayed, and the process of drawing is not shown. The result is the appearance of smooth animation.

The technique is also used when transferring data between computer and peripheral to ensure the slowest part of the operation (the peripheral) is operational throughout the process. Assuming the transfer is from computer to peripheral:

- the computer fills the first buffer
- the peripheral starts to empty the first buffer and the computer fills the second buffer
- as soon as the first buffer is empty the peripheral moves onto the second buffer which will already be full (the computer fills the buffer faster than the peripheral empties it)
- when the computer receives the signal (handshaking) that the peripheral has moved onto the second buffer it fills the first buffer and waits for the peripheral to empty the second buffer.

This process continues until the data transfer is complete.

double-clicking: pressing and releasing a *mouse button* twice without moving the mouse. Double-clicking is a means of rapidly selecting and activating a program or program feature. A single click may have one effect and a double click may have another.

double precision: using two computer words to represent a number; contrast this with single precision which uses only one computer word to represent a number.

down time: the time during which a computer system or associated hardware is not available. Although down time can occur because hardware fails unexpectedly or through a communications failure, it can also be a scheduled event, as when a *network* is shut down to allow time for *maintenance*.

download: to transfer a copy of a *file* or program from a remote computer to the requesting computer by means of a *modem* or *network*.

DPA: see *Data Protection Act*.

draft quality: a low grade of printing that can be printed quickly. For example, it is generated by the draft mode on *dot-matrix printers*. Draft quality varies among printers, ranging from suitable for most purposes to nearly useless.

drag: in *graphical user interface* environments, to move an image or block of text from one place on the screen to its new location by pulling it using the *mouse*. The mouse pointer is positioned over the object, and the mouse button is pressed and held while the mouse is moved to the new location. Before this can take place the image or text has to be selected in some way, either by highlighting the text or selecting the image. It can also refer to highlighting a range of *cells* in a *spreadsheet*.

drag-and-drop editing: performing operations in a *graphical user interface* by dragging objects on the screen with the *mouse*. For example, in a word processing package, text can be highlighted and then dragged and dropped into a new location. To delete a document, a user can drag the document icon across the screen and drop it on the trashcan icon (Macintosh OS) or in the Recycle Bin (Windows). It is also possible to move text or a graphical item from an application running in one window to a different window running another application. Both applications need to support *object linking and embedding*.

DRAM: see *dynamic RAM*.

drawing package: a package, using *vector graphics* for manipulating object-oriented graphics, as opposed to manipulating *pixel* images such as are used in most Paint packages. In a drawing package, for example, the user can manipulate an element, such as a line, a circle, or a block of text, as an independent object simply by selecting the object and moving it. Objects can be resized, rotated or grouped together to be treated as a single entity for the purpose of moving or copying and can then be ungrouped. Objects can be laid on top of other objects and remain in separate layers.

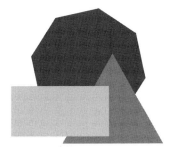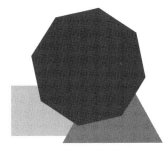

dry run: to execute a program by hand, writing values of variables and other run-time data on paper, in order to check its operation or to track down a *bug*. A dry run is an extreme form of desk check and is practical only for fairly simple programs and small amounts of data.

DTP: see *desktop publishing.*

dual in-line socket: a socket that can be soldered onto a circuit board and is capable of taking the most common forms of integrated circuits (ICs or chips). The dual in-line package for this type of IC is rectangular with vertical pins equally spaced down the two long sides.

dummy variable: a variable that exists in a program, but whose contents are not used for any significant purpose by the programmer. The following segment of Pascal code makes use of a dummy variable 'keyentry'

```
Writeln ('Press any key to continue');
        Readln (keyentry);
```

The term is also used when a variable is used as a temporary holding area for some data. The following segment of Pascal code is used to swap the contents of the two variables ('firstdata' and 'seconddata')

```
        dummydata := firstdata;
        firstdata := seconddata;
        seconddata := dummydata;
```

The variable 'dummydata' can be described as a dummy variable since its contents are never used after the swap has taken place.

dump: a large mass of information about a problem, or the state of a system, giving the contents of each byte of memory, mass storage, or some *file.*

duplex: in a communications system, the ability to simultaneously transmit and receive data.

dynamic IP address: a temporary *IP address* allocated by an *Internet service provider* to a computer, which does not have a static IP address, when it connects to the *Internet* using its services. A static IP address is a dotted quad number that is assigned to a computer by an Internet service provider to be its permanent address on the Internet. Computers use IP addresses to locate and talk to each other on the Internet. When a user wants to visit a web site a request is made for the correct dotted quad number from a *domain name system* server and the answer is used to connect to the required web site.

It would be simple if every computer that connects to the *Internet* could have its own static IP number, but when the Internet was first conceived, the architects didn't foresee the need for an unlimited number of IP addresses. Consequently, there are not enough IP numbers to go around. To overcome this problem, many Internet service providers limit the number of static IP addresses they allocate, and economise on the remaining number of IP addresses they possess by assigning a dynamic IP address from a pool of IP addresses to a user for the duration of the connection.

dynamic RAM (DRAM): a type of computer *memory* that is stored in capacitors on a chip and requires a refresh signal to be sent to it periodically. Most computers have DRAM chips, because they provide a lot of memory at a low cost.

EAROM: acronym for electrically alterable *read-only memory*.

ease of maintenance: a term used to describe how well a program or system has been written or produced to allow modifications to be made easily and cheaply.

ease of use: a term used describe how well a program can be operated with a minimum of training and support. Applications across a suite of programs can be designed with similar menu structures and tool bars to ensure that users feel comfortable with them and do not need to learn too many new operations.

echo: 1 A feature of *data transmission* in which a signal is transmitted back to the sender to check the original signal. *Network* connections can be tested by sending an echo back to the main computer.

2 To echo input by displaying data on the screen as it is received from the keyboard.

e-cash: a form of *electronic funds transfer* via the *Internet*. There are several systems being developed to allow the public to pay for goods purchased on the *World Wide Web*.

e-commerce: the use of computers and electronic communications through an online information service, web sites, a digital television or a *wireless application protocol* (WAP) telephone for individual commercial activity such as banking, shopping and gambling and also business-to-business transactions. Many businesses, such as supermarkets, booksellers, travel agents, car dealers and numerous others, now sell their products or services through web sites. Advantages are lower prices for goods and services, the ability to view and select products from home, pay for them electronically and have them delivered frequently within 24 to 48 hours. E-commerce can allow products to be purchased directly from other countries. It can considerably benefit those people that for one reason or another cannot get to shops, such as the elderly or those living in remote areas. The main drawbacks are the inability to view and handle actual products and the poor backing provided by delivery services that often cannot deliver larger items when people are home. Various methods are being trialled such as central collection points and secure boxes attached to people's homes, where goods can be left.

Business-to-business e-commerce can provide considerable savings, as orders can be taken on-line and invoices and settlements completed electronically. This can reduce costs and improve efficiency.

edit: to make a change to an existing file or document. Changes to the existing document are saved in memory or in a temporary file but are not added to the document until the program is instructed to save them. Editing programs typically provide safeguards against inadvertent changes, for example by requesting confirmation before saving a file under an existing filename.

editor: see *text editor*.

e-form: (short for electronic form) an online document that contains blank spaces for a user to fill in with requested information. It can be submitted through a *network* to the user or organisation requesting the information.

eight-to-fourteen modulation (EFM): the conversion of 8-bit binary codes to 14-bit codes. In magnetic media, a byte commonly has eight bits, whereas optical media such as CD-ROM disks use a 14-bit byte, a modification necessary because of the way data is stored and *read* with lasers, using the pits (indentations) and lands (spaces between indentations) on the disk. In transferring from magnetic to optical media, the 8-bit byte has to be modulated to a 14-bit byte and demodulated when data is read back. See *modulation* and *demodulation*.

e-learning: taking a course or training via the *Internet*. There are many training courses available; one of the most frequently used in the UK is Learndirect (www.learndirect.co.uk).

electronic data interchange (EDI): a system that allows users to exchange business documents, such as purchase orders and invoices, between computers. The aim of EDI is the elimination of paperwork and a reduced response time. For EDI to be effective, users must agree on certain standards for formatting and exchanging information. It is a system that is in use by schools and colleges with examination boards to transfer data such as entries and examination results.

electronic funds transfer (EFT) is the use of computer *networks* to transfer money. Most companies now pay their employees by electronic funds transfer into their personal bank or building society accounts. Banks use this method where transfer of money is required between branches of the same bank or between different banks. The banks can also be in different countries.

electronic funds transfer at point-of-sale (EFTPOS): is an alternative to payment by cheque or credit card, used by retail stores. The purchaser has a debit card that is processed in a similar fashion to a credit card, but the money in the purchaser's account is transferred directly to the retailer's account.

electronic signature: a short text file that has the name of the user and contact information, which is automatically attached to *e-mail* messages and *newsgroup* postings. Some people include ASCII art, slogans, etc. in their signatures

e-mail (or email): 1 Short for electronic mail. The sending of text messages and/or computer files from user to user over a communications *network*, such as a *local area network*, the *Internet*, a television with a digital service or a WAP telephone. The message is typed and the sender gives giving the recipient's *e-mail address*. The message is transmitted through various gateways and servers to the recipient's mailbox. The next time that the recipient logs on, he or she will be told that a message is waiting or being received and will then be able to read it, print it or look at the attachments.

2 An electronic text message.

3 To send an e-mail message.

E-mail is relatively cheap, extremely quick compared to normal post ('snail-mail') and is proving to be a major way of communicating both within offices, around the country and between countries. Users do not have to be at their machines to receive messages. Messages can be less formal and replies can be sent by clicking on a Reply button. Disadvantages are that not everyone has the necessary equipment. E-mail is often used when a telephone conversation would be more appropriate. Using e-mail can abdicate responsibility for taking action. Companies are frequently now putting in place codes of conduct for the use of e-mail as there are issues of security and libel associated with its use.

e-mail address: a string that identifies a user so that they can receive *e-mail*. An e-mail address typically consists of a name that identifies the user to the mail server, followed by @ (an 'at' sign) and the *host* name and domain name of the mail server. For example, if Bob Penrose has an account with an *Internet service provider* called msnaol, he might have an e-mail address bp@msnaol.com.

embedded object: an object, such as a *graphic*, which has been placed in a document from another file.

employee code of conduct: see *codes of conduct*.

em space: a typographic unit of measure which is the same as the width of a capital M in a given font. See *en space*.

emulation: the process of a computer, or a program imitating the function of another computer or program. It can allow software designed for one computer (X) to be run on a different type of computer (Y) if an emulator of X is present on Y. This can extend the range of software available to a type of machine. However, emulation will almost always run at a slower rate than on a machine for which it was designed.

en space: a typographic unit of measure which is the same as the width of a capital N in a given font. See *em space*.

encapsulation: 1 The technique used by layered *protocols* in which a layer adds header information to the protocol data unit (PDU) from the layer above. For example, in *Internet* terminology, a *packet* would contain a header from the physical layer, followed by a header from the network layer (IP), followed by a header from the transport layer (TCP), followed by the application protocol data. See *open systems interconnection seven layer model*.

2 In *object oriented programming* the technique of keeping together *data structures* and the methods (procedures) which act on them. This involves the inclusion within a program object of all the resources needed for the object to function, i.e. the object is self-contained. The object is said to 'publish its interfaces' and other objects that want to use the object use these interfaces without having to be concerned with how the object carries out its task. The underlying principle is 'don't tell me how you do it; just do it'.

encryption: the process of encoding data to prevent unauthorised access, especially during transmission. This adds a level of security to data transfer. Encryption is usually based on encoding and decoding *algorithms* using one or more keys or codes. It is essential for decoding (returning the data to readable form) that both users have a copy of the key. Generally a single cipher key is sufficient for most purposes, although, where extra protection is required, it is possible to have different enciphering and deciphering keys. Encryption is used to protect e-mail messages, credit card information, and corporate data. One of the most popular encryption systems used on the *Internet* is *Pretty Good Privacy* because it is effective and free. See *public key cryptography*.

end key: a cursor-control key that moves the cursor to a certain position, usually to the end of a line, the end of a screen, or the end of a file, depending on the program.

end-of-file (EOF) marker: a special character or sequence of characters that marks the end of a file. There are two methods *operating systems* use to keep track of where every file ends. The first puts a special end-of-file marker at the end of each file, the second keeps track of how many characters are in the file.

enter key: the key that is used at the end of a line or command to instruct the computer to process the command or text. In word processing programs, the Enter key is used at the end of a paragraph to start a new paragraph. It is also called the Return key.

entity: an item to be represented in a database. The item could be a customer, video, supplier, etc. See also *data model.*

entity relationship: a connection (relationship) between items (*entities*) in a database. A student, for example, takes many courses and each course is taken by many students. See also *data model.*

entity-relationship diagram: a diagrammatic way of showing *entity relationships.* This is a simple example of a many-to-many relationship:

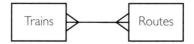

The above diagram shows two entities, Trains and Routes. See also *data model.*

envelope: see *volume envelope.*

equivalence (EQ) gate: see *XNOR gate.*

erasable programmable read-only memory (EPROM): a memory chip onto which data can be written and subsequently erased. EPROMs are manufactured as blank chips but data can be written onto them with an EPROM programmer or EPROM burner. Like ROMs, EPROMs retain their data when power is removed. See *read-only memory.*

error detection and correction: methods for detecting and correcting errors in transmitted or stored data, such as *parity* bits and the cyclic redundancy check.

error message: a message that appears on the computer screen to let the user know the computer cannot carry out an instruction, or there is some other problem.

escape key (Esc): a key on the keyboard that sends the escape (Esc) character to the computer. In many applications, the Esc key *exits* the program or moves the user back one level in the menu structure.

Ethernet: the most popular type of *local area network*, which sends its communications through radio frequency signals carried by a *coaxial cable.* Each computer checks to see if another computer is transmitting and waits its turn to transmit. If two computers accidentally transmit at the same time and their messages collide, they wait and send again in turn. Software protocols used by Ethernet systems vary, but include Novell Netware and transmission control protocol/Internet protocol (TCP/IP).

Each computer has a network card with its own Ethernet address (the physical *address* of the Ethernet controller board, expressed as a 48-bit number in hexadecimal notation) that enables the computer to connect to the Ethernet network.

European Article Number (EAN): a numbering system used to identify products. The number is usually represented by a *bar code*. Another method of representing product numbers is the *universal product code* (UPC).

European Union Data Protection Directive: a directive passed by the European Union in 1995 in order to harmonise and strengthen data protection laws throughout the member states of the EU. It led in the UK to revisions to the *Data Protection Act* (1998) phased in for 2001.

European Union Health and Safety Regulations: a directive passed by the European Union in 1992 in order to control health problems associated with the use of computer equipment. See *health and safety*.

even parity: see *parity*.

event-driven program: a program that waits for events to occur and responds to them, instead of going through a prearranged series of actions. In this context an event is an occurrence that is significant to a program, and which may call for a response from the program, e.g. a user clicking a mouse somewhere on the screen, or entering a keyboard command.

exception reports provide management with information on items where some action may need to be taken. For example, it could be a list of stock that has fallen below expected sales. It is not necessary to print out all stock items, which may run to thousands, but only those that do not meet the sales targets.

exclusive-NOR gate: see *XNOR gate*.

exclusive-OR gate: see *XOR gate*.

executable program: to execute a *program* is to start it running. An executable program is a file that is capable of being executed or run as a program in the computer. In the MS-DOS or *Windows* operating systems, an executable file usually has a file name extension of .bat, .com, or .exe.

execute: 1 To run a program.

2 A computer has a fetch cycle, when it is locating its next instruction, and an execute cycle, when it is carrying out the instruction

execution error: an error that occurs while a program is running. This type of error can occur, for instance, when the program cannot find a file specified by the program, when a program tries to close/open a file that is already closed/open, or when an attempt is made to divide by zero, etc.

executive information system: a set of tools designed to organise information into categories and reports for senior managers and directors. Because the emphasis is on information, an executive information system differs from a *decision support system* (DSS), which is designed for analysis and decision-making. An executive information system should allow senior personnel to move from high-level information down the more detailed information on which the high-level information is based. In such a system, data can be manipulated, comparisons can be made and presentations can be prepared. The systems are generally designed to be user friendly, as executives often have only limited IT skills. See also *management information system.*

exit: 1 An option on a menu that allows the user to quit a program.

2 In a program, to move from a called routine back to the calling routine. A routine can have more than one exit point, thus allowing termination based on various conditions.

expert systems: an application program that attempts to emulate human reasoning in some specialised field. The software makes decisions or solves problems in the particular field, such as finance or medicine, by using knowledge and analytical rules defined by experts in the field. It uses two components: a knowledge base containing the facts and rules provided by human experts and an inference engine designed to form conclusions. Such systems can help decision makers by improving the speed at which certain tasks are done, providing consistent recommendations in similar sets of circumstances and providing a volume of knowledge not necessarily available to the user. However, these systems can make mistakes. If the appropriate knowledge programmed in is inaccurate, is not built in or has changed, then the decisions can be inaccurate. Users can feel undervalued for their own skills and therefore be reluctant to learn. The systems do not learn by their mistakes. These systems are also known as *knowledge-based systems*.

exponent: in a floating point number, the numeric value which indicates the power of the radix (base) to be used. For example, in $2\,746\,000 = 2.746 \times 10^6$, 2.746 is the mantissa, 10 is the radix, and 6 is the exponent.

export: to move a *file* created using one application from that system or program to another so that it can be read by other software. There are standard formats for data transfer between packages to reduce the problems of moving information. Files that consist of text only can be exported in ASCII (plain text format). For files with graphics, however, the receiving system or program must offer some support for the exported file's format. The process of reading or accepting a file produced by some other software is called *importing*. This is a different process from that of *cut and paste*.

extended binary coded decimal interchange code (EBCDIC): an 8-bit binary code normally used only on mainframe computers in which each *byte* represents one alphanumeric character or two decimal digits. EBCDIC also contains control commands along with codes for all the characters found on a *QWERTY keyboard*. EBCDIC is similar to ASCII code, which is used on most other computers.

extended graphics array (XGA): a *super video graphics array* (VGA) system that can provide up to 1024×768 *pixels* and 65,536 colours. The actual resolutions available depend on the combination of XGA card and monitor.

extended industry standard architecture (EISA) bus: a PC *bus* that extends the ISA bus from 16 bits to 32 bits, but can still be used to plug in ISA expansion cards. The ISA bus is a PC expansion bus that is used for modems, video displays, speakers, and other peripherals. PCs with ISA commonly have some 8-bit and some 16-bit expansion slots.

external modem: a *modem* that is outside the computer case and is plugged into the *serial port*.

extranet: the part of a company or organisation's internal computer *network* that is available to outside users, for example, information services for customers. The extranet forms an extension of a company's *intranet* out onto the *Internet*, e.g. to allow selected customers, suppliers and mobile workers to access the company's private data and applications via the *World Wide Web*. The extranet is usually in addition to the company's public web site that is accessible to everyone. The difference can be somewhat blurred, but generally an extranet implies *real-time* access through a *firewall* of some kind. Such facilities require very careful attention to security but are becoming an increasingly important means of delivering services and communicating efficiently.

e-zine: an electronic magazine. Many e-zines are online versions of printed magazines.

facilities management is the contracting to an outside agency of the computer operations and IT support for an organisation. The facilities management company runs the operations, employs its own staff and guarantees that breakdowns in the service are dealt with quickly and efficiently. The operations can involve hardware support and maintenance and software development. The organisation generally pays a fixed monthly or annual fee and hopes to avoid the breakdowns and repairs associated with purchasing and administering its own equipment.

The advantages to the organisation are not having to employ and train IT personnel, breakdowns are the responsibility of the facilities management company and backup and recovery are also their responsibility.

The disadvantages are that the organisation is totally dependent upon an outside agency that may increase its fees, it could fail to deliver what was agreed, and the data belonging to the organisation could be at risk, as it is being handled by an outside agency. If the facilities management company goes out of business, the cost of transferring or setting up an IT department could be extremely high.

facsimile machine: see *fax machine.*

false: one state of a *Boolean variable* which can hold only one of two values: True or False.

fan-fold paper: continuous paper with holes on the edges, folded like a fan with each page folded in the opposite direction to the page before. Fan-fold paper is used in *tractor-feed dot-matrix printers.* After printing, the pages are separated along the perforations and the edge strips torn off.

FAST: see *Federation Against Software Theft.*

fax (facsimile) machine: a device that scans and digitises pages, and transmits the image through a telephone line. A fax machine at the receiving end decodes the images and prints them on paper.

An alternative type of fax operation makes use of a *fax modem* within a computer. This allows faxes to be sent from one computer to another, with a fax modem eliminating the need to scan a paper copy. The documents are sent as graphics, however, and cannot, therefore, be transferred directly to a word processing application without some form of *optical character recognition* scanning software. The advantage is that faxes arriving this way can be received automatically by the fax modem and stored until a suitable time when they can be read.

fax modem: a *modem* that has the capability of sending and receiving fax documents. Text and graphic documents can be converted into fax format by special software usually provided with the modem; paper documents must first be scanned in. Fax modems may be internal or external and may combine fax and conventional modem capabilities. See also *fax (facsimile) machine.*

feasibility study: an evaluation in depth of a prospective project for the purpose of determining whether or not the project should be undertaken. Feasibility studies normally consider the time, budget, and technology required for completion and decide whether or not the project is cost effective. Technical issues that may indicate that the project is not feasible should be considered, e.g. poor response times. The economic considerations are more difficult to judge, in that it may be possible to determine a reasonable estimate for the cost of the project but not to determine accurately whether the benefits from implementation are enough. Factors such as changes, loss of jobs, levels of service, customer satisfaction, prestige, etc. are almost impossible to quantify. The social effects of job loss, deskilling and job satisfaction are also points to consider. A feasibility study would normally be presented to the management of the organisation as a report describing the costs, benefits, possible alternatives and recommendations.

Federation Against Software Theft (FAST): an organisation that pursues breaches of software *copyright* and tries to prevent the illegal use of software. It works on behalf of major software companies and has a policy of prosecuting anyone found to be in breach of copyright law.

feedback: a control system that monitors its inputs and modifies its outputs to control the way the system works. For example, for a thermostat the input is the actual temperature and the set value is the required temperature. The output of the thermostat turns a heater on or off. By monitoring the actual temperature and adjusting the output (turning the heater on or off) the thermostat tries to equalise the actual and required temperatures.

Computer *disk drives* use feedback control to position the *read/write heads* accurately on a recording track.

fetch execute cycle: see *instruction cycle*.

fetch phase: see *instruction cycle*.

fibre-distributed data interface (FDDI) is a standard for *data transmission* on *fibre-optic cables* that can extend in range up to 200 km (124 miles). The FDDI protocol is based on the token ring protocol. In addition to being geographically large, an FDDI *local area network* can support thousands of users. An FDDI network contains two token rings, one for possible backup in case the primary ring fails. The primary ring offers up to 100 Mbps capacity. If the secondary ring is not needed for backup, it can also carry data, extending capacity to 200 Mbps. The single ring can extend the maximum distance; a dual ring can extend 100 km (62 miles). See also *token-ring network*.

fibre-optic cable: a cable made up of glass (or plastic) threads (fibres) that carries laser light, encoded with digital signals, rather than electrical energy. Fibre-optic cables can transmit large amounts of data per second and cannot be tapped by remote sensing equipment because they do not emit electromagnetic radiation.

The main advantage of using fibre optic cables is that data can be transmitted digitally (the natural form for computer data) rather than in analogue form.

The main disadvantage of fibre optics is that the cables are expensive to install because they are more fragile than wire and are difficult to split.

field: 1 A location in a *record* at which a particular type of data is stored. For example, CUSTOMER_RECORD might contain fields to store First_name, Last_name, Address, City, Post_Code and so on. Individual fields are characterised by their maximum length and the type of data (for example, alphabetic, numeric, date or financial) that can be placed in them.

2 In an on-screen form, a space where a user can enter a specific item of information.

field name: the designation given to each *field*, (e.g. Last_name) that identifies the data in the field and makes it clear what type of data is being processed.

field separator: a character, such as a comma or tab, used to separate the *fields* in a database *record*.

field type identifies the type of data stored within a *field*, e.g. alphabetic, numeric, date or financial. This allows for limited validation and specifies the types of operation that can be performed on that field.

FIFO (first in, first out): a method of processing a *queue*, in which items are removed in the same order in which they were added. The first item in is the first out. A typical FIFO set up would be a list of documents in a print queue, waiting to be printed.

fifth-generation computers are still as yet undefined and are yet to appear, although they are expected to combine *very-large-scale integration* (VLSI) with sophisticated approaches to computing, including *artificial intelligence* and true distributed processing. In addition, new methods of interaction with computers, such as more sophisticated speech and touch, could be incorporated.

file: a complete, named collection of related information, such as a *program*, a set of data used by a program, or a user-created document. Traditionally, files are thought of as collections of identically structured *records*, made up of *fields* contained as a single unit. See also *file extension*.

file access: see *direct access, index sequential access method, sequential access*, and *serial access*.

file-allocation table (FAT): a table or list held on disk by some *operating systems* to maintain and manage disk space used for *file* storage. Files are stored on a disk, as space allows, in fixed-size groups of bytes (characters), rather than from beginning to end as an undivided string of text or numbers. A single file can be broken up into clusters over many separate storage areas. The file allocation table maps and links together the pieces of a file. This is done with a *pointer* at the end of each entry that points to the next cluster relating to that file. The last entry has a special indicator to show that this is the last part of the file. In Windows 98, there is a FAT32 file system, an enhancement of the file allocation table (FAT or FAT16) file system formats. When the hard drive is in this format, it stores data more efficiently, creating up to several hundred megabytes of extra disk space on the drive.

file attribute: a *label* attached to a *file* that describes and regulates its use, for example, hidden, system, read-only and archive. In MS-DOS, this information is stored as part of the file's *directory* entry. (See illustration on page 69.)

file directory: see *hierarchical directory structure*.

file extension: a set of characters added to a filename that serves to extend or clarify its meaning or to identify a *file* as a member of a category. An extension may be assigned by the user or by a program. In MS-DOS, for example, .com or .exe are used for executable programs that can load and run. A list of file extensions can be found in an appendix at the back of this book.

file format: the structure of the contents of a *file* that defines the way it is stored and laid out on the screen or in print. This determines which software can be used with the file and whether an applications package can load and run it. The format can be fairly simple and common, as are files stored as ASCII text, or it can be quite complex and include various types of control instructions and codes used by programs, printers, and other devices. Examples of the latter include RTF (Rich Text Format), CSV (comma separated variable), DIF (data interchange format), TSV (tab separated variable), TIFF (tagged image file format), and EPSF (encapsulated PostScript format). See also *file extensions.*

file operations: the activities that can be performed on a data file, such as *read*, *write*, insert, *append*, read-only and *update.*

file server: a file-storage device on a *local area network* that is accessible to all users on the *network.* A file server has software that manages the files and allows network users to access their own files and make changes to them from any station on the network. On local area networks, a file server is often a computer with a large hard disk that is dedicated only to the task of managing shared files.

file sharing: the public or private sharing of computer *data* or space in a *network* with various levels of access rights. *File* sharing allows a number of people to *read*, view, *write*, modify or *print* the data in the same file at the same time.

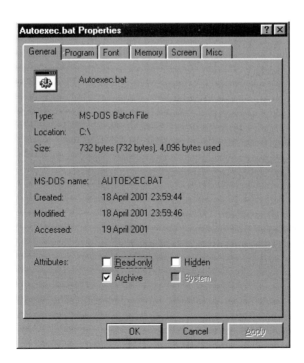

File attribute (see page 68)

file transfer: the process of moving or transmitting a *file* from one location to another, for example between two programs or over a *network*.

file-transfer protocol (FTP): a standard *Internet protocol*, FTP uses the *Internet's transmission control protocol/Internet protocols* and is the simplest way to exchange *files* between computers on the Internet. FTP is commonly used to transfer *web page* files from their creator to the computer that acts as their server for everyone on the Internet. It is also commonly used to download programs and other files to a user's computer from other servers.

file type: see *file format* and *file extension*.

filter: an option in an application that allows a user to *import files* from or *export* files to another application. Examples are documents in WordPerfect, WordStar or earlier versions of Word that can be imported into the latest version of Word without losing any work.

firewall: a *security* system intended to protect an organisation's *network* against external threats, and prevent unauthorised access, such as *hackers*, coming from the *Internet*. A firewall is usually a combination of hardware and software, and is placed between the network *file server* and the external network, thus preventing computers in the organisation from communicating directly with computers external to the network and vice versa. All communication is routed through the firewall and the firewall decides whether it is safe to let a particular message or *file* pass through to the organisation's network. An access log can be created to keep a record of all attempts to access the network. This can be checked to see if any attempts at unauthorised access have been made.

firmware: *software* that is inserted into programmable *read-only memory*, thus becoming a permanent part of a computing device. Firmware is created and tested like software and when ready can be distributed like other software. Using a special user interface it is installed in the programmable read-only memory by the user. Firmware is sometimes distributed for printers, modems, and other computer devices.

first in, first out: see *FIFO*.

first normal form: see *normalisation of data*.

fixed-point notation: a notation system that allows real numbers to be held in *binary* form with the decimal point in its correct position. When calculations are carried out the position of the point is normally maintained. Using this notation the number 13.75 would be held in binary, with eight bits before the point and eight bits after the point as:

00001101.11000000

flag: a *field* or bit sequence setting in a small data area that is used by a program either to remember something or to leave a sign for another program. For example, a procedure could set a flag to indicate if a search had been successful.

flash memory: a type of constantly-powered non-volatile *memory* that can be erased and reprogrammed in units of memory called *blocks*. It is a form of electrically erasable programmable *read-only memory* (EEPROM). However, whereas EEPROM is erased and rewritten byte by byte, flash memory is reprogrammed in blocks, which is faster than EEPROM updating. Flash memory is often used to hold control code such as the *basic input output system* (BIOS) in a personal computer. Updating BIOS is quick if flash memory has been used. However flash memory cannot be used as RAM since for this use individual bytes need to be addressable.

flatbed plotter: an output device that draws lines on paper. The paper is held on a flat platform and a pen moves along both axes, travelling across the paper to draw an image. This method is slightly more accurate than that used by drum plotters, which move the paper under the pen. Flatbed plotters can also accept a wider variety of media because the drawing surface does not need to be flexible.

flatbed scanner: a *scanner* with a flat transparent surface that holds the image to be scanned. This is usually a book or other paper document. A scan head below the surface moves across the image.

flat file: a *file* consisting of *records* of a single record type in which there is no embedded structure information governing relationships between records. It can be kept in a single table. The following is an example of a flat file:

Members

Last name	First name	Address
Brown	Tom	10 Margate Road, Anytown
Jones	Dick	25 Culver Close, Anytown
Smith	Mary	36 Acacia Avenue, Sometown

flat file database: a database that takes the form of a single table. It is the electronic equivalent of a card index file. A flat file database can work only with one file at a time. It has a limited use in that a user can only do simple sorts and searches.

flexibility: see *program features*.

floating-point notation: a notation system where *real numbers* are expressed using three parts: the sign (plus or minus), the *mantissa* which is the digits that are meaningful, and the *exponent* which determines the place to which the decimal point floats. By increasing the size of the exponent the range of numbers that can be held is increased, whereas increasing the number of bits allocated to the mantissa increases the accuracy with which the numbers are held. Because the total number of bits available to store a number is normally fixed, increasing the range reduces the accuracy with which the numbers are held, and increasing the accuracy reduces the range of numbers that can be held. Generally, floating point numbers are normalised which means that the exponent is adjusted and the point 'floated' until it is in front of the most significant bit in the mantissa of a positive number. Thus:

$$0.1001000 \times 2^{00001011} \text{ is normalised}$$

whereas

$$0.0001001 \times 2^{00001000} \text{ is not normalised}$$

Normalising ensures that the maximum precision is achieved and multiplication can be carried out more accurately.

floating-point unit: a separate microprocessor, or special circuitry in a more general microprocessor that manipulates numbers more quickly than the basic microprocessor. The floating-point unit has a special set of instructions that focus entirely on large mathematical operations.

floppy disk: a *random access*, removable data storage medium that can be used with personal computers. Also called a '3.5 inch diskette', it can store up to 1.44 megabytes (Mb) of data. Although most personal computers today come with a 3.5 inch diskette drive pre-installed, some *network* computers now omit them. Floppy disks are convenient for storing individual *files* and small programs.

floppy disk drive: an electromechanical device that writes data to and reads data from *floppy disks*. Generally designated as drive A:, and B: where a second floppy drive is in use.

flowchart: see *program flowchart.*

folder: in the Macintosh *operating system,* 32-bit versions of Windows, and some other operating systems, it is a container for programs and *files.* It is an alternative name for a *directory.* In *graphical user interfaces,* it is symbolised on the screen by an icon of a file folder.

font: a set of printing or display characters of the same typeface (such as Arial or Courier), style (such as *italic*), and weight (such as **bold**). Fonts are used by computers for on-screen displays and by printers for hard-copy output. In both cases, the fonts are stored either as *bitmaps* (patterns of dots) or as outline fonts (defined by a set of mathematical formulae). See also *TrueType font.*

footer: one or more identifying lines printed at the bottom of a page. A footer may contain a variety of information such as a page number, a date, the document title and/or the author's name. Once entered, the information repeats on each page within the document or section as specified. It is possible to exempt the first page of a document and have different footers in each section or for odd and even pages. See also *header.*

footprint: the amount of space a particular unit of hardware or software occupies. With hardware, this is physical space; with software it is the amount of memory or processing power that the software needs.

Marketing brochures frequently state that a new hardware unit or desktop display has a 'smaller footprint', meaning that it occupies less desk space than a comparable version produced by another company.

Software footprints have become steadily larger as more features are added to software packages. This means that they require more memory, faster processors and greater amounts of backing storage space.

FOR loop: a *loop* construct available in all high-level programming languages that repeats a block of instructions a fixed number of times determined by the loop control variable.

```
FOR count := startvalue TO endvalue
Block of Instructions
```

In the above example the block of instructions will be executed the number of times indicated by the contents of the variables 'startvalue' and 'endvalue'.

foreground/background processing: organisation of the tasks being processed by a computer system into foreground and background tasks. The foreground tasks are the important ones and are given access to the processor whenever they require it, whereas background tasks make use of the processor whenever it is not being used by foreground tasks. On personal computers printing is often carried out as a background task, allowing the user to continue word processing (foreground task) whilst the printing happens. Only when the user is not typing, spell checking, etc., will the data from the document to be printed be transferred to the printer.

foreign key: a *field* in one *table* of a *relational database* that is also a *primary key* in another table. It is not a key in its own table. The format of the foreign key must be identical to that of the primary key in the linked table. Foreign keys are used to establish relationships between tables. See also *normalisation of data*.

form feed: a printer command that tells a printer to move to the top of the next page. In the ASCII character set, the form-feed character has the decimal value 12 (hexadecimal 0C). Form feed is also used for ejecting a page from a printer.

form letter: a letter created for printing and distribution to a group of people whose names and addresses are taken from a database and inserted by a *mail merge* program into a single basic document.

format:

1 (i) The layout of data storage areas (*tracks* and *sectors*) on a disk.
   (ii) To prepare a disk for use by organising its storage space into a collection of tracks and sectors, each of which can be located by the *operating system* so that data can be sorted and retrieved. When a previously used disk is formatted, any information already on it is lost.
2 The specifications for text on a page or in a paragraph. See *formatting*.
3 (i) The attributes of a *cell* in a *spreadsheet*, such as its being alphabetic or numeric, the number of digits, the use of commas, and the use of currency signs.
   (ii) To change the appearance of selected text or the contents of a selected cell in a spreadsheet.
4 The arrangement of data within a document file that typically permits the document to be read or written by a certain application. Many applications can store a file in more than one format.
5 The order and types of fields in a database.

format toolbar: a *toolbar* within an application used for modifying the format of the text and paragraphs within the document being displayed. This can include changing the font, font size or characteristic, justification, indenting, etc.

formatting: 1 The elements of style and presentation that are added to documents through the use of *margins*, *indents* and different *font* sizes, styles and characteristics.

2 The process of initialising a *floppy* or *hard disk* so that it can be used to store information.

forms dialogue: a user *interface* where the screen is set up to look like a paper form. The computer prompts for inputs in each field. This can be text, selections from a drop-down list or check boxes. Entries can be changed at any stage until the user is satisfied and the form can be processed.

formula: a mathematical statement that describes the actions to be performed on numeric values. A formula sets up a calculation without regard to the actual values it is to act upon. An example would be $(13 + (X * Y))$, with X and Y representing whatever values the user designates. Through formulae, users of applications such as *spreadsheets* gain the power to perform complex calculations that can include cell references, simply by changing selected values and having the program recalculate the results. Sophisticated applications may include many built-in formulae for performing mathematical and business calculations such as SUM, MAX, MIN, AVERAGE, etc.

forward compatible describes a system that is designed in such a way that it will fit with planned future versions of itself. 'Forward compatible' usually implies that dependent systems, such as application programs developed for a specific *operating system*, will work in a satisfactory way in future as well as in the current, forward compatible system.

fourth-generation computers are those commonly used today. There are no individual technological advances that distinguish fourth-generation computers from third-generation computers, except the greater use of *large-scale integration* of components on chips. There has also been a considerable increase in the speed of machines and the capacity of internal and external storage.

fragmentation: the storing of parts of the same disk *file* over different areas of the disk. Fragmentation occurs as files on a disk are deleted and new files are added. Such fragmentation slows disk access and the overall performance of disk operations, although usually not severely. *Utility programs* are available for rearranging file storage on fragmented disks.

frame: 1 A single, screen-sized image that can be displayed in sequence with other, slightly different, images to create animated drawings.

2 The storage required to hold one screen-sized image of text, graphics or both.

3 A rectangular space containing, and defining, the proportions of, a graphic.

4 A rectangular section of the page displayed by a *web browser* that is a separate HTML document from the rest of the page. *Web pages* can have multiple frames, each of which is a separate document. Associated with each frame are the same capabilities as for an unframed web page, including scrolling and linking to another frame or *web site*; these capabilities can be used independently of other frames on the page. Frames, which were introduced in Netscape Navigator 2.0, are often used as a table of contents for one or more HTML documents on a web site. Most current Web browsers support frames, although older ones do not.

fraud: see *computer crime.*

freedom of information acts: these are the equivalent in other countries of the UK *Data Protection Act* and place similar constraints on organisations using computer data to respect the rights of individuals.

freeware: programs that are offered for use at no cost but are not free of *copyright.* Hence they (or their code) cannot be included in any software being developed.

frequency modulation (FM): a method of impressing data onto an alternating-current carrier wave by varying the instantaneous frequency of the wave.

friction feed: a means of moving paper through a printer that does not have *tractor-feed* holes. The paper is gripped either between the printer's platen and pressure rollers or (in printers that do not have a platen) between two sets of rollers.

front-end processor: a computer system, normally associated with large mainframe computers, that handles all the communications devices. The front-end processor takes all incoming messages from the communications devices and removes unnecessary details before passing the data onto the mainframe processor. Data to be passed to other devices is passed to the front-end processor that packages them before transmitting them. In this way the mainframe processor is used only to carry out the complex processing, leaving the smaller front-end processor to deal with the routine tasks.

full adder: see *adder*.

full duplex: a data transmission system that allows data to be transmitted in both directions at the same time on a signal carrier. See *half duplex, simplex*.

full justification: in *word processing*, and *desktop publishing* applications, the process of aligning text evenly along both the left and right margins of a column or page.

This paragraph is an example of fully justified text. Notice that the text starts from the left-hand margin and goes right up to the right-hand margin and is aligned so that there is no space between the text and the right-hand margin.

See also *right alignment* and *left alignment*.

function: a named *subprogram* that performs a distinct service and normally returns a single value. The language statement in a program that requests the function is called a function call. Standard functions are normally provided as part of a programming language. These provided functions are sometimes referred to as *library routines*. Some functions are self-sufficient (SIN, COS) and can return results to the requesting program without help. Other functions (FILEEXIST) need to make requests of the *operating system* in order to perform their work.

function key: any of the ten or more keys labelled F1, F2, F3 and so on, that are located across the top of a keyboard. Function keys are used in application programs or the *operating system* to provide either a shortcut for a series of common instructions (such as calling up a program's on-screen help facility, frequently F1) or a feature that is not otherwise available. In some instances the meaning of a function key can be defined by the user.

functional programming: a style of *programming* that emphasises the evaluation of expressions rather than the execution of commands.

functional specification: a description of how an information-handling *system* should behave, including the scope, objectives, and types of operations that are to be considered in the development of the system.

functionality: the features offered by a software application, e.g. as well as standard features, a *word processing* package might include the ability to *mail merge*, to build an index, to insert hyperlinks, etc.

future proofing is the notion of trying to ensure that a computer system has a reasonable lifespan and does not need major upgrades or to be totally replaced too soon. This is even more crucial with *network* systems within building and across offices that may involve cabling, *routers, servers*, etc.

fuzzy logic: an approach to computing based on 'degrees of truth' rather than the usual 'true or false' Boolean logic on which the modern computer is based. The idea of fuzzy logic was developed from attempts to get a computer to understand *natural language* that does not easily translate into Boolean values.

Fuzzy logic includes 0 and 1 as extreme cases of truth ('fact') but also includes the various states of truth in between so that, for example, the result of a comparison between two things could be not 'tall' or 'short' but 'tallish'.

Fuzzy logic seems closer to the way our brains work and is used in *artificial intelligence, neural network* design and *expert systems.* See also *Boolean algebra.*

G: see *giga.*

Gannt chart: a Gantt chart consists of horizontal bars indicating when individual activities will take place within the timescale of a project. Gantt charts are frequently used in project management since they provide a graphical illustration of a schedule that helps to plan, coordinate, and track specific tasks in a project. Gantt charts may be simple versions created on graph paper or more complex automated versions created using project management applications such as Microsoft Project.

A Gantt chart is constructed with a horizontal axis representing the total timespan of the project, broken down into increments (for example, days, weeks, or months) and a vertical axis representing the tasks that make up the project. Horizontal bars of varying length represent the sequences, timing, and timespan for each task. The bars may overlap 'in time'. As the project progresses, secondary bars, arrowheads, or darkened bars may be added to indicate completed tasks, or the portions of tasks that have been completed. Gantt charts give a clear illustration of project status but don't indicate task dependencies – you cannot tell how one task falling behind schedule affects other tasks (*PERT charts* give this type of information). Here is an example:

	Jan	Feb	Mar	Apr	May	Jun
Analysis	▓					
Design	▓	▓				
Program A		▓	▓			
Program B			▓	▓		
Test program A			▓	▓		
Test program B				▓	▓	
Documentation	▓	▓			▓	▓
Implementation						▓

garbage collection: the recovery of computer *memory* that is being used by a program when that program no longer needs the storage. This frees the memory for use by other programs (or processes within a program). Some programming languages such as Java provide built-in garbage collection so that the programmer does not have to write code for it.

garbage in garbage out (GIGO): the idea that if the data put into a computer or program is not good, the result the program comes back with will not be worth much.

gate: see *logic gate.*

gated: capable of being switched on and off.

gateway: a *network* point that acts as an entrance to another network. The network software and the *protocols* used on the two networks being joined do not have to be the same when a gateway is used. Within an organisation a network server acting as a gateway *node* is often also acting as a *proxy server* and a *firewall* server. A gateway is often associated with both a *router*, which knows where to direct a given *packet* of data that arrives at the gateway, and a *switch*, which provides the actual *path* in and out of the gateway for a given packet.

general protection fault: a message that users of PCs see when an *applications program* they are running tries to access memory that is not designated for use with that application. If an applications program were to be able to write outside its allocated memory area, it could overwrite instructions and data belonging to other applications or the *operating system*.

generic software: another name for general purpose software. It is software designed to be used for a wide range of applications. A word processing package is a generic piece of software since it can be used across a range of areas such as personal letters, official reports, writing books, etc.

geographical information system (GIS): allows the user to query or analyse geographic data and receive the results in the form of a map. A GIS can have many uses: weather forecasting, sales analysis, population forecasting and land use planning. In a GIS, geographic information is described explicitly in terms of geographic coordinates (latitude and longitude or some national grid coordinates) or implicitly in terms of a street address or postal code.

GISs are able to:

- accept geographic input in the form of scanned-in and digitised map images (often this data is supplied by a source that owns maps and has already digitised them)
- rescale or otherwise manipulate geographic data for different purposes
- make use of query and analysis programs to retrieve answers to simple questions, such as the distance between two points on a map or more complicated questions that require analysis, such as determining the traffic pattern at a given intersection
- provide answers visually, usually as maps or graphs.

GIF images: one of the two most common *file formats* for graphic images on the *World Wide Web* (WWW) since it allows graphic files to be stored in a compressed form. Compressed files download much quicker and hence are attractive to website owners. The other common file format on the World Wide Web is the JPEG (see *joint photographic expert group*).

giga: in general terms a prefix meaning one billion (10^9) but when applied to computer memory it means 1 073 741 824 (2^{30}). It is abbreviated to G.

gigabit: in data communications, a gigabit is one billion *binary digits*, or 1 000 000 000 (that is, 10^9) bits. It is commonly used for measuring the amount of data that is transferred in a second between two telecommunication points.

Some sources define a gigabit as 1 073 741 824 (that is, 2^{30}) bits. Although the bit is a unit of the binary number system, bits in data communications are discrete signal pulses and have historically been counted using the decimal number system. For example, 28.8 kilobits per second (Kbps) is 28,800 bits per second.

global variable: a variable that has value and meaning throughout the program in which it is declared.

gopher: an *Internet* application *protocol* in which hierarchically organised file structures are maintained on servers that themselves are part of an overall information structure. Gopher was popular, especially in universities, and provided a way to bring text files from all over the world to a viewer on a user's computer. Although most gopher browsers and files are text-based, gopher browsers (notably HyperGopher) were also developed to display graphic images.

graph plotter: a device that draws images using ink pens that can be raised, lowered and moved over a page. Lines and curves are drawn on the page by a combination of horizontal and vertical movements of the pen. The plotter uses *vector graphics*, making an image out of a series of lines.

graphical user interface (GUI): a graphical rather than purely textual user interface to a computer. The term came into existence because the first interactive user interfaces to computers were not graphical; they were text-and-keyboard oriented and usually consisted of commands you had to remember and computer responses that were very brief (MS-DOS is an example). An intermediate step in user interfaces between the command line interface and the GUI was the non-graphical, menu-based interface, which let the user interact by using a mouse rather than by having to type in keyboard commands. Windows is an example of a graphical user interface. The use of a *WIMP* system (windows, icons, mouse, pull-down menus) is now almost universal. Windows is an example of a GUI:

See also *bitmapped* and *vector graphics*.

graphics: there are two different kinds of graphics: pixel-based graphics, known as bitmapped, and vector-based graphics, also known as object-orientated. Bitmapped images are produced by scanners and paint programs. Bitmapped images are collections of individual *pixels* that each have a colour or attribute. Editing is, therefore very difficult. Also bitmapped images give jagged edges and white spaces, especially when enlarged.

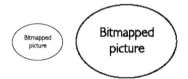

Vector-based graphics are made up of geometric mathematical data. A line is defined by its end points, width, colour, etc., and is, therefore, device independent. Vector-based graphics can be scaled and stretched without distortion. Vector-based graphics are used in CAD programs, as the degree of accuracy that can be achieved ensures that objects can be moved precisely, lines at angles are exact and zooming in on objects for greater precision is achieved with no loss of clarity.

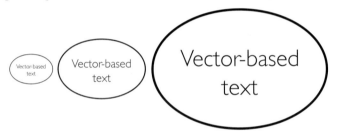

See also *bitmap, vector graphics.*

graphics adapter: a circuit board that enables a computer to display information on its screen. The *resolution,* number of colours, and *refresh rate* of a monitor are determined by the kind of graphics adapter used, plus the limitations of the monitor itself. Other names used for a graphics adapter are: graphics card, display adapter, or video adapter.

graphics pad or tablet: a device used to input line drawings into a computer. A flat rectangular pad or tablet is equipped with a pen (also called a stylus) and sensing electronics report the position of the pen to the computer, which translates the data into a cursor position on the screen. Lighter or darker lines can be produced by varying the pressure. The pen or stylus allows for freehand drawing. A device called a *puck* (a small disk shaped device) can also be used to trace drawings.

greeked text: used in a mock-up of a page layout, to represent text as abstract lines or symbols, just to give an impression of where the text blocks will be. In traditional graphic design, such text areas were sometimes represented in Greek lettering. Some *desktop publishing* programs can be set up to do greeking.

greyscale: a sequence of shades ranging from black through to white, used in computer graphics to add detail to images or represent a colour image on a monochrome output device. Like the number of colours in a colour image, the number of shades of grey depends on the number of bits stored per *pixel*. Greys may be represented by actual grey shades, by halftone dots, or by dithering.

group: in a drawing or desktop publishing program, to select multiple objects and transform them into a single entity for the purpose of editing, moving, scaling, etc. See also *ungroup*.

groupware: software for people working together on a project. Groupware makes it possible for several people to work over a *network* on the same *file* at the same time. It also helps with scheduling meetings and other kinds of group planning. Lotus Notes is a popular groupware package.

guiltware: freeware or shareware that has a message attached, asking for payment. It attempts to make the user feel guilty until they make the payment.

Gzip: a free downloadable *compression*–decompression utility from GNU for use with *Unix*.

hacker: a term traditionally used to mean 'a clever programmer' but by the media to mean 'someone who tries to break into computer systems.' In the traditional sense a hacker:

- enjoys understanding the detail of a programming language or system
- enjoys finding neat solutions to difficult programming problems
- appreciates the programming skills of other programmers
- is often an expert at a particular programming language or system.

The hacker referred to by the media is a proficient programmer with enough technical knowledge to be able to identify the weak points in the *security* aspects of a computer system and is prepared to misuse these skills to access and possibly to damage the computer systems used by an organisation.

half adder: a logic circuit in the *arithmetic logic unit* (ALU) of a computer system that adds two bits together, producing a sum and a carry bit. A half adder consists of an *XOR gate* and an *AND* gate. See *full adder*.

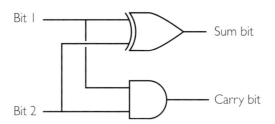

half duplex: a *data transmission* system that allows data to be transmitted in both directions on a signal carrier, but not at the same time. For example, a *local area network* using half duplex transmission would allow one workstation to send data on the communications line and then immediately receive data on the same line. See *full duplex, simplex.*

hand-held scanner: a *scanner* that is held in the hand and passed across the image to be scanned. Hand-held scanners are rarely used, since desktop scanners are now relatively cheap and produce better images than hand-held scanners that require a steady hand to get a clear image.

handshake: the exchange of information passed between two devices (e.g. printer and computer) when data is being transmitted. Handshaking is used to check that a device is ready to receive data before the originator starts transmission. In telephone communication, handshaking is the exchange of information between the two *modems* and the resulting agreement about which *protocol* to use before actually starting data transmission, as well as the constant exchange required during transmission.

handwriting recognition: the ability of a computer system to accept handwritten information and turn it into digital data that can be stored and processed by the computer system. Because people's handwriting changes with time and stress, this is difficult to implement but, like *voice recognition*, when fully implemented will free users from using the keyboard.

hang: an unexpected halt of a computer system, usually caused by a software fault in the application being used, the *operating system* or the interface between them. It is apparent when a system is hung since it will not respond to either mouse or keyboard. Once a system is hung, usually the only remedy is to restart the computer system.

hanging indent: a paragraph in which the first line begins at the left margin, and the rest of the lines are indented. The next paragraph starts with a hanging indent:

- Hanging indents are sometimes used with bullet points or numbered lists, when the first line begins with a bullet or a number and the lines that follow are indented to line the text up.

hard copy: the paper version of a document, as opposed to the version on disk or tape.

hard disk: the part of the hard disk drive made up of a set of stacked disks, each with two *read/write heads*, one on each side. The disks store large amounts of data on concentric tracks that cover each surface. Disk *access time* is measured in milliseconds, with each physical location being identified by its cylinder, *track*, and *sector* locations.

hard disk drive: the mechanism in a personal computer that controls the positioning of the *read/write heads* and the reading, and writing of data on the hard disk. Although the hard disk drive and the *hard disk* are not the same thing, they are packaged as a unit and so either term is often used to refer to the whole unit. It is also known as the hard drive.

hard return: a character input by the user to indicate that the current line of text is to end and a new line is to begin. In word-processing programs that automatically break lines within the margins of a page, a hard return indicates the end of a paragraph.

hard space: a space character that is regarded by the software as a letter. Hard spaces are used when the user does not want a line break in the middle of a phrase or multiple-word proper name. It is also called a fixed space.

hardware: the physical part of computers and other information technology devices. The term is used to distinguish the electronic circuitry and components of a computer from the software that controls the hardware. Hardware not only includes the computer, display, keyboard, mouse, audio speakers and printers but also the cables, connectors and power supply units.

hardware compatibility: the capability of one hardware device to work with another. A printer would be described as compatible with a particular type of computer if the necessary driver is available and printouts were possible using this combination of hardware.

hardware documentation: the instructions that come with a piece of hardware explaining how to connect the device to a computer system and maintain it in the future.

hardware failure: a term used whenever part of the hardware that makes up a computer system does not function as expected.

hardware platform: the CPU family which is the basis for a particular machine. Each hardware platform has its own *machine code*, and all the software it uses must be in that language.

hard-wired: a function or capability that is controlled by the wiring of a system, rather than the software, and cannot be modified.

hash function: see *hashing*.

hash table: see *hashing*.

hash total: a *validation* check where the contents or part of the contents of a numeric field are added together to produce the hash total for the file. In future processing of the file the hash total can be re-generated for comparison with the original hash total to ensure that all the records in the file have been processed.

hashing: the process of generating the location *address* to be used to store a *record* in a *random access* file. The address is generated by putting the contents of the *key field*, or a combination of fields including the key field, through a mathematical formula known as the hash function. The hash function should ensure an even distribution of records throughout the file and deal with any collisions (two records requiring the same space) that occur. The technique can also be used to generate the position within a data structure known as a hash table that stores the data in the computer's memory rather than on disk. An example of a hash function for a file that has 500 blocks of disk storage space and a numeric key field is:

- divide key field of record by 500
- use remainder plus one as the block number for the record
- if block full, use next available block.

Assuming that initially every location is available and only one record will fit into each block using this hash function for the records with the following key fields:

Record	Key field contents	File location used
A	765	265
B	1766	266
C	1265	267

Record C cannot be placed in its intended location 265 since it is occupied by the record with key field content 765. Location 266 is also occupied so it is placed in location 267 (the next available location).

Records can be unintentionally lost in this type of file (physical removal of record 1766 would make it impossible to find record 1265 unless the whole file was to be searched) if the deletion of records is not handled sensibly. One method of deleting records involves marking the record as deleted but not removing it. If this method is used the file will need periodic reorganisation if accessing records is not to become very slow.

head crash: accidental contact between a disk and its *read/write head*, causing physical damage and loss of recorded data. When a disk is working normally the read/write head does not touch the surface of the disk but hovers just above it.

header: in general a header is something that goes in front of an item and is usually repeated for each occurrence of that item. Examples of the ways headers are used in IT/computing include:

- In a document, a header is some combination of text and images that appears at the top of each page when displayed or printed; it may include a page number, date or title; it can also be different for the first page of a document and have different information on odd and even pages.
- In an *e-mail*, the header is the part of a message that indicates who wrote the message, who it is addressed to, any users copied in, message priority, etc.
- In a computer file, a header is a record that appears at the start of a file and includes the name of the file, originator, date and time created, any passwords, etc.
- In *network* transmissions, it is the part of a *packet* that contains control information such as source, destination, sequence number, and priority level.

headset: 1 An input and output device consisting of a microphone and earpiece combination, used to input and listen to speech.

2 An input and output device, like a helmet, worn in *virtual reality* systems. It consists of small video screens in goggles worn by the user to provide vision and headphones to provide sound. It gives a strong impression to the user of being within a computer-generated environment. The headset senses movement of the head and changes the scene accordingly as though the user is moving or looking around a real environment.

Health & Safety (Display Screen Equipment) Regulations 1992: a set of regulations incorporated into the Health and Safety at Work Act of 1974, introduced by the European Union in order to try to prevent health and safety problems associated with the use of computers and VDUs.

Employers must comply with the following. They must:

- assess and evaluate the health and safety risks associated with workstations and display screen equipment and take steps to reduce any risks found
- ensure that workstations and the working environment conform to minimum standards suitable for the work undertaken. This means ensuring that workstations are not cramped, that lighting is adequate, that chairs are adjustable and have footrests and that screens are tiltable and have anti-glare screen filters
- ensure that employees take regular breaks or changes in activity
- provide training and information for users of display screen equipment
- pay for regular eyesight tests for users of display screen equipment and pay for glasses where necessary.

Employees have a responsibility to:

- use workstations and display screen equipment correctly and as directed
- bring problems to the notice of their employer.

These regulations apply only to offices and do not apply to students in schools and colleges.

heap: a common pool of free memory usable by a program. This area of memory can be allocated dynamically with blocks of memory being used in an arbitrary order.

help desk: a point of contact in an organisation that an IT user can call to get help with a problem they are encountering with either hardware or software. A help desk can be as small as one person or can consist of a group of experts with their own software system for logging and tracking the status of problems and other special software to help analyse problems, e.g. the status of the organisation's *network* cabling system. Some common names for a help desk include: computer support centre, IT response centre, customer support centre, IT solutions centre, resource centre, information centre and technical support centre.

heterogeneous network: a *network* in which the hardware and the software come from different organisations. Heterogeneous networks are possible because of all the different international standards covering hardware and software interfaces, thus allowing different products to communicate with each other. The *Internet* itself is an example of a heterogeneous network.

heuristics: a method of solving problems by intelligent trial and error. This approach can be adopted in testing software where intelligence and previous experience are used to determine the actions to be taken.

hexadecimal (hex): a base-16 number system. Since 16 characters are needed to represent each of the 16 hexadecimal 'digits' the numbers 0–9 and letters A–F are used. Hexadecimal is a convenient shorthand way of expressing the eight bits in a byte, since one hexadecimal digit can represent four binary digits. Hence only two hexadecimal digits are needed to represent the eight binary digits in a byte.

Binary	Decimal	Hexadecimal
0000	0	0
0001	1	1
0010	2	2
0011	3	3
0100	4	4
0101	5	5
0110	6	6
0111	7	7
1000	8	8
1001	9	9
1010	10	A
1011	11	B
1100	12	C
1101	13	D
1110	14	E
1111	15	F

The byte 0 0 1 0 1 0 1 1 is represented by the hexadecimal number 2B.

hidden file: a *file* that is not normally visible when the file *directory* is inspected. The essential files of an *operating system* are often hidden to prevent inexperienced users from deleting or changing them. Some file *utility programs* also allow users to hide files. See also *file attribute*.

hierarchical directory structure: a method of organising the files on a hard disk so that files are collected into logical groups. Each group of files is placed in a separate folder (*subdirectory*) and the structure is then represented as a tree.

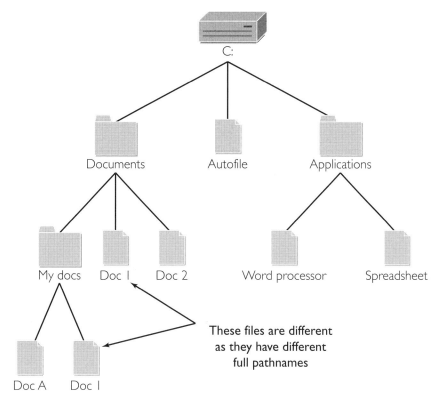

A hierarchial directory structure

high-level language: a language for programming computers that does not require detailed knowledge of how a computer works, unlike a *low-level language*. Programs written in a high-level language are easier to read and easier to maintain than those written in low-level languages.

high resolution: the large number of dots per square inch required to produce a high-quality image in printing or on a computer display screen; the higher the resolution, the finer the image quality.

highlighting: selecting text or graphics for moving, editing, or deletion. Text, images, etc. can be selected by dragging the mouse pointer over the areas to be highlighted. The highlighted area appears in reverse video (also known as inverse video) i.e. text is white with a black background.

hit: a single file request during the updating of a file. Each transaction involves a separate hit on the file (see *hit rate*). The term is also used to describe the accessing of a web site or the number of files that have to be transferred when a web site is accessed, e.g. a web site with three graphic images requires four hits during a user's access of the site (three for the images and one for the page data).

hit rate: the percentage of records in a file that are accessed in an updating run.

home page: the first *web page* that is displayed after starting a *web browser* like Netscape's Navigator or Microsoft's Internet Explorer. Initially the first page of the manufacturer of the browser's web site is set as the home page, however this setting can be changed by the user.

From a web site developer's point of view, the home page is the first page presented when a user selects the site being developed.

homogenous network: a *network* in which the hardware and the software come from the same vendor.

hop: in a *packet-switching network*, a hop is the name given to each stage in a *packet's* journey from sender to receiver. Each move a data packet takes from one *router* or intermediate point to another in the network is called a hop. On the Internet, the number of hops a packet has taken toward its destination, called the 'hop count', is kept in the packet header and any packets with a large hop count are discarded.

host: a main computer system in a *network* to which several computers are connected. The term is often used to describe a computer that is used to store several web sites, in which case the host has a specific local number that, together with the network number, forms its unique *IP address*.

host computer: see *host*.

hosting service: (also known as *web site* hosting and web hosting) the business of storing, delivering to users, and maintaining files for one or more web sites. As well as providing storage space for the web site, the host must provide a fast connection to the *Internet*. An organisation hosting its own site would require an expensive, fast connection and hence many small organisations use a hosting service that effectively lets them share the cost of the fast Internet connection. Hosting services will sometimes describe the service they offer as virtual hosting. This type of hosting allows each web site to have its own *domain name* and set of *e-mail addresses*. Dedicated hosting is the provision of a separate server for each web site and is often used for very busy sites.

hot key: (sometimes called a shortcut key) a key or combination of keys on a computer keyboard that, when pressed at one time, perform a task (such as starting an application) more quickly than by using a mouse or other input device. The function keys at the top of the keyboard are often used as hot keys and many software packages use F1 as the hot key to call up online help.

hot spot: a spot in a *web site* that contains a *hyperlink*.

hot swapping: the replacing of a hard drive, CD-ROM drive, power supply, or other device with a similar device while the computer system using it remains in operation. Hot swapping works by providing a rack or enclosure for the device that makes it appear to the computer's bus or I/O controller that the device is still there while it is being removed and replaced with another device. A hot swap arrangement is sometimes provided where multiple devices are shared on a *local area network*.

hub: like the hub of a wheel, in *network* technology, a hub is a central device that connects together several computers or other network devices (e.g. printers). Data arrives at the hub from several different places (the network *nodes* or network *servers*) and is forwarded out in one or more other directions. A hub is generally regarded as a non-intelligent piece of hardware. An intelligent hub is usually called a *switch* and is capable of determining how, when and to which node a *packet* of data should be forwarded.

human–computer interaction: the study of how humans interact with computers. The information gathered by this type of study is used to design computers and their software interfaces so that they are easy for humans to use.

human–computer interface: a phrase used to describe the interaction between a user and a computer. It is the method by which the user tells the computer what to do and the way in which the computer responds. This covers all of the ways in which users interact with 'computers', from PCs to cash machines. The interface must be appropriate for the user. A child learning arithmetic at a screen would need a different interface from a computer programmer or an interactive application for customers in a travel agents. Interfaces can be command-line, menus, graphical (GUIs), forms and dialogue, natural language or speech (voice recognition). It is common for a suite of applications or software packages from the same company to have a consistent user interface to facilitate ease of use when moving from one application or package to another. See *graphical user interface*.

HyperCard: an information-management software tool, designed for the Apple Macintosh, that allows for interactive storage and retrieval of on-screen 'cards'. It implements many *hypertext* concepts. A HyperCard document consists of a series of cards, collected into a stack. Each card can contain text, graphical images, sound, video clips, buttons that enable travel from card to card, and other controls. Programs and routines can be coded as scripts in an *object-oriented language* called HyperTalk.

hyperlink: a highlighted word or picture within a *hypertext* document that, when clicked, takes the user to another place within the document or to another document altogether. Hyperlinks are common on *web sites* where they are used to navigate between and within *web pages*.

hypertext: text that includes links to other documents or within itself, allowing the reader to move easily from one section of text to related sections in a non-linear fashion. The text has to be organised into sections of information that can then be linked into a series of connected units by the originator of the data. The connections are often in the form of *hyperlinks*. Hypertext is extensively used on the *World Wide Web*, which has an enormous amount of information connected by an enormous number of hyperlinks.

hypertext database: an alternative concept in database design is known as *hypertext*. In a hypertext database, any object, whether it be a piece of text, a picture, or a film, can be linked to any other object. Hypertext databases are particularly useful for organising large amounts of disparate information, but they are not designed for numerical analysis.

hypertext mark up language (HTML): the hidden codes in text documents, *web pages* and *e-mails* that allow the reader to move quickly about the document, or jump to another document by clicking on 'links' that appear as coloured, highlighted words, phrases or graphics. Documents are normally set up in this form, ready for use on the *World Wide Web* where the markup commands tell the web browser how to display the data provided for the user. Each individual markup command is correctly called an element, but 'tag' is becoming the more commonly used term. Some elements come in pairs (e.g. turn bold on and turn bold off) that indicate where some display effect is to begin and where it is to end.

hypertext transfer protocol (HTTP): the set of rules for exchanging files (text, graphic images, sound, video and other multimedia files) on the *World Wide Web*. Relative to the TCP/IP suite of protocols, HTTP is an application protocol. HTTP provides the language that web stations and servers use when they are communicating with each other. It allows users of the web to transfer hypermedia documents successfully. When a web user types in or selects a *uniform resource locator* (URL), their browser builds an HTTP request and sends it to the *Internet protocol address* indicated by the URL. The request is analysed by the destination server's daemon (a program designed to wait for HTTP requests and process them when they arrive) and the appropriate file returned. See also *transmission control protocol/Internet protocol* (TCP/IP).

I

icon: in a computer's *graphical user interface* an icon is an image that represents an application, a function of the software package, or some other concept with meaning for the user. An icon is selectable by moving the mouse pointer over the icon and either single or double clicking a mouse button.

identifier: the name chosen by the *programmer* to represent a variable, constant or *label* within a program. All *programming languages* have rules that determine the characters and their arrangement that are permitted within that language in building up an identifier name. Good programming practice means that the names chosen as identifiers should be as meaningful as possible, to make a program as readable as possible and help in future maintenance.

IEEE interface: an interface largely used to connect scientific instruments to a computer that has been developed by the Institute of Electrical and Electronics Engineers. The IEEE describes itself as 'the world's largest technical professional society – promoting the development and application of electrotechnology and allied sciences for the benefit of humanity, the advancement of the profession, and the well-being of our members.'

IF statement: a conditional branch construct found in all high-level programming languages. The IF statement allows one of two blocks of instructions to be executed, depending on the result of a condition.

```
IF condition THEN
    block 1
ELSE
    block 2
```

Instructions in block 1 are executed if the result of the condition is true and those in block 2 if the result is false.

ill-behaved: software is said to be ill-behaved if it has been designed to bypass normal *operating system* functions. These non-standard routines may result in better performance but make the software less portable and more likely to be restricted to specific hardware. Contrast this with *well-behaved software*, which uses the operating system in the expected way for such tasks as screen display, keyboard input, disk input/output, etc.

image: a picture (visual representation of something) that has been created or copied and stored in either *bitmap* or *vector graphic* form. The term image can also describe an area of memory (RAM) that is an exact copy of another area of memory.

image compression: minimising the size of a graphics file without degrading the quality of the image to an unacceptable level. The reduction in file size reduces the time required for images to be sent over the *Internet* or downloaded from web pages. Image files can be compressed using JPEG or GIF format. See also *lossless compression*.

image editing: making changes to an image using a variety of tools normally provided with art packages, e.g. colour changes, pixel-by-pixel editing to smooth jagged lines, image reversal, etc.

image recognition: an *artificial intelligence* (AI) application involving the identification of objects in an image. This process involves locating lines, regions and areas with certain textures before interpreting them as everyday objects, e.g. cars on a road, boxes on a conveyor belt or cancerous cells on a microscope slide. This application of computers involves AI because an object can have a totally different appearance when viewed from different angles: it is difficult to decide which lines, areas, etc. are part of the object and which are background or shadow. The human eye and brain carry out these tasks without the person being aware it is happening but the software involves complex techniques, and a high power processor is required in the computer being used.

immediate access store (IAS): see *RAM*.

immediate addressing: an addressing mode where the *operand* part of an instruction contains the data to be used by the *operator*. This type of addressing requires no memory accesses since the data is already part of the instruction. Immediate addressing is used to load constants into the accumulator in low-level programming.

immediate mode: the direct entry of a programming command without the need to compile the command. This type of facility is normally only available with interpreted languages.

impact printer: a printer that prints by mechanical impact, e.g. a *dot-matrix printer*. The character is printed when the print head strikes a print ribbon and transfers the ink to the paper.

imperative language: a language where the programmer specifies the exact sequence of steps to follow to produce the desired result. Common *procedural languages* include Basic and *Pascal*. See also *declarative language*.

implementation: 1 In small scale project work, the actual software solution to a problem carried out in whatever application(s) is chosen. It is the stage following on from the analysis and design of a problem.

2 Part of the *system life cycle*. It is the installation and setting up of a system after the analysis, design, development and testing have been undertaken and completed satisfactorily. There are various types of systems installation. See *direct changeover, parallel running, phased conversion* and *pilot conversion*.

import: to convert a file from one system or application to the format of the system or application being used.

in-house: used to describe a program or package solution to a problem that has been created by employees of the organisation concerned.

incompatible: not able to work together. The term is used when referring to combinations of *hardware* and *software*.

incremental backup: making a copy of only the files that have changed since the last backup was carried out. This type of backup is normally carried out during the week instead of backing up every file, which would be done at weekends. Incremental backup saves a lot of time and can save storage space.

incremental plotter: see *plotter*.

indent: aligning a portion of text a greater distance in from the edge of the paper than the surrounding text. The first line of a paragraph is often indented from the left margin.

index file: a small file, usually associated with a large *direct access file*, which contains *records* made up of the *key field* for each record held in the large file, together with its location in the large file. This file can often be held in *arrays* in the computer's memory, allowing very fast access to the individual records.

index register: the register that holds the base *address* when index addressing is used.

indexed sequential access method (ISAM): a file management system that allows *records* to be accessed either sequentially (in the order they were entered) or randomly (with an index). Each index defines a different ordering of the records. A product file might have several indexes depending on the different ways it needs to be accessed. One index might allow direct access by product code, whereas another could allow access by product name and yet another by manufacturer.

index sequential file: a method of organising *records* within a file stored on a hard disk, that allows both sequential access and direct access to the records.

The records are organised sequentially using the *key field* for the record to determine the sequence, but indices are provided at the start of each file and at the start of each cylinder to allow *direct access*. The index at the start of the file holds the cylinder index that indicates the key field value for the last record in each cylinder. This index can be used to determine the correct cylinder for any record being updated.

The index at the start of each cylinder indicates the key field value for the last record in each track in that cylinder. This index allows the correct track to be selected and the required record can then be found as the disk revolves.

indexed addressing: an *address* in memory that is described in terms of its displacement from a base address. The base address is held in the *index register*.

indirect addressing: an addressing mode where the *operand* part of an instruction contains the *address* of a memory location that in turn contains the address of the data. This type of addressing requires two memory accesses – one to fetch the address of the data and another to read or write the actual data. However, since all the bits in a memory location can be used for the address, a greater range of memory locations is accessible.

industry standard architecture (ISA): a standard *bus* architecture that is associated with the IBM AT *motherboard*. It allows 16 bits at a time to flow between the motherboard circuitry and an expansion slot card and its associated device(s).

industry structure model (ISM): a structure designed by the *British Computer Society*, setting out, as a series of competencies, the expectations of a person performing computer-related tasks at each stage of a career pathway. This is a comprehensive set of standards for all the people working in ICT. The ISM defines over 200 different jobs in IT, each at one of ten different levels of technical expertise and responsibility. This can assist:

- in producing job descriptions from standardised tasks
- applicants to know what jobs to apply for
- employers knowing what experience and abilities applicants should have

- in planning career development
- in establishing training needs both for individuals and organisations.

The ISM is regularly reviewed to ensure that it is up-to-date and reflects the changing nature of the ICT industry. The BCS web site is http://www.bcs.org.uk.

inference: a process of deriving new facts from known facts by means of the rules of logic.

inference processor: the search engine of an *expert system*. This is the piece of software that searches the knowledge base of a knowledge-based expert system.

infinite loop: a program loop that will repeat itself forever, unless it is interrupted from outside the program. An infinite loop can be caused by a *bug* in the program, or may be intentional, as with a screen saver that repeats itself until the user interrupts it by touching the mouse or keyboard.

infix notation: the method of writing mathematical calculations used by mathematicians. For example, $4 * (x + y)$ means add the contents of x and y together and then multiply the result by 4. See *reverse Polish notation, postfix notation* and *prefix notation*.

informatics refers to the development in recent years of all aspects of computer communication. It includes *e-mail*, fax, *teletext*, viewdata, *video conferencing, telecommuting* and the *Internet*. These developments have made use of electrical signals through wires at ever increasing *bandwidths*, radio waves (including satellite communication) and *fibre-optic cables*. Processing speeds have increased, as well the speeds of modems, and ISDN has been introduced. It is now possible to send not only text but graphic images and videos with sound. See also *telematics*.

information can be regarded as organised facts and figures that have meaning within a context that is intended to be interpreted by people. *Data* consists of facts and figures, which become information when seen in context and convey a meaning. Computers process data without any understanding of what the data represents. For example, 'Helen, Lucy, Sunaya, Theresa, 37, 56, 76, 21' is data because it has no context. The computer can work out an average from the figures but it means nothing. It is just a set of figures. However, if put into the context of marks for a test then it becomes information, and the average becomes an average mark for the four pupils (see also *coding information*).

Name	Mark for geography test
Helen	37
Lucy	56
Sunaya	76
Theresa	21

In a business sense, information is a commodity and, as such, has a value. It has to be kept accurate, up-to-date and complete. It is a crucial area for management in planning and decision making. References to information occur throughout this book and are too numerous to itemise here. However, from an organisational perspective, see also *channels of communication, corporate information systems, corporate plan, decision support system (DSS), management information system*.

information processing: the acquisition, storage, manipulation, distribution and presentation of data, particularly by electronic means. The term covers activities that are central to the whole concept and use of computers.

information retrieval: the process of finding, organising, and displaying meaningful information from stored data, especially where the data is maintained in a large database.

information service: an online service that provides access to many kinds of *information*.

information system: a computer system that processes, generally, large amounts of data to produce meaningful information. The information can be used to assist management in decision making. In contrast, a *data-processing* system is designed to process data used in day-to-day operations, such as accounts, invoices and stock control. The major difference is that an information system produces useful reports or output for a user.

information systems manager: the person who manages the *information system* of an organisation and acts as the interface between a computer system and the users of the system.

information technology (IT): a term that encompasses all forms of technology used to create, store, manipulate, exchange, and use *information* in its various forms (business data, voice conversations, still images, motion pictures, multimedia presentations, and other forms). The subject is also referred to as information and communications technology (ICT) to emphasise the recent increase in the importance of communications networks.

infra-red communication: the use of infra-red waves to communicate data. Infra-red wavelengths are longer than those of visible light, but shorter than those of radio waves. Infrared communication is used in a variety of applications where cables would be inconvenient, for example:

- home-entertainment remote-control boxes
- wireless *local area networks*
- links between notebook computers and desktop computers
- cordless *modems*.

inheritance: in *object oriented programming*, inheritance is the concept that subclasses of a class carry the definitions of data and methods that were applied to the class when it was set up. This speeds up program production.

initial value: the value given to a variable at the start of a program or subprogram.

initialisation is the process of locating and using the defined values for the initial contents of the variables in a computer program. When the operating system or an application program is first loaded into memory, part of the program performs this initialisation. In Windows these values are held in files with extensions INI and include all the initial settings that the user has specified for the start position of the screen – which icons appear, the background to be used, the tunes to be played when the computer is ready for use, etc.

ink cartridge: the cartridge that supplies ink for an *inkjet printer*.

inkjet printer: a printer in which the image is made by tiny ink droplets which are sprayed from a nozzle onto a piece of paper. Inkjet printers can produce *high resolution* colour or black and white images.

input device: a peripheral device that is used to enter commands or information into a computer, such as a *keyboard, mouse, joystick, modem, scanner,* or *touch screen.*

input/output device (I/O device): a peripheral that is capable of both sending data to a computer and receiving data from a computer. Typical I/O devices are *hard disks*, diskettes and re-writable *CD-ROMs.*

install: to load and configure a piece of *software* on a computer.

instruction: an order given to the central processing unit (CPU) by a computer program. At the lowest level a *machine code* instruction is a sequence of 0s and 1s and corresponds to a single action. In a *low-level language* an instruction corresponds to a single processor instruction but is written in a more intelligible form. In *high-level languages* an instruction corresponds to multiple processor instructions and is written in an easily understood form.

instruction address register (IAR): see *program counter.*

instruction cycle: each time a computer is given a *machine code* instruction the CPU carries out a four-step cycle:

- fetch the instruction from memory
- decode it
- execute it
- store the result.

These four steps are sometimes called the *fetch execute cycle* and make extensive use of the following registers within the CPU:

- *program counter*
- *instruction register*
- *memory address register*
- *memory buffer register.*

instruction decoder: the part of the control unit of a processor that decodes an instruction and works out what the next steps are.

instruction register (IR): this register is part of the central processor and holds the actual instruction that is being executed by the processor and hence is sometimes known as the 'current instruction register'.

instruction set: the complete collection of *instructions* that are available for *machine code* programming a particular processor.

integer: a whole number that can be positive, negative or zero. Numbers that are integers include 5, –4, 3452, 0, 67, –2, whereas 1.6, 5.7, –4.2, 0.07 are not integers.

integrated circuit (IC): a semiconductor wafer on which millions of tiny resistors, capacitors, and transistors are fabricated. Integrated circuits are manufactured to carry out a variety of tasks. They may act as:

- amplifiers
- timers

- computer memory
- microprocessors
- counters.

They are classified as linear (analogue) or digital.

Linear ICs produce a continuously varying output that is dependent on the input signal level. Linear ICs are used as audio-frequency and radio-frequency amplifiers.

Digital ICs are capable of only a limited number of different output states (normally the two binary states) and are used in computers and computing equipment.

ICs are sometimes called chips or microchips. See also *logic gates.*

integrated drive electronics (IDE) interface: a standard interface between the buses on a computer's motherboard and its hard disk drives, where the disk drive controller is built into the logic board on the disk drive. The IDE interface is based on the IBM PC industry standard architecture (ISA) 16-bit bus standard, but it is used in computers that contain other bus standards. There is an improved IDE interface called the enhanced integrated drive electronics interface (EIDE).

integrated package: one that combines a number of distinct applications within a single package. These applications frequently consist of a word processor, spreadsheet and database, but can also include communications software. The intention is consistency for the user, including similar menus in the same style of toolbar, and ease of exchanging data between individual applications.

integrated services digital network (ISDN): a set of CCITT/ITU standards for digital transmission over ordinary telephone copper wire as well as over other media. ISDN is the integration of both analogue (or voice data) together with digital data over the same network. Home and business users who install an ISDN adapter instead of a modem get a significantly improved data transmission rate (up to 128 Kbps) over that available when a modem is used (up to 56 Kbps). This increase is most noticeable when accessing a web site that includes many graphic images.

integration generally means combining parts so that they work together or form a whole. In information technology, the term is used in a variety of ways:

- during product development combining separately produced components or subsystems and dealing with the problems of their interaction
- an activity carried out by companies that specialise in bringing different manufacturers' products together into a single working system.

Products are said to be integrated if:

- they share a common purpose or set of objectives
- they observe the same set of *protocols*
- they are designed at the same time with a unifying purpose and/or architecture
- they share some of the same programming code.

integrity: the assurance that data can only be accessed or modified by those authorised to do so. Integrity can be ensured by:

- making sure rooms that contain network terminals and servers are kept secure

- restricting access to data by controlling user rights
- making servers accessible only to *network administrators*
- keeping transmission media (i.e. cables and connectors) protected to ensure that they cannot be tapped
- documenting system administration procedures and maintenance activities
- creating disaster recovery plans for occurrences such as power failure, server failure, and virus attacks.

intellectual capital: knowledge that can be exploited for money-making. The term combines the idea of the intellect with the economic concept of capital. Intellectual capital can include:

- the skills and knowledge that an organisation has acquired whilst developing its goods or services
- individual employees or groups of employees whose knowledge is deemed critical to a company's continued success
- the documentation produced to cover manufacturing processes
- research results
- other information that might have value for a competitor and is not common knowledge.

intelligent agent: an *Internet* program that gathers information or performs some other service without the user's immediate presence according to a regular schedule. Using parameters provided by the user, an agent program searches all or part of the Internet, gathering information ready for the user to access. An agent is sometimes called a bot (short for robot).

intelligent knowledge-based system (IKBS): see *knowledge-based system.*

intelligent terminal: a terminal that is part of a larger system and uses a main computer for the storage of data, but has its own processing capability.

intelligent time division multiplexer: a time division *multiplexer* that allocates time to each transmission, proportional to the activity involved in the transmission.

inter-block gap (IBG): the gaps left between *blocks* of data on a tape. When data blocks are transferred between tape and computer the tape has to be stopped between successive blocks, to allow the data to be processed, and re-started and accelerated to the working speed before the next transfer begins. This starting and stopping takes a few thousandths of a second and a blank space must be left on the tape to allow for it; these gaps are called inter-block gaps.

interactive processing: computer software that requires input from the user while it is running. Examples of interactive software are:

- games that wait for the user to take an action, then responds to that action
- holiday booking software.

The interaction between software and user can be done by:

- typing commands
- voice commands
- mouse clicks.

The opposite of interactive processing is *batch processing*, where the software can run without stopping for input from the user.

interactive video: video in which the user can control which part of a program to view, or interact with certain parts of the program.

intercast: see *multicast*.

interface: the physical components and software drivers that support the attachment of any peripheral to a computer. The term is also used to describe how a user interacts with a software package. See *human–computer interface*.

interface card: the necessary hardware to connect a peripheral to a computer. The interface card is normally a separate circuit board that is inserted in one of the expansion slots on the motherboard of the computer. It is also known as an interface board.

interference: the introduction of unwanted signals to the main signal being transmitted. Interference is usually the result of faulty connections or a fault on some part of the hardware circuits being used. Outside interference can be generated by equipment (such as electric motors) in close proximity to the computer or connected to the same mains electricity circuit.

interlaced scan: a display technology in which electron beams scan alternately all the even numbered lines then all the odd numbered lines, so that the whole screen is covered in two vertical scans. See *scanning*.

interleaving: to arrange parts of one set of data so they alternate with parts of another set of data. Audio files, video images or any large data files may be stored in alternating blocks on disk to allow fast retrieval in the future. When a file is retrieved, the system puts the right segments back together again. The term is also used to describe the splitting up of large programs into segments so that only part of a program needs to be in memory at a particular time. The interleaving of programs is used in *multiprogramming* environments.

intermediate code: the code produced by the *parser* ready for conversion into *machine code*.

internal character code: see *character set*.

international standard book number (ISBN): a unique number assigned to a book title by its publisher for tracking and ordering purposes. The ISBN allows publishers, retailers, libraries, and readers to specify a particular book without confusion. An example ISBN is:

    ISBN 0-340-77214-X

which is the ISBN for THE COMPLETE A–Z BUSINESS STUDIES HANDBOOK.

international data encryption algorithm (IDEA): an encryption *algorithm* that uses a block cipher with a 128-bit key, and is generally considered to be very secure.

International Standards Organisation (ISO): a world-wide federation of national standards bodies with each of over 100 countries having one representative. The standards it is responsible for include the *open systems interconnection seven-layer model* for communication protocols.

Internet: a world-wide *network* of computer networks that allows computer users on one network to retrieve information from any other computer linked to any network within the system, provided they have the necessary rights. It was originally developed as *ARPAnet* by the Advanced Research Projects Agency (ARPA) of the US government in 1969. ARPAnet was intended to create a network that would allow users of a research computer at one university to be able to access information held on research computers at other universities. The technology was set up so that the network could continue to function even if parts of it were destroyed or not functioning for some reason. The Internet today is a public facility that is accessible to hundreds of millions of people world-wide and uses existing public telecommunication networks to link together all the networks and users. The Internet, organisations' *intranets* and *extranets* all use the *transmission control protocol/Internet protocol* (or *e-mail*) set of standards to control their data transmissions.

Probably the most commonly used application on the Internet is electronic mail, which has almost replaced the postal service for short written messages. Using Internet Relay Chat it is possible to carry out 'conversations' with other online computer users.

The *World Wide Web* (often abbreviated to 'the web' or WWW) is the most widely used part of the Internet. The WWW makes extensive use of *hypertext* (*hyperlinks*) as a method of cross-referencing pages and sites on the web. Hyperlinks on *web sites* often appear as words, images or phrases in different coloured text from the main text or as underlined text. Selecting one of these hyperlinks by moving the mouse pointer over the hyperlink and clicking transfers the user to the related site or page. Hyperlinks can also be identified by watching the mouse pointer as it moves over the screen. If the pointer changes from its usual shape of an arrow to a hand it has moved over a hyperlink. By surfing (web browsing using a *web browser*) it is possible to access millions of pages of information.

Internet access provider (IAP): a company that provides individuals and other companies with access to the *Internet*. See *Internet service provider*.

Internet Architecture Board (IAB): the group responsible for the technical development of the *Internet*. The IAB supervises:

- the Internet Engineering Task Force responsible for the development of *transmission control protocol/Internet protocol* (TCP/IP)
- the Internet Research Task Force responsible for overseeing work on network technology
- the Internet Assigned Numbers Authority which assigns *IP addresses*
- the Internet registry, which manages the recording and registration of domain names.

Internet Network Information Centre (InterNIC) was responsible for registering and maintaining the top level domain names (com, net, org) on the *World Wide Web*. Since 1998 the Internet Corporation of Assigned Names and Numbers (ICANN) has taken over the responsibility of registering the organisations able to register domain names. ICANN's responsibility ultimately is derived from the Internet Assigned Numbers Authority that inherited responsibility for Internet root naming and address assignment from the originator of the *Internet*, ARPA.

Internet phone: technology for sending *real-time* voice communication over the *Internet*.

Internet protocol (IP): the rules or *protocol* according to which data is sent from one computer to another on the *Internet*. Each computer on the Internet has at least one *IP address* that uniquely identifies it from all other computers on the Internet. Using IP, a message (data) gets divided into *packets* each of which contains both the sender's and the receiver's Internet address. Each packet is first sent to a gateway computer that understands a small part of the Internet. The gateway computer *reads* the destination address and forwards the packet to an adjacent gateway computer that in turn reads the destination address.

This continues until one gateway computer recognises the packet as belonging to a computer within its immediate neighbourhood. That gateway then forwards the packet directly to the computer whose address is specified. The various packets that represent the complete message do not all take the same route across the Internet nor do they necessarily arrive in sequence. The packets are returned to their original sequence by the transmission control protocol (TCP).

Internet protocol address (IP address): a string of four numbers separated by full stops, e.g. 205.188.146.146, used to represent a computer on the *Internet* (this is the web address of the Internet Society). The format of the *address* is specified by the Internet protocol, currently IP version 4 but being replaced by IP version 6, which will allow for more users of the Internet. The number version of the IP address is usually represented by a name or series of names called the domain name. When a PC accesses the Internet through an *Internet service provider*, it sometimes receives a temporary *IP address* rather than having its own address.

The 28-bit IP address has two parts: the identifier of a particular network on the Internet and an identifier of the particular device (which can be a server or a workstation) within that network. Since networks vary in size, there are four different address formats for IP addresses:

- **class A** addresses are for large networks with many devices
- **class B** addresses are for medium-sized networks
- **class C** addresses are for small networks (fewer than 256 devices)
- **class D** addresses are *multicast* addresses.

Class	Number of network bits	Number of local address bits
A starts with 0	7 bits	24 bits
B starts with 10	14 bits	16 bits
C starts with 110	21 bits	8 bits

Class D starts with 1110 and has 28 bits allocated to the multicast addresses.

The binary IP address is usually expressed as four decimal numbers, each representing eight bits, separated by full stops. The huge increase in users of the Internet means that the number of addresses available under version 4 of IP would soon be used up, but version 6 allows 128 bits for each address.

Internet relay chat (IRC): a system for chatting with other users on the *Internet* that involves a set of rules and conventions, and client/server software. Sites like Talk

City or IRC networks such as the Undernet help users to download an IRC client. Users initially join an existing chat group but can later create their own group. Some groups encourage users to register a nickname for regular use and offer space for a personal profile, picture, and personal *home page* link.

Internet service provider (ISP): a company that provides access to the *Internet*. The company provides the user with a software package, username, password and access phone number allowing access to the Internet and *World Wide Web*. ISPs are connected to one another through network access points (NAPs). ISPs are also called IAPs (*Internet access providers*).

Internet shopping: purchasing items from *web sites* on the *Internet* using credit or debit cards. The benefits of this type of purchase are:

- easy comparison of prices on several sites
- wider variety – users in rural areas are not restricted to just purchasing from local stores
- lower prices – vendors do not have the overheads of high street stores and hence can offer goods at lower prices.

See also *e-commerce*.

Internet Society (ISOC): the Internet Society is an international non-profit organisation that acts as guide and conscience for the *Internet*. It was founded in 1992 and supports the *Internet Architecture Board*, which supervises technical Internet issues. The web address is http://www.isoc.org/

interpreter: a language translator that executes program *source code* by reading it one line at a time and performing each instruction immediately. Unlike a compiler, an interpreter does not produce an *object code* version of the program. An interpreter is often used during the development of a program, as it allows the programmer a more interactive approach than does a compiler.

interrupt: a signal informing the operating system/program that something has occurred that requires its attention. When the operating system/program receives an interrupt signal, it takes a specified action (which can be to ignore the signal). Interrupt signals arise from a variety of sources, e.g. a peripheral (disk transfer complete, printer out of paper), software (arithmetic overflow, program terminated).

Hardware interrupts are normally associated with individual bits in an interrupt register. By regularly checking the interrupt register (IRQ) to ensure it contains zero the operating system can tell when an interrupt has occurred (when the contents of the interrupt register are non-zero) and instigate appropriate actions.

Prior to *plug and play* devices, users often had to set IRQ (interrupt request) values manually when adding a new device to a computer.

Software interrupts are normally associated with an interrupt vector table, with each interrupt having a specific value. This value is 'looked up' in the vector table, which contains the address of the start point for the corresponding interrupt routine.

intranet: a private version of the *Internet*, normally with access to the Internet through a *firewall*. The main purpose of an intranet is to share company information, procedures and knowledge confidentially with employees. An intranet uses the same *protocols* as the Internet. See *extranet*.

inverse video: see *highlighting*.

inverter: see *NOT gate*.

iteration: a noun that means repetition. The term is used in two significant ways in computing/IT.

1 In computer programming, iteration describes the process of repeating a set of instructions as part of a *loop* command. Each pass through the set of instructions is called an iteration.

2 An iterative approach to software development is when an application is designed heuristically, with each section developed called an iteration. After completion, each iteration is reviewed and commented on by the software team and a focus group of end-users. The comments raised during this review determine the next iteration. Documentation is produced at each iteration indicating what has been tried, approved, or discarded. The main advantage of using iterative development is that the end-user is involved in the development process. The software is often made available before it becomes a final product. In fact it might never become a final product and hence iterative development is sometimes called circular or evolutionary development.

J

jabber: any *network* device that is handling electrical signals improperly, usually affecting the rest of the network. A jabber is usually the result of a bad *network interface card* but can occasionally be the result of outside electrical interference.

Jackson structured development (JSD): a methodology developed by Michael Jackson for the analysis and design of solutions to problems that can then be implemented using a computer.

Jackson structured programming (JSP): a structured programming technique that uses diagrams to represent the *algorithm* that is to be used in the production of a program. The JSP approach produces well-organised programs that are easier to maintain than those created using traditional flowcharts.

jaggies: the jagged edges that appear in graphics on diagonal or curved lines. The stepped appearance is the result of trying to create a diagonal or curved line out of rectangular shapes. Jaggies can be reduced by producing a large version of the image and then reducing it to the required size or by *anti-aliasing*, which means putting *pixels* along the jagged edge which are of an intermediate colour between the background and the image.

jam: a signal on an *Ethernet network* from one device to all other devices announcing that a collision has occurred. The jam signal results in additional collisions in any other packets that are in the process of being transmitted and warns non-transmitting devices to wait. A jam signal forces all devices to restart any bids to get control of the network cable.

jargon: the specialised or technical language of a trade; for example, 'computerese'.

Java: a cross-platform programming language that can be used to create animations and interactive features on *World Wide Web* pages. Java programs are embedded into HTML documents and have the 'look and feel' of the C++ language. Java is simpler to use than C++ and enforces an *object-oriented programming* model. Java can be used to create complete applications that may run on a single computer or be distributed among servers and clients in a network. It can also be used to build a small application module or *applet* for use as part of a web page. The major characteristics of Java are:

- The programs created can be run anywhere in a network on a server or client that has a Java *virtual machine*. This means platform-specific versions of programs are no longer needed.
- The code is robust since it cannot contain references to external data. This means that an instruction cannot contain the address of a data location used by another application which would cause the program to crash.

Java applet: a small program written in *Java* that can be embedded into an HTML document.

Java chip: a microchip that can be incorporated into a computer to improve the execution times of *Java* programs (including *Java applets*).

Java database connectivity (JDBC): a specification for the interface to connect an application program written in *Java* to the data in popular databases.

JavaScript: a cross-platform *World Wide Web* interpreted scripting language from Netscape Communications that is simple and easy to learn and can be included in an HTML file by using the tag <script language='JavaScript'>. JavaScript is used when developing web sites that:

- automatically change a formatted date on a web page
- cause a linked-to page to appear in a popup window
- cause text or a graphic image to change during a mouse rollover.

Jaz drive: a small, portable, removable cartridge, hard disk drive made by Iomega Corporation. Jaz drives are mainly used to *backup* and archive data on PCs. The Jaz drive uses the *small computer systems interface* (SCSI) and requires a SCSI controller. The Jaz drive is different from a Zip drive in that the computer recognises it as another hard disk, which allows the user to install and use applications from the Jaz drive.

job: a unit of background work (batch programs) that can be run without requiring user interaction, e.g. payroll.

job-control language (JCL): a command language for mainframes and mini-computers, used for starting applications. The JCL describes the tasks to be carried out in the execution of a *job*. JCL statements mainly specify the input files that must be accessed, the output data files to be created or updated, what resources must be allocated for the job, and the programs that are to run, using these input and output data files. A set of JCL statements for a job is itself stored as a data file and can be started interactively.

job-control program: the set of *job-control language* instructions that specify the steps to be taken to complete a *job*. Since the job can involve running several different programs the instructions will cater for any of the programs failing and hence possibly not producing the output required as input for subsequent programs.

job queue: the line up of *jobs* that have been loaded into a computer system and are to be run.

job scheduling involves determining which *jobs* in a job queue should be given highest priority. To ensure most efficient use of the resources in a computer system, processor-bound programs should be given lowest priority and peripheral-bound programs highest priority.

job swapping: the process of moving a *job* out of the processor and giving use of the processor to the highest priority program available.

John von Neumann: the person who originally came up with the idea that programs and data could be stored and not entered each time a program is run – machines that work like this are generally referred to as stored-program computers.

Joint Academic NETwork (JANET): the main backbone network for the UK university system of academic and research computers. It was re-named SuperJANET after it was upgraded to higher speed links. It is operated by UKERNA (United Kingdom Education & Research Networking Association), a non-profit group, under contract from the Joint Information Systems Committee (JISC) of the UK Higher Education Funding Councils.

joint photographic expert group (JPEG): part of the International Standards Organisation responsible for devising software *compression* systems. Picture files using these compression techniques are referred to as JPEG files and are commonly used on *Internet* pages, as their small size reduces download times. When a JPEG image is created the user is asked to specify the quality of image required. The highest quality yields the largest *file* and hence a trade-off occurs between image quality and file size. Formally, the JPEG file format is ISO standard 10918.

journal: a daily, or regular, record of events and transactions. A computer journal includes a record of changes made to files, messages transmitted, etc. It can be used to recover previous versions of a file before updates were made, or to reconstruct the updates if an updated file gets damaged.

journalled file system: a file system in which updates to the master file are automatically recorded in a *journal*. If the new master file is corrupted in any way it can be recreated using the information in the journal file and a copy of the *master file* taken before processing began.

joystick: a hand held stick like the joystick in an aeroplane, which is used as a pointing device in arcade games and video games. The joystick can move an object on screen in any direction. It usually has one or more push buttons for shooting, jumping, etc.

Jscript: a script *language* from Microsoft that is expressly designed for use within *web pages* and is similar to Netscape's more widely used *JavaScript*.

jump: an instruction within a program that changes the sequence in which instructions are executed by making the next instruction to be obeyed the one indicated in the jump instruction, either unconditionally (unconditional jump) or subject to some condition (conditional jump).

jumper: a pair of prongs that are electrical contact points set into a computer circuit board. To set a jumper, the user places a plug on the prongs which completes a circuit. Jumper settings are used to adjust the configuration of a computer. *Plug and play* technology does not require manual setting of jumpers.

justification: in *word processing*, and *desktop publishing* applications, alignment of text with both the left and right margins, except for last lines of paragraphs, which are only left-justified. Also referred to as fully justified.

This paragraph is an example of justified text. Notice that the text starts from the left margin and goes right up to the right margin and is aligned so that there is no space between the text and the right edge margin.

See also *right alignment* and *left alignment*.

just-in-time compiler: a program that turns *Java* byte code into instructions that can be sent directly to the computer's processor. The *source language* statements of a Java program are compiled into bytecode rather than *machine code*. This bytecode is platform-independent code and can be sent to any *platform* and run on that platform after putting it through the just-in-time compiler. The Java just-in-time compiler at the particular system platform compiles the bytecode into the system code required on that platform.

In the past, most programs written in any language have had to be recompiled, and sometimes, rewritten for each computer platform. One of the biggest advantages of Java is that you only have to write and compile a program once.

K (kilo): abbreviation for the prefix kilo – which normally represents 1000 but in computing stands for 1024, i.e. 2^{10}. It is often used to identify an amount of memory or size of file, e.g. 1 K meaning 1024 *bytes* of memory.

kangaroo code: a term used to describe clumsily-written, disorganised computer program code that has been created by a novice and is difficult to follow because it jumps around in an illogical way. Also known as spaghetti code.

Karnaugh map: a two dimensional grid that can be used to represent a Boolean expression with four or fewer variables. Once the representation is transferred to the map, simplification can be carried out using visual inspection techniques. Karnaugh maps provide an easier way of simplifying Boolean expressions than the algebraic approach but do not always arrive at the simplest expression. (The one requiring the least number of gates to implement the expression as a logic circuit.)

Example of a Karnaugh map:

The expression $R = A.B.C.\bar{D} + A.B.C\bar{D} + \bar{A}B.C\bar{D} + A.\bar{B}.C\bar{D} + \bar{A}.B.C\bar{D}$ is represented on a Karnaugh map as:

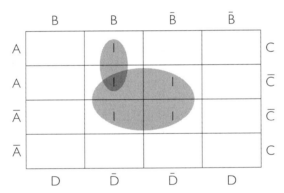

and this simplifies to:

$$R = \bar{C}.\bar{D} + A.B.\bar{D}$$

See also *Boolean algebra.*

Kermit: a *file transfer* and terminal emulation program produced by Columbia University, USA. Kermit is very versatile and freely available for many different types of computer. Some advantages of Kermit are:

- the user can write a script that will allow a sequence of file transfers to happen with a single command
- the user can transfer an entire file directory and its subdirectories with a single command
- text and binary files can be sent in the same file transfer
- character-sets can be translated as part of the transfer (for example, from EBCDIC to ASCII).

kernel: the essential part of an *operating system* that is responsible for carrying out its basic functions. Typically, the kernel of an operating system includes the *interrupt* handler, a *scheduler* that determines which programs use the processor, and a *supervisor* that actually gives each process use of the processor when it is scheduled. The kernel may also include a manager of the operating system's address spaces in memory, sharing these among all components and other users of the kernel's services. A kernel's services are requested by other parts of the operating system or by applications software through a specified set of program interfaces sometimes known as system calls.

Because the code that makes up the kernel is needed continuously, it is usually loaded into the computer's memory in an area that is protected so that it will not be overlaid with other less frequently used parts of the operating system.

kerning: reducing the spacing between certain pairs of letters in a proportional-pitch font to improve the appearance of a line of text. For example, A and V look better with a smaller space between them than the space that would be appropriate between A and B. Proportional-pitch fonts often have automatic kerning of certain letter pairs which can then be adjusted by the operator, according to their preference.

key: a variable value that is applied to a block of text to encrypt the text for security purposes. The length of the key generally determines how difficult it will be to decrypt the text in a given message. See also *encryption*.

key escrow: a policy of the United States government, allowing strong *encryption* technology to be exported pending the approval of the Commerce Department and under the condition that the company exporting the technology offer a third key to the government. Some United States companies, including Hewlett Packard, Novell and Cisco Systems Inc., have agreed to participate in the key escrow system.

key field: the *field* in a *record* whose contents are used to uniquely identify a record in a database or file. The field is often used to determine the order in which the records are organised in the file.

key frame: a *frame* in an animated sequence of frames that was drawn or otherwise constructed directly by the user rather than generated automatically, e.g. by *tweening*.

keyboard: a peripheral for data entry that is made up of a set of keys that resemble a typewriter keyboard, but with a few extra keys for computer commands and (usually) a numeric keypad added. Pressing a key on a computer keyboard sends an electrical signal to a microprocessor, which sends a scan code to the computer's *basic input output system* (BIOS). The BIOS translates the scan code into the ASCII code for the character pressed and the operating system or applications software then displays the character on the screen. See *QWERTY keyboard*.

keyboard shortcut: a key combination that, when pressed, executes a task. Normally keyboard shortcuts are alternative methods of selecting options from drop-down menus using a mouse. A commonly used keyboard shortcut in Windows or Macintosh is Control + S, which is a quick way to save a file.

keypad: a *keyboard* with a restricted set of keys. The term can also refer to the keys on the numerical keypad on a computer keyboard.

An example of a laptop keyboard

keystrip: a piece of plastic or card placed over or above the *function keys* to indicate the operations performed by each key within a specific application. It is useful as a reminder to a user of what certain function keys do. For example, F3 may represent Save in certain applications.

keyword search: conducting sort or search operations on *records* in a database by using a characteristic word, phrase, or code that is stored in a *key field*.

kill file: a *file* used by some *e-mail* software that filters out unwanted messages, usually from a particular author or on a particular subject.

knowbot: short for **know**ledge ro**bot**. A knowbot is a program that automatically searches *Internet* sites and gathers information according to a set of rules that is specified by the user. A knowbot is different from a *search engine* crawler that gathers information according to a generalised set of rules which can then be indexed and made available to several users. An example of a knowbot search would entail visiting major news-oriented web sites each morning and providing a digest of stories for a personalised news page. A knowbot is also known as an 'intelligent agent'.

knowledge acquisition: the process of collecting knowledge from humans for use by an *expert system*.

knowledge base: a database of knowledge about a particular subject that is used in *artificial intelligence* applications. The knowledge base for an *expert system* is acquired partly from human experience and partly from the computer's accumulated experience in solving problems. Before it can be used by an expert system the knowledge base must be expressed in a formal knowledge representation language.

knowledge-based system (KBS): a computer system that is programmed to imitate the problem-solving procedures human experts carry out. For example, in a medical system the user might enter data such as the patient's symptoms, lab reports, etc., and derive from the computer a possible diagnosis. The success of a knowledge based system depends on the quality of the data provided to the computer, and the rules programmed into the computer for making deductions from that data. See also *expert systems*.

knowledge domain: a specific area of knowledge covered by a *knowledge-based system*.

knowledge engineer: an engineer who obtains knowledge from human experts and organises it into a *knowledge base* for an *expert system*.

label: an identifier in a program that is used with unconditional and conditional *jumps*. The label is placed at required points in a program and can then be used as the *operand* in a jump instruction. The instruction below:

    Jump LoopStart

when executed would transfer execution to the next instruction after the label 'LoopStart'.

LAN: See *local area network*.

language: a formal language in which computer *programs* are written. The definition of a particular language consists of the *syntax* rules and its *semantics*. Languages are classified as low level if they are close to machine code and high level if each language statement corresponds to many machine code instructions and the source program is easily understood by humans. Another major distinction is between *imperative languages* and *declarative languages*.

language-based editor: a software application that is designed to allow the user to *write* and *edit* programs in a particular programming language. The editor has the *syntax* rules of the language built into it, and can check for mistakes as programs are written or edited.

language translator: see *translator, interpreter*.

Laplink: a program from Travelling Software Inc. that transfers data between laptops and desktop computers.

laptop computer: a battery-powered personal computer, generally weighing less than 3 kg and smaller than a briefcase, that can easily be transported and conveniently used in temporary spaces such as on aeroplanes, in libraries, temporary offices, and at meetings. Laptop computers cost more than comparable desktop computers with the same capabilities because they are more difficult to design and manufacture. There are several different methods of integrating a mouse-type device into laptop computers, e.g. *touchpad, trackball* and pointing stick.

large-scale integration (LSI): the use of *integrated circuits* with between 100 and 10 000 logic gates.

laser disk: a technology and the physical medium used in storing and providing programmed access to a large database of text, pictures, and other objects, including motion video and full *multimedia* presentations. The laser disk itself is 30 cm in diameter and holds much more information than a *CD-ROM*. It is also known as a video disk.

laser printer: a popular type of personal computer printer that uses a non-impact photocopier technology. When a document is being printed on a laser printer a laser beam 'draws' the document on a selenium-coated drum using electrical charge. After the drum is charged, it is rolled in dry powder toner. The toner sticks to the charged image on the drum and is then fused to the paper with heat and pressure. After the document is printed, the electrical charge is removed from the drum and the excess toner is collected. The printed image from a laser printer will not smudge unlike *inkjet printer* output, which uses liquid ink.

Laser printers vary considerably in price, which is determined by:

- print capacity and speed: the cheapest laser printers are designed for 'home' use and can print up to eight pages per minute (ppm). Top end laser printers can print up to 700 ppm and are used by commercial printers who use them 24 hours a day, seven days a week
- resolution: the most common resolution for laser printers is 600 dots per inch (dpi) which is adequate for everyday printing, including small desktop publishing jobs. A top-end printer might have a resolution of 2400 dpi.

last in first out (LIFO): a method of storage in which the data item stored last will be retrieved first. See also *stack*.

latch: a digital logic circuit used to store a bit. A latch has a data input, a *clock* input and an output. When the clock input is active, data on the input is stored and transferred to the output either immediately or when the clock input goes inactive. The output will then retain its value until the clock goes active again.

latency: 1 In a *network*, latency is the time it takes for a packet of data to get from one designated point to another. There are several contributors to network latency:

- propagation – the time it takes for a packet to travel between one place and another
- gateway – each gateway takes time to examine the header in a packet before determining its onward route.

2 On a *disk drive*, latency is the time it takes to rotate the disk until the correct sector is under the *read/write head*. This is generally regarded as half the time taken for the disk to complete one complete revolution.

launch: to load a *program* and start it running.

layout: the design and formatting of a page for publication, which can include the specifications for margins, indents, column widths, word wrap, tabs, etc. Layout is done onscreen, using a computer program and a hard copy of the page may never be made.

leading: the vertical spacing between lines of type or other design elements, usually measured from baseline to baseline. Leading and fonts are measured in points and leading is normally set at 120% of the font size of the text, e.g. a 10 point font would normally have 12 point leading. Leading can however be adjusted to any desired setting. Simple word processors allow only for single-, space-and-a-half and double-spacing, whereas desktop publishing packages allow finer leading adjustments.

leading zeros: zeros on the left side of a number that have no effect on the value held but are used to fill in a *field* or *register*. For example, the zeros in 0002347.

leaf: a *node* in a *tree* data structure that has no descendants. The term is also used to identify the lowest level of file in a hierarchical file system. The *hierarchical directory structure* is described as a tree with a descending system of directories similar to roots, branches, and leaves.

leased line: a telephone line that has been leased (rented) for private use. In some contexts, it is called a dedicated line.

least significant bit (LSB): the bit of a *binary* number that is farthest to the right. This bit position is designated as bit zero.

left alignment: text that is aligned on the left margin. It is sometimes known as 'flush left'.

This paragraph is an example of left-aligned text. Notice that text runs from the left margin and is aligned so that there is no space between the text and the left margin, but the right edge of the text is ragged.

legacy application: an application that has been in use for a long time, usually on a mainframe or minicomputer.

letter quality (LQ): printing quality as good as, or better than, the best typewriters. *Laser printers* and most modern *inkjet printers* produce letter quality printing.

lexical analysis: the first stage of processing a program in which a lexical analyser takes the *source program* and groups characters into elemental units of the language which can then be sent on to the *parser*.

library: a collection of compiled *subroutines, functions* and *subprograms* stored in one or more areas, ready for linking with other programs. Libraries are normally created to group together routines of a similar type, e.g. file handling, graphic, mathematical, etc.

library program/routine: a program held in an organisation's software *library*.

licence agreement: a legal statement which indicates the terms under which a user may make use of a software product. The license to use does not transfer ownership of the software product. In many cases the licence is worded so that installation or use of the product indicates agreement to the terms stated.

Usually the license agreement is in effect with retail software once the user opens the software package. If the software is bought for use on a *network*, then a single copy is provided together with a licence to use the software on a certain number of machines. This is generally cheaper than buying individual copies for each machine. The unauthorised use of software that has not been properly purchased with a licence is illegal, as is using the software on more machines than specified by the licence. Copying software that has been bought by someone else is, therefore, highly likely to be illegal.

light-emitting diode (LED): a semiconductor device that emits visible light when an electric current passes through it. The light is normally of a single wavelength (single colour) and not particularly bright. Some LEDs emit infrared energy and are known as infrared-emitting diodes (IRED).

Advantages of LEDs and IREDs, compared with incandescent and fluorescent light devices, include:

- low power requirement – most types can be operated with battery power supplies
- high efficiency – most of the power supplied to an LED or IRED is converted into radiation in the required form, with minimal heat production
- long life: an LED or IRED can function for decades.

Typical applications include:

- indicator lights – on/off lights on peripherals and computers
- remote control – most home-entertainment 'remotes' use IREDs to transmit data to the main unit.

light pen: a light-sensitive device that can be used to draw on a screen by moving it over the screen's surface.

line art: see *vector graphics*.

line break: see *hard space, soft return*.

line noise: extraneous characters that appear in a computer transmission because of electrical noise in the communications link. Line noise can be as a result of a poor connection, electrical storms, or other problems.

line printer: a printer that prints one line at a time. It is commonly used with large mainframe computers where vast amounts of computer printout are required at high speed. Line printers are expensive compared to *character printers*.

linear search: a *search* that is carried out by starting with the first item and inspecting each item in turn until either the required item is found or the end of the data is reached, in which case the required item does not exist. The search can be made more efficient by sorting the data items into search field order before the search commences. Using sorted data means the non-existence of the required item is established when the search field of the data item being considered has a value greater than the required item. This type of search can be used to search files of data as well as data held in arrays in memory, unlike the binary search which requires the data to be sorted and held in memory.

link: a selectable connection from one word, picture, or graphic image to another. In a *multimedia* environment such as the *World Wide Web* the links are selected by moving the mouse pointer over the object and clicking the mouse button.

link editor: see *linker*.

linked list: a list in which each *node* of data has a *pointer* to the next node in the list. The data elements may be in non-contiguous storage locations but need a start pointer to identify the first node in the list and the use of a *null pointer* to indicate the end of the list.

linker: a computer program which accepts the *object code* files of one or more separately compiled program segments (*subprograms*) and links them together into a complete executable program, resolving references between the subprograms.

linking: the process of combining *subprograms* together to form a single program using a *linker*.

linking error: an error that occurs during the linking process. Examples of linking errors include:

- a *routine* specified is not present in the *library*
- the wrong number or type of parameters are provided.

Linux: is a *Unix*-like *operating system* that was designed to provide personal computer users with a free or very low-cost operating system comparable to traditional, and usually more expensive, Unix systems. Linux has a reputation as a very efficient and fast-performing system that includes a *graphical user interface*, an X window system, TCP/IP, the Emacs editor, and other components usually found in a comprehensive Unix system. Although copyrights are held by various creators of Linux's components, Linux is distributed on the legal basis that any modified version that is redistributed must in turn be freely available.

liquid-crystal display (LCD): a type of display used on digital watches, calculators, and laptop computers. LCDs are light and use considerably less power than other computer displays. Liquid crystals are rod-shaped molecules which spiral when they are exposed to an electrical charge. Polarised light passing through the layer of liquid crystal cells is twisted along the spiral path of the molecules. The light then passes through a series of filters that block light vibrating at certain angles and allow light vibrating at other angles to pass through; thus the colour of each *pixel* can be controlled.

LISP (an acronym for list processing) is a *programming language* that was designed for easy manipulation of data strings. It is a commonly used language for *artificial intelligence* programming.

list: 1 An ordered set of data items.

2 To display a program line by line.

list box: a scrollable area within a *dialogue box* where the user can choose from a list of items.

listing: see *program listing*.

listing file: a *file* created during the compilation process that contains the program listing and a list of any errors that have been found during compilation.

literal: a constant, or part of an instruction in a computer program that remains unchanged. The contents of the literal are defined at compilation and cannot be modified by the user whilst the program is running. For example in Pascal the instruction:

```
Writeln('The answer is ',result);
```

has a literal 'The answer is' which does not change once the program is running and a variable 'result' which can change during execution.

loader: the part of the *operating system* that locates a given program on disk, transfers it into memory (RAM) and gives it control of the processor. The program loaded may itself contain components that are not initially loaded into memory but can be loaded if and when needed.

local area network (LAN): a group of computer systems (*network* stations) and associated peripherals that are located within a small geographic area (for example, within an office building). The computer systems on the LAN share a communications cabling system and the resources available on the network *server*. Normally the server holds all the software applications available and these can be downloaded to the individual network stations when required. Each user of the network has their own data storage area but many LANs provide a shared data storage area that is available to all users. Printing facilities are normally available as one of the shared resources, which means that each user does not need their own local printer. The main advantages of LANs are:

- shared hardware
- shared data
- shared software.

Common *network topologies* for the communications cabling are:

- *bus*
- *ring*
- *star.*

local area wireless network (LAWN): a technology from O'Neill Communications, Inc., for wireless networking using a radio transmitter/receiver.

local bus: an extra *bus* in addition to the main bus in a computer that provides a fast data path connecting the central processing unit (CPU) with memory and peripherals. The local bus is designed to run at the same speed as the CPU. The most common local buses are VLB (VESA local bus) and PCI (*peripheral component interconnect*).

local variable: a *variable* that only has value and meaning in the *subprogram* in which it is declared. The local variable is normally defined inside its subprogram and only comes into existence when the subprogram is entered. On exit from the subprogram the contents of the local variable are destroyed, along with any indication of its whereabouts in memory. The use of local variables can make a subprogram self-standing, allowing its use in other programs.

log file: a *file* that is used to record the activities carried out on a computer. Log files are normally used on *networks* to record time of connection, user ID of the person logging on, applications used, files accessed and disconnection time, etc.

log in/log on: the procedure used to gain access to a network or application in a remote computer. Almost always the user is required to have a login identity ID and *password* to gain access to the facilities. The login ID can be freely known and is visible when entered at a keyboard or other input device, whereas the password must be kept secret (and is not displayed as it is entered). Logging onto a *network* will normally give the user access to some of the resources available on the network and to a protected work space that cannot be accessed by other users of the network.

log off/log out: to exit from a *network* or remote system in an orderly way.

logic bomb: code that was not intended by the user to be included in a program but is hidden in a program or system by its programmer and is executed when the user performs a certain action or when certain conditions are met. A logic bomb may destroy data, violate system security, or totally erase the contents of a hard drive. It is not the same as a *virus* because the logic bomb executes once, or at periodic intervals, whereas the action of a virus is ongoing. A logic bomb could be set up by a programmer to destroy vital data files if the programmer's record is removed from a company's payroll in an attempt to guarantee employment for the programmer.

logic error: see *logical error.*

logic gate: a basic building block in a digital logic circuit. Logic gates normally have two inputs and one output, with each input being in one of the two binary conditions (0 or 1) at any given moment. The inputs to the gate often change as the circuit processes data and hence can produce different outputs. There are seven basic logic gates: *AND, OR, XOR, NOT, NAND, NOR,* and *XNOR.*

Using combinations of these logic gates all the complex operations required in a computer are performed. As integrated circuit (IC) technology advances, the amount of space required for each logic gate decreases and digital devices of the same or smaller size become capable of performing ever-more-complicated operations at ever-increasing speeds.

logical address: a memory location accessed by an application program in a system with *virtual memory* such that intervening hardware and/or software maps the virtual *address* to a real physical memory location. During the course of execution of an application, the same virtual address may be mapped to many different real memory locations, as data and programs are paged in and out.

logical equivalence: two logic circuits are described as being logically equivalent when the output from one is identical to the other for the same inputs.

logical error: an error that occurs in a program when the result is not what was expected even though the program runs successfully. A trivial example would be a program that was intended to add two numbers together which output the result 3 when the two numbers 8 and 5 were entered (the programmer probably entered a minus sign when a plus sign should have been entered).

logical operator: one of the Boolean operators *AND, OR* and *NOT.*

logical record: a term used to describe the actual information held in a *record,* unlike the physical record which is the term used to identify the block holding the logical record.

logical shift: a *machine code* instruction that moves the bits in a register either one place left (left logical shift) or one place right (right logical shift). A logical shift discards any bits that 'fall off' the register and does not preserve the sign of the number held in the register. A zero is placed in the 'empty' bit position in the register.

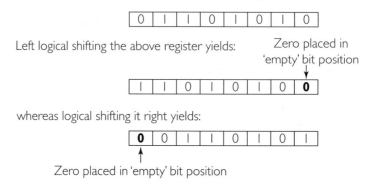

Left logical shifting the above register yields:

whereas logical shifting it right yields:

Zero placed in 'empty' bit position

lookup table: a table used to convert one set of values into another. A lookup function, often built into *spreadsheet* programs, is used where a previously constructed table of values called a lookup table is searched for a desired item of information. A lookup table consists of rows and columns of data. A lookup function examines the table either horizontally or vertically and then retrieves the data that corresponds to the argument specified as part of the lookup function.

The following simple worksheet shows the use of a lookup table (the grading table) to insert the appropriate grade into column C. The formula in *cells* C4 to C7 would use the mark in B4 to B7 to compare values in E4 to E7 and return the grade in the corresponding cell in F4 to F7.

In Excel, this formula would be =VLOOKUP(B4,$E$4:$F$7,2). B4 gives the mark, $E$4:$F$7 gives the range and 2 returns the value in the second column, i.e. column F.

	A	B	C	D	E	F	G
1	Grading a test						
2							
3	Name	Mark	Grade		Grading table		
4	Anne	76	Merit		0	Fail	
5	Bill	35	Pass		35	Pass	
6	Dave	90	Distinction		60	Merit	
7	Myna	14	Fail		80	Distinction	
8							

loop: a sequence of program instructions that is repeated until a certain condition is reached. A loop is a fundamental programming concept that is commonly used in writing programs. There are three essential constructs: *while loops* where the condition is tested at the start of each execution of the loop, *repeat until loops* where the condition is tested at the end of each execution of the loop and *for loops* where the loop is executed a prescribed number of times. See also *infinite loops*.

loop network: see *ring network*.

loopback: a test signal, in telephone systems, that is sent to a *network* destination and returned as received to the originator. Loopback is used to help determine the cause of a fault. Loopback is similar to PINGing on the *Internet*.

lossless compression: a *compression* method in which no data is lost. With lossless compression, a large file can be compressed to take up less space, and then decompressed without any loss of information, e.g. graphics and video files can be compressed and decompressed without any loss of resolution.

low-level language: a computer programming language that is close to *machine code*. Low-level languages are sometimes called *assembly languages* and are translated into machine code by an *assembler*. Each low-level (assembly) language instruction corresponds to one machine code instruction, but low-level (assembly) language is easier for the programmer to understand (and hence to use) than machine code.

low resolution: a small number of dots or lines per inch. Low-resolution images use less memory but result in a lower print or display quality.

MacBinary: *Macintosh* files that prevent loss of the resource fork when transferring the file to a non-Macintosh computer, by attaching the resource and data forks together in a single data file. Macintosh files have a resource fork and a data fork, unlike files that have been produced on other types of computer, which hold data only. If Macintosh files are put on a non-Macintosh machine, the resource fork is stripped off, which makes the files unusable. MacBinary files must be transferred using an 8-bit, binary mode. They often have '.bin' as a filename extension.

machine address: an *address* that is permanently assigned by the maker of the machine to a specific storage location in a computer's memory.

machine code: the basic *language* of computers, consisting of 0s and 1s. This is the lowest level computer language and all programs produced in higher level languages must be translated into machine code before they can be executed.

machine cycle: the cycle carried out by a computer's central processing unit (CPU) each time a *machine code* instruction is obeyed:
- fetching the instruction from the main memory
- decoding it
- executing the instruction.

machine-dependent program: a program that runs only on one type of computer, unlike a machine-independent program, which is a program that can run on many different types of computer.

machine language: see *machine code*.

machine learning: the ability of software to recognise patterns that have occurred several times and use this information to improve performance based on this past experience.

machine-oriented language: a computer *programming language*, which is specifically written for a particular processor. See *machine code*.

machine readable: data that can be transferred directly to a computer without anybody having to carry out any data preparation. OMR, OCR, MICR are all methods of producing machine readable data.

Macintosh: a personal computer made by Apple Corporation. The Macintosh (often called 'the Mac') was the first widely sold personal computer with a *graphical user interface* (GUI) giving users a natural, intuitively understandable computer interface. The Macintosh has its own *operating system*, Mac OS.

Macintosh user interface: the *graphical user interface* (GUI) used by *Macintosh* personal computers. The interface is modelled on an actual desktop with icons of file folders, a trash can for deleting files, etc. The interface is designed to be easy to use for users who are not experts and uses *pull-down menus*, point and click, and a *drag and drop* approach to loading files and starting software.

macro: a simple programming function used to automate frequently used commands and functions. Within software applications (Microsoft Word) a macro represents a recorded sequence of commands or keystrokes which is stored and then recalled with a single command or keystroke. In *assembly language* programming, a macro definition defines how to expand a single instruction into a number of instructions. The macro statement contains the name of the macro definition and usually some variable parameter information.

macro call: an instruction that requests a section of code that already exists (the macro) to be executed or incorporated into a program.

macro virus: normally a relatively harmless computer *virus* that 'infects' application software packages such as Microsoft Word and causes a sequence of actions to be performed automatically when the application is started. Typical effects of macro viruses include letters falling down the screen and collecting at the bottom of the screen or the insertion of some comic text at certain points when text is entered in a word processor. Macro viruses are often spread by attaching themselves to *e-mails*.

magic cookie: a file created by *Microsoft Explorer* and *Netscape Navigator* and kept in the preferences folder. The file stores data about the web sites visited by a user as well as the actual pages within the web site. This information can then be used by the servers storing the web sites for marketing analysis or to include the user in mailing lists.

magnetic disk: the main method of storing data on personal computers. Data is magnetically recorded onto the disk's surface and hence can also be erased and re-recorded. The data is organised in concentric rings called *tracks*, which are further divided into *sectors*.

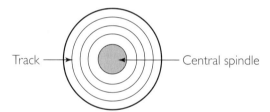

Data is transferred to the disk using *read/write heads* attached to the end of a mechanical arm. As the disk rotates the mechanical arm moves the read/write heads back and forth across the disk's surface. The heads write data by aligning magnetic particles on the disk's surface, and reads data by detecting the polarities of particles that have already been aligned.

magnetic-ink character recognition (MICR): a character recognition system used on bank cheques. Special ink that can be magnetised for automatic reading is used in the printing of the characters on the cheques.

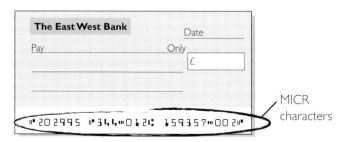

magnetic-strip card: a plastic card with a magnetic strip (stripe) on the back that holds data that can be read by computer peripherals. Magnetic strip cards are used for credit cards, debit cards, library cards, shop loyalty cards, etc.

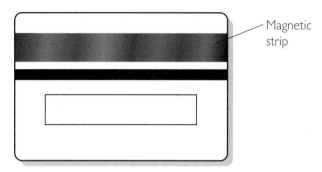

Magnetic strip

magnetic tape: a data storage medium used for backing up computer files and systems. The tape is made of a thin plastic strip with a magnetisable oxide coating on one side. Tapes are available in reels and cartridges of various sizes and data is transferred using a *read/write head* as the tape drive winds the tape from one reel to another. The data is written in *blocks* whose maximum size is determined by the size of the buffer in the interface with *inter-block gaps* between them. Tapes can only be used to store sequential or serial data files since it is necessary to read the tape from the beginning until the block containing the required record is reached.

magneto-optical disk: a plastic or glass disk coated with a chemical with special properties that make it rewritable. A combination of magnetic and optical methods is used to write data to the disk. A high-intensity laser heats the material up to its Curie point, the temperature at which molecules can be realigned by a magnetic field. A magnet is used to make changes in polarity, which remain after cooling. The disk is read by directing a low-intensity laser at the disk and interpreting variations in its reflected light, which result from differences in polarity of the stored magnetic field.

mail bomb: the sending of a huge amount of *e-mail* to a specific person or system. The intention is to fill up the recipient's disk space on the server or to generate so much data that the server stops functioning.

mail exploder: part of an electronic mail system used by mailing lists. The user sends *e-mails* to a central *address* where the mail exploder delivers the e-mails to all the individual *mailboxes* in its list.

mail filter: a program that can sort and process incoming *e-mail* for the recipient, based on the mail headers. For example, all e-mail referring to a certain subject in the header could be put into a particular folder.

mail merge: a facility provided in many *word processors* allowing individually customised letters to be produced. The letter is stored in one file and a name and address list in another. Each name and address is taken in turn and incorporated into the letter at designated merge points before printing and clearing ready for the next name and address. Other data can also be inserted at chosen points as specified by the user.

The following diagrams show the set up for a simple mail merge letter in Word. The standard (form) letter is shown on the next page.

The letter requires a source of data with the same field names. This can be set up in Word as here or can come from another source, such as a database or an address book.

Title	FirstName	LastName	Address1	Address2	City	PostalCode
Mr	John	Morgan	1 The Avenue	Greenfield	Anytown	AN1 2JK
Miss	Aseema	Amla	1 The Close	Whitelea	Anytown	AN3 5RT
Mr	Paul	Wilson	1 The Copse	Woodlands	Anytown	AN6 8GH

The data is then merged either completely or selectively into the standard letter to produce individual letters as shown below.

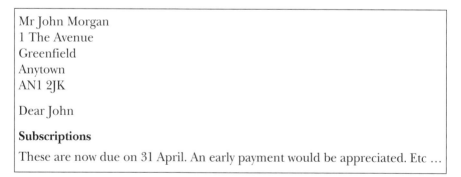

An example of an individual letter produced by mail merge

mailbox: a box (disk storage area) assigned to hold incoming *e-mails*. The service provider acts in a similar way to a post office, storing messages in transit and those waiting to be retrieved when a user logs on.

mailing list: a list of the *e-mail addresses* of people who subscribe to a periodic mailing distribution on a particular topic. Mailing lists have become a popular way for *Internet* users to keep up with topics they are interested in. Many software and hardware producers are now using them as a way to keep in touch with customers.

main store: the main area in a computer in which data is stored for quick access by the computer's processor. On microcomputers this area is generally called RAM (*random access memory*).

mainframe: an industry term for a large computer that is normally produced by one of the large computer manufactures such as IBM. Traditionally the mainframe computer is associated with centralised rather than distributed computing.

maintenance: the activities that keep the software and hardware of a computer system operational.

maintenance documentation: the necessary documentation to allow a programmer or maintenance engineer to understand and make changes to an existing computer system (both hardware and software).

man–machine interface (MMI): see *human–computer interface* (HCI).

management information systems (MIS): a general term for the computer systems in an organisation that provide information about its business operations. The term is used in a number of contexts and includes: *decision support systems*, resource and people management applications, *project management*, and data *retrieval* applications.

The intention of MIS is to take data from various sources, either internal or external, and convert it into information in an appropriate form for use by the managers of an organisation. This is in order that they can make operational, tactical and strategic decisions and plan for the short- and long-term future. MIS should provide information that can assist in planning, organising, decision-making, co-ordinating activities and controlling the way operations are carried out.

MIS should be flexible and provide different ways of presenting information. The information should be provided at an appropriate level of detail for the person intending to use it.

mantissa: in a floating point number, the numeric value which is multiplied by the number base raised to the power of its *exponent*. For example, in $2,746,000 = 2.746 \times 10^6$, 2.746 is the mantissa, 10 is the radix, and 6 is the exponent.

many-to-many relationship: see *data model, entity relationships, entity relationship diagram* and *relationships*.

margin: the space between the text and the edge of the page. Most word processors and desktop publishing programs provide a way of adjusting the size of the margins.

mark sense reader: a peripheral capable of reading optical mark recognition (OMR) documents. See *optical mark reader*.

markup language: a language that has codes within a text file for indicating layout, type styling (bold, italic, underline, etc.), placement of graphics, or other information that will be interpreted by the system used to *read* the document, e.g. HTML.

mask: this is used to manipulate individual bits in a *register*. Masking allows the programmer to hide part of a register so that the remainder is visible. In control technology masks are very important, being used to:

- ascertain the contents of a bit
- set an output bit low

- set an output bit high
- reverse certain bits.

A mask is combined with the contents of a register using a *logical operator*, to produce the desired effect on the register.

Masking rules:

- **Ascertaining the contents of a bit** – use a mask with zeros in every bit position except the required bit position and apply the *AND* operator. For example use 0 0 0 0 0 1 0 0 as the mask together with the AND operator to look at the contents of bit 2. A non-zero result indicates bit 2 is set high(1) in the register, a zero result indicates bit 2 is low(0).
- **Setting an output bit low** – use a mask with a 1 in every position except the position required, which should contain a zero and apply the AND operator. For example use 1 1 0 1 1 1 1 1 as the mask and apply AND operator to set bit 5 low (i.e. to 0).
- **Setting an output bit high** – use a mask with zeros in every bit position except the required bit position and apply the *OR operator*. For example, use 0 0 1 0 0 0 0 0 as the mask and the OR operator to set bit 5 high (i.e. to 1).
- **Reversing the contents of bits in the register** – use a mask with zeros in every bit position except the required bit positions and apply the XOR operator. For example, use the XOR operator and the mask 0 0 1 0 1 0 0 0 to reverse bits 3 and 5.

mass storage: a large-capacity *backup* storage such as an external *hard disk* or *magnetic tape*.

master file: a main file of data for a system. The records in the master file are regularly updated using *transaction* records.

master page: a template that sets up certain design elements that will appear on every page of a printed document, such as *headers*, *footers* or logos.

maths coprocessor: a circuit inside a computer that is capable of carrying out high-speed floating point arithmetic operations. The maths coprocessor is used whenever fast accurate calculations are needed in a program, e.g. in *computer-aided design* and *spreadsheet* applications. Well written software will make use of a maths co-processor if it is present but continue by using the central processing unit (CPU) if one is not available. For software where speed of calculation is essential a maths co-processor must be present for it to run. The maths co-processor may be on its own separate chip, or on the CPU chip.

matrix: see *array*.

maximise: enlarging a window in a *graphical user interface* to full size. This is done by clicking the mouse on the 'maximize' icon in Microsoft Windows. In a Macintosh file maximising is achieved by clicking on the little box in the upper right-hand corner of the window. The reverse effect minimises the window.

mean time between failures (MTBF): a figure that provides an estimate of the reliability of a piece of equipment. The higher the MTBF, the longer the equipment should last.

media: the collective name used for the material used to store *data* in computer systems. Examples of media include: *magnetic tape*, *magnetic disk*, *CD-ROM* and computer printout.

media access control address (MAC address): the physical *address* of a device connected to a *network*, expressed as a 48-bit *hexadecimal* number.

medium access control protocol (MAC protocol): in a *local area network*, the protocol that determines which device has access to the transmission medium at a given time.

medium-scale integration (MSI) has 20 to 100 *logic gates* on a chip.

mega (M): a prefix normally meaning 1 million (10^6), but in computing it often means 1 048 576 (2^{20}). A one megabyte file holds 1 048 576 bytes of data.

megaflops: one million floating-point operations per second. A unit used to measure the performance of computers when carrying out calculations.

memory: the storage medium used by computers to hold data. The memory of a computer consists of *read-only memory* (ROM) and *random access memory* (RAM).

memory address register (MAR): a register in the central processing unit that holds the *address* of the memory location currently being accessed, either to retrieve an item of *data* or store data. The data is either placed in the *memory buffer register* (MBR) or taken from the MBR and placed in the location specified.

memory buffer register (MBR): a register in the central processing unit that holds the *data* retrieved from *memory* or about to be stored in memory. The location of memory accessed is determined by the contents of the *memory address register* (MAR).

memory cache: a *memory* area between the main memory and the central processing unit that allows the computer to read data and execute instructions faster. See *cache* and *disk cache*.

memory data register (MDR): see *memory buffer register*.

memory dump: a printout of an area of *memory* usually in *hexadecimal* form. When problems are being analysed, or programs *debugged*, a memory dump of the area of memory involved can sometimes prove useful. Dumps also contain other information about the computer's operation, such as the *address* of the instruction that was being executed at the time the dump was initiated.

memory management: strategies for providing sufficient *memory* to all the active processes in a computer system are carried out by the *memory management unit*.

memory management unit (MMU): a hardware device that translates virtual *addresses* into physical addresses and is used to manage *virtual memory*.

memory protection: a system used to prevent one program from corrupting another program running at the same time, and to prevent corruption of the *operating system*. The hardware *memory management unit* and parts of the operating system are used to ensure that instructions within one program are not able to accidentally influence another program.

memory refresh: the process of reading the contents of a memory location and writing it back to the same location that is used by dynamic RAM to ensure the contents are not lost.

memory resident: see *resident program.*

menu: an on-screen list from which the user can choose an operation to be performed. Items from the menu may be selected by keyboard commands or by pointing and clicking with a mouse.

See also *pull-down menu.*

menu bar: a bar across the top of the computer screen or window, which has the names of the available pull-down menus, such as 'File', 'Edit', 'View', 'Insert', 'Window', etc. Clicking the mouse on a menu bar item makes its *pull-down menu* appear.

Menu bar

Pull-down menu

menu selection interface: a user *interface* that provides menus from which the user selects the desired options. Rather than having a single line where a command must be typed in or *icons* to click on the user has a list of items to choose from, and can make selections by moving the mouse pointer over one and clicking the mouse button. This kind of interface is easier to use than a command-line interface, but does not have all the visual elements of a graphical user interface. For example, for a simple record managing menu the following might be used:

1 Print a record

2 Edit a record

3 Delete a record

Select 1,2 or 3.

merge: the combining of two ordered *data* structures to create one structure. The term is often used when two files sorted into the same order are combined to create one file, which will be in the same order as the original two files.

message: in *object-oriented programming*, a message is the way that one program object requests an action from another object. A message specifies the name of the object to which the request is made, the action (or method) to be performed, and any parameter or value that needs to be specified for this request.

message switching system: a computer communications system that is capable of receiving, storing and forwarding messages to workstations connected to the system.

metropolitan area network (MAN): a *network* that interconnects users with computer resources over a large geographic region. The term is used to describe the interconnection of networks in a city into a single larger network or the networks set up on large university campuses.

microchip: a unit of packaged computer circuitry that has been manufactured from a material such as silicon at a very small scale. Microchips are made for logic chips, microprocessors and memory.

microcode: see *micro program, micro instruction.*

microcomputer: a stand-alone small computer that has its own central processing unit, memory and all the necessary interfaces to link it to a variety of peripherals. The term has gradually come to include a small computer with a hard disk, DVD, keyboard, mouse, speakers and monitor with interfaces allowing printers, scanners, etc., to be linked.

microfilm: a high resolution photographic film on which records are kept of documents or other material, in greatly reduced size. Microfilm makes it possible to store a great amount of material in a small amount of space.

micro instruction: an instruction that activates the necessary circuits to carry out an operation that is specified by the *machine code* instruction.

micro program: a set of micro instructions that make up the necessary steps to complete a *machine code* command. A programmer cannot access the micro programs since they are built into the microprocessor when it is manufactured. Whenever a machine code command is executed the corresponding micro program is used by the CPU to carry out all the steps involved in completing that command.

microprocessor: a single *chip* containing all the features of a central processing unit. The first microprocessor was created by Intel and led to the development of the personal computer.

Microsoft Disk Operating System (MS-DOS) was the Microsoft-marketed version of the first widely installed *operating system* in personal computers. It was essentially the same operating system that Microsoft developed for IBM (Personal Computer Disk Operating System (PC-DOS)). Most users of either DOS system simply referred to their system as DOS. DOS is a non-graphical, line-oriented, command-driven operating system with a simple, but not user-friendly, *interface.* Original versions of Microsoft's Windows ran on top of DOS to provide a *graphical user interface.*

microwave transmissions: short wavelength electromagnetic radio transmissions that operate at high frequencies. These transmissions are restricted to distances of approximately 50 km because the two stations involved must have 'line of sight' and the Earth's curvature restricts the distance. The stations are often placed on towers or large hills to allow the distance between stations to be increased.

milli (m): one thousandth. For example, 5 milliseconds is 5 thousandths of a second.

million instructions per second (MIPS): a unit used to measure the speed at which a processor executes instructions. This value does not always allow comparisons of program execution time as different computers need a different number of instructions to do the same thing.

MIME: an acronym for multipurpose *Internet* mail extensions. A *protocol* widely used on the Internet that extends the SMTP (*simple mail transport protocol*) to permit data, such as video, sound, and binary files, to be transmitted by Internet *e-mail* without having to be translated into ASCII format first.

minicomputer: a term for a computer between a *mainframe* and a *microcomputer* in size; the term is no longer much used. Minicomputers normally have several terminals connected and are used by small to medium sized organisations, with each terminal using the same software.

minimise: to make a *window* in a *graphical user interface* (GUI) as small as possible. Once minimised the window appears as a single icon. The reverse effect is achieved by maximising the window.

Minitel: a European videotext firm funded by the French national telephone company. Using Minitel, it is possible, for example, to make train and aeroplane bookings, check telephone directory listings, and find out what is on at cinemas and theatres.

mirror: to create a duplicate of either a hard disk or an entire web site. The duplicate disk ensures data can be recovered quickly if one disk fails. Mirror web sites provide users with an alternative site to access when one site is very busy. The closest *mirror site* to the user will provide the fastest access.

mirror site: a mirror site is an exact replica of an original *web site* and is usually updated frequently to ensure that it reflects the content of the original web site. Mirror sites are created to reduce network traffic and ensure better availability of the web site. Mirroring is the practice of creating and maintaining mirror sites. A popular web site in one country may have a mirror site in another country, a site with a low-speed connection to the *Internet* may arrange for a mirror site at a larger site with a higher-speed connection and perhaps closer proximity to a large audience.

mnemonic: (from ancient Greek 'mnemon' for mindful; pronounced neh-MON-ik) is a word, abbreviation, rhyme, or similar verbal device to help the user to remember something. In *assembly language*, a mnemonic is an abbreviation for an operation. For example, ADA for 'add to accumulator'.

mobile phone: see *cellular phone*.

model: an attempt to create a set of rules that can be implemented on a computer to simulate a real situation. The model can then be used to predict future events.

modem: a peripheral that allows a *microcomputer* to be connected to a telephone line. A modem modulates the outgoing *digital signal* from the computer to an *analogue signal* for transmission over the telephone line, and *demodulates* the incoming analogue signal and converts it to a digital signal for the microcomputer. Most new personal computers come with 56 Kbps modems. With a digital *integrated services digital network* (ISDN) adapter instead of a conventional modem, the same telephone wire can now carry up to 128 Kbps.

modular design: the division of a large program into several small programs, each of which is converted into a program *module*. These modules can then be combined to produce a solution to the overall problem.

modulation: the adjustment of the amplitude, frequency or phase of the carrier wave being used in a data transmission so that the wave holds the data signal being transmitted.

module: a part, segment or *subprogram* of a computer program or system that performs a particular function. Modular programming is the concept that similar functions should be contained within the same unit of programming code and that separate functions should be developed as separate units of code so that the code can easily be maintained and modules reused by different programs. Each module can be produced and tested by a different programmer using a different programming language with a *linker* used to connect together the resulting sections of machine code to form the final program. *Object-oriented programming* embraces the basic ideas of modular programming.

monitor: a term used to describe a computer display and related parts that can be separated from the computer, unlike the displays on *laptop* and *notebook* computers which are an integral part of the system. The terms monitor and display are used interchangeably.

monochrome monitor: a black and white *monitor*, or a monitor that has one foreground colour and one background colour (such as green and black). Greyscale displays have more shading variation, but are sometimes described as monochrome monitors.

morphing: the transformation of one image into another by a gradual process, which allows animated sequences to be created from a limited number of original images.

Mosaic: the first widely distributed graphical *browser* or viewer for the *World Wide Web*. It is generally regarded as being the software that introduced the World Wide Web to a wide general audience.

most significant bit (MSB): the bit that is farthest to the left, and has the greatest weight in a binary number.

motherboard: the main circuit board in a microcomputer that contains the computer's basic circuitry and components. The computer components included on the motherboard are:

- the *microprocessor*
- any coprocessors
- *memory* (RAM)
- the *basic input output system* (BIOS)
- expansion slots
- interconnecting circuitry.

Additional components can be added to a motherboard through its expansion slots. The electronic interface between the motherboard and the smaller boards or cards in the expansion slots is called the *bus*.

motion picture expert group audio layer 3 (MP3): a popular format for storing music. MP3 is one method used extensively for storing music on the *Internet*. The music can be downloaded for use on an MP3 player. MP3 produces almost CD-quality music in a compressed file that can be transferred quickly, and played on any multimedia computer with MP3 player software. The technology creates sound files a tenth the size of standard CD music files with very little loss of sound quality.

mouse: a small peripheral that is used in a *graphical user interface* to launch programs and select and move text, images, etc. As the mouse is moved across the surface of a desk the mouse pointer on screen moves across the display area. Clicking or holding a mouse *button* down selects one or more actions to take place from that position. The most common type of mouse consists of a plastic casing, a ball that sticks out of the bottom of the casing and is rolled on a flat surface, one or more buttons on the top of the casing, and a cable that connects the mouse to the computer. As the ball is moved over the surface in any direction, a sensor sends impulses to the computer. The impulses are used by the software to determine the changes that are required in the mouse pointer. Mouse design continues to evolve and mice without leads and mice that use infrared sensors instead of a ball are now available.

mouse pointer: the screen symbol that is moved by the *mouse*. The mouse pointer can take the form of a hand, an arrow, a cross, and various other symbols depending on the software being used and the task being carried out.

moving picture experts group (MPEG): (pronounced EM-peg) a group that develops standards for compression of digital video and digital audio files. The group is part of the International Organisation for Standardisation.

multi-access: a computer system is described as being a multi-access system if it is possible for several users to have access to the resources of the system at the same time.

multicast: two-way communication between a single sender and multiple receivers on a *network*, as in videoconferencing or sending a communication from one site to a group of selected receivers. Most of the communications on the *Internet* involve one user requesting *files* from one source at another Internet address (unicast). However, *Internet protocol* (IP) also supports multicasting, the transmission of data *packets* to multiple addresses. Multicasting is different from broadcasting, which involves sending a transmission to everyone who has the equipment or connection to receive it. The receivers of a multicast are selected or are part of a restricted group with the rights to receive the transmission. One commercial use of multicast is the updating of travelling sales staff from head office with the company's latest prices and discounts, etc.

multicast backbone (MBONE): a *network* of *Internet* sites that supports *Internet protocol* multicasting for a limited number of users. MBONE provides a faster technology than the *Internet* for transmitting *real-time* audio and video programs, and for videoconferencing. The Rolling Stones made history with the first major multicast concert on the MBONE.

multimedia is a combination of different presentation media:

- text
- spoken audio
- music
- still images
- animated images
- multiple display areas
- video.

CD-ROMs are often used to store multimedia presentations since they require large amounts of data and hence large files.

multipart stationery: continuous stationery for a printer. It has several layers separated by sheets of carbon-coated paper. Impact printing on the top layer results in as many copies as there are layers to the stationery used.

multiple address instruction: a *machine code* instruction consisting of an *operator* and at least two *operands*.

multiplexer: a hardware device that enables two or more signals to be transmitted over the same circuit by temporarily combining them into a single signal. At the receiving end the signal is split to form the original signals by a demultiplexer. Analogue signals are generally multiplexed using frequency-division multiplexing (FDM), in which the carrier bandwidth is divided into subchannels of different frequency widths, each carrying a signal at the same time in parallel. Digital signals are generally multiplexed using time-division multiplexing (TDM), in which the multiple signals are carried over the same channel in alternating time slots.

multipurpose internet mail extension: see *MIME*.

multiprocessor system: a computer with several *processors* which work together, often with each processor dedicated to a specific type of task, e.g. calculations.

multiprogramming: the ability to create the impression that several programs are running on a computer at the same time. Initially computers were only capable of running one program at a time, which meant that a *processor bound* program that took one hour to run and a *peripheral bound* program that took one hour to run would take a total of two hours to run. *Operating systems* were developed that allowed the interleaved execution of both programs.

The peripheral bound program would start and whenever it required an I/O operation the processor bound program would make use of the processor. The total execution time for the two jobs would then be a little over one hour. The next improvement was to give each program of the multiple programs submitted by users use of the processor for a short time. The programs took turns to use the processor for a short time.

To users it appeared that all of the programs were executing at the same time. Both these methods of multiprogramming had problems with resource allocation, which could result in *deadlock*.

multiscan monitor: a monitor that can scan at more than one frequency, making it possible to work with various kinds of equipment and video modes. It is also known as a multisync monitor.

multisession CD: a *CD* that can be written to several times until it is completely full. Once an area of the CD has been used it cannot be re-used but any unused areas of the CD can be used at a later time.

multi-tasking: a multi-tasking *operating system* allows a user to perform more than one computer task (i.e. running more than one application program, at a time). The operating system is able to keep track of each of these tasks independently and go from one to the other without losing information. Using a web browser and a word processor at the same time is an example of multi-tasking that many users carry out regularly on a personal computer. Each task requires an area of the system's memory and other resources so for any particular computer system a limit is imposed on the number of tasks possible, dependent on the resources available.

multi-user dungeon (MUD): an inventively structured social experience on the *Internet*, managed by a computer program and often involving a loosely organised context or theme, such as a rambling old house with many rooms. MUD participants adopt a character when they connect to a MUD and describe this character to the other participants.

musical instrument digital interface (MIDI): a way of communicating music instructions from one electronic device to another, e.g. from a synthesiser to a computer to an electronic keyboard. MIDI includes the devices, the necessary interfaces and the software to transfer the data. A MIDI file does not store sound as a wave file but stores information on how to create the sounds, including pitch, loudness, timbre, and length of a note. MIDI instructions can be edited in a variety of ways, e.g. one instrument can be changed to another. MIDI files require less storage space than files that store actual sounds.

MySQL: (pronounced 'My Ess Cue El') a true multi-user, multi-threaded, structured query language (SQL) database server. The main features of MySQL are its speed, robustness and ease of use when working with very large databases.

n (nano): a prefix meaning one billionth (10^{-9}).

nagware: software that is available as shareware but constantly reminds the user of the need to pay when used extensively.

name table: see *symbol table.*

NAND gate: a logic gate which is a *NOT(AND)* gate. All outputs are 1 except when both inputs are 1s when a zero is produced. The symbol for a NAND gate is:

The truth table that represents the actions of the NAND gate is :

Input A	Input B	Output
0	0	1
0	1	1
1	0	1
1	1	0

NAND operator: a logical operator having the property that, if P is a statement, Q is a statement, R is a statement, ..., then the NAND of P, Q, R ... is true if at least one statement is false, false if all statements are true.

nanosecond: one billionth of a second; the symbol is ns.

narrow band: frequently used to describe fractions of a broadband channel but also used to describe bandwidths which are smaller than the smallest broadband *bandwidth.*

natural binary coded decimal (NBCD): see *binary coded decimal.*

natural language: a language used by humans as opposed to a computer language. Natural languages have vocabulary, rules and a grammar that have evolved over long periods of time, whereas computer languages have a grammar, vocabulary and rules that have been designed, then immediately used.

natural-language processing: the use of computers to process *natural languages.* This involves recognising and generating speech.

navigate: a term used to describe moving around *web sites* or *hypertext* documents.

navigation map: used in production of *web sites.* Colourful graphics overlay a hidden grid which contains *hypertext* links. A person visiting the web site navigates by moving their mouse cursor over an image and clicking the mouse. This sends a map reference to the web site which activates a link. This method of developing sites allows easy development and is more attractive to users.

near letter quality (NLQ): the best quality of printing possible on a *dot matrix printer*. Cheap laser and inkjet printers have resulted in dot matrix printers now being rarely used in the production of letters. See *print quality*.

negative numbers: represented within the computer by a variety of methods including : sign and magnitude, *one's complement, two's complement*.

Neq gate: see *exclusive–OR (XNOR) gate*.

nerd: a slang term for a person who spends more time interacting with computers than with people. Geek is similar in meaning.

nested structure: when a programming structure (*loop, procedure, function*, etc.) is held within another structure of the same type the whole is referred to as a nested structure. Thus programmers will talk about nested loops where one loop is contained within another loop.

net abuse: the name given to actions which upset other users of *newsgroups*, etc.

net police: self-appointed users of Usenet who monitor messages that are posted in newsgroups and send angry messages to users who breach *netiquette*.

NETBUI: a protocol (set of rules) developed by Microsoft for controlling *network* access and data exchanges on Microsoft's network *operating systems*.

Netfind: a search engine that is designed to find personal *e-mail addresses*. Users provide the name of the required person and Netfind produces a list of options.

netiquette: the term is derived from 'Internet etiquette' and covers the guidelines that have been evolved by users of the Internet to cover appropriate behaviour, i.e. the standard of conduct expected of users on the Internet.

Netscape: the company that produces Netscape Navigator, a very popular web *browser*.

Netware: the *local area network operating system* produced by Novell.

network: the name given to a group of computers that have been joined together to allow users to share hardware (printers, etc.), software and data. Cables, satellites, microwaves and radio transmission media are used to connect the network hardware. See *wide area network* and *local area network*.

network accounting software: a utility or an application that provides data and statistics about the use of a network. Occasionally, this can be provided by the *network* software itself. This tracking can be required to charge users or departments within an organisation for the network time or to monitor the various uses of the network, including access to the *Internet*. Various types of information can be collected, such as logging on times and dates for each machine as well as user names, connection and processor times, printer use, e-mail use, Internet access and which sites are visited. The benefits can include improved security (recording attempted logging in at particular stations or attempts to access restricted files) and data about the effectiveness of the network to provide information for future development or expansion of the network. The data can be presented in a variety of forms including charts, graphs and tables. This can also assist the *network manager* in optimising the system.

network accounts are required by users to access a *network*. Each user account has a user name, a password, access privileges (levels of access) to the network, frequently an allocation of disk space as well as a range of other parameters. The network accounts are created by the *network manager* or administrator. A user will then have access to the software and *files* on the network to which they are authorised, together with the files in their own user area.

network adapter: the interface for linking a *network* device to all other resources on the network. The adapter, commonly called a network card, is fitted into an expansion slot inside each workstation and other network device. A different type of adapter is required for each type of network; an adapter for a *token ring network* is different from one used on an *Ethernet* bus network.

network administration involves ensuring the efficient and reliable running of the *network*, monitoring activity levels on the network, regular backups of the data, monitoring space utilisation on *network drives* and monitoring attempted breaches of security.

network architecture: the design of a communications *network* that includes details of the *network topology*, the network *operating system* and hardware to be used.

network basic input/output system (NETBIOS): a *protocol* (set of rules) developed by IBM controlling network access and data exchanges on IBM's network *operating systems*. It provides a *session layer* interface between network applications running on a PC and the underlying protocol software of the transport and network layers on the *open systems interconnections* (OSI) model.

network computer: see *network station*.

network controller: a computer responsible for the overall organisation of a computer *network*. It is solely responsible for handling the communications between users and the shared resources, such as printers and drives.

network directory: a directory on a disk on a *local area network* that is located on a computer other than the one being operated by the user. A network directory differs from a *network drive* in that the user has access only to that directory. The rest of the disk may only be accessible to the user if access rights have been granted by the *network manager* or administrator. On the Macintosh, a network directory is referred to as a shared folder.

network drive: a disk drive on a *local area network* whose disk is available to other computers on the network. Access to a network drive might not be allowed to all users of the network; a *network administrator* can grant or deny access rights to part or all of a network drive. If users have two drives and a CD-ROM drive on their own machine, these could be designated C:, D: and E:. Network drives may, therefore, start from F: or G: and run up to Z: if required.

network front-end processor: see *front-end processor*.

network interface card (NIC): the interface to link a *workstation* to all other resources on the *network*. The interface card is fitted into an expansion slot inside the workstation. See also *network adapter*.

network manager: sometimes called the network administrator, the person responsible for the smooth running of a *network*. This person's responsibilities include user access (providing unique network identifiers and passwords), ensuring each user has access to only the shared resources they need to carry out their tasks and that all parts of the network are functioning correctly.

network news transfer protocol (NNTP): network news transport protocol is used with the *Unix to Unix copy program* (UUCP) to transfer news across the *Usenet*.

network operating system (NOS): software which allows workstations connected to a *network* to communicate with the server and each other.

network protocol: the common set of rules that computers on a *network* use when communicating and exchanging data with each other.

network security: the ways in which a *network* can be protected from hazards, *viruses*, unauthorised access and any other catastrophes. This is more difficult than on a stand-alone system, since with a network there are multiple points of access. Security will combine physical and logical controls. Physical controls will include access to buildings, to rooms, even locks on machines. Logical security concerns the use of *user names, passwords, access controls*, virus checkers and *firewalls*. There is also likely to be a *code of conduct* for employees. If a network is large then any disruption will cause enormous problems for the organisation. See also *contingency plan* and *security*.

network station: a microcomputer and associated equipment connected to a *network*.

network terminal: see *network station*.

network time protocol (NTP): a *protocol* that ensures accurate local timekeeping with reference to radio and atomic clocks located on the *Internet*. This protocol is capable of synchronising distributed clocks within milliseconds over long time periods.

network topology: the geometrical layout of the cables used to connect the computers together to form a *network*. See *ring network, star network, bus* network.

neural network: a collection of processors connected together that attempts to mimic the structure of nerve cells in living organisms. The main characteristic of neural networks is their ability to take large amounts of imprecise data and decide whether they match a pattern. Neural networks are likely to be used to match fingerprints and develop vision systems for robots but are unlikely in the forseeable future to imitate the human brain.

new master file: the latest version of the file that holds the main data for an application. This term is generally used when a *transaction* file is used to update an existing *master file*. The master file being read from is referred to as the old master file while the master file created becomes the new master file. These two files are also known as the parent (father) file and the child (son) file.

new media: a general term that embraces the latest electronic storage systems. These include *CD-ROM*, the *World Wide Web* and *multimedia* in general.

newbie: insulting term used for a new user of a *Usenet* newsgroup whose contributions are regarded as naïve or who is asking questions already covered in the newsgroup's frequently asked questions (FAQ) section.

newline character: one or two *bytes* that denote the end of a line. In DOS, a newline character is two bytes: a carriage return and a linefeed. In *Unix*, a newline character is one byte: a linefeed.

newsgroup: bulletin boards and discussion groups on the *Usenet*, part of the *Internet*. Newsgroups exist on almost every topic imaginable, serious and frivolous. These groups are self-regulating and can contain comments that some people find offensive. They are forums for discussing subjects; the title of the newsgroup will hopefully indicate the subject area for discussion. Each discussion topic is known as a thread.

newsreader: a program that gives access to *Usenet newsgroups* providing a simple user-friendly interface. Newsreader programs have been largely replaced by web browsers that include this feature.

news server: the computer that stores the messages posted in *newsgroups*.

Newton: a small portable computer produced by Apple. See *personal digital assistant*.

next instruction register: see *program counter*.

NeXTStep: an *operating system* based on *Unix*, originally created for NeXT workstations but also available for the PC.

nexus: a name sometimes used for the central computer in a *star network*. It has a separate connection to each device on the network.

nibble/nybble: half a *byte*, i.e. four bits.

nil pointer: see *null pointer*.

no carrier: the error message generated by a *modem* when it loses its telephone line, normally because of *noise* on the line.

node: any device connected to a *network*, including *routers*, *bridges* and *hubs* as well as the computers.

noise: the random signals, interference and variations in electrical voltage that occur during transmission of data. Noise can cause data arriving at the receiving computer to be corrupted.

non-binary tree: a tree structure in which one or more *nodes* have more than two branches coming out of the node. The non-binary tree provides a hierarchical method of structuring data for use in applications.

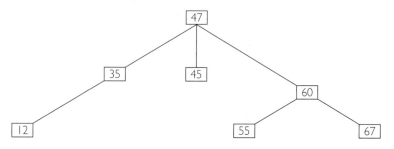

A non-binary tree can be held in memory using either two *arrays* – one for the data and one for the *pointers* or a single array of *records*. The above tree would be stored in two arrays as:

	Data	Eldest child pointer	Next sibling pointer
row 1	47	2	0
row 2	35	6	4
row 3	60	5	0
row 4	45	0	3
row 5	55	0	7
row 6	12	0	0
row 7	67	0	0

where 0 is used as the *null pointer*.

non-breaking space: a special character which prints as a space and is often seen on screen as a space, but has the additional property that it cannot be used as a line break. This ensures that the two words it separates always remain together and are not printed on separate lines. It would be used between Elizabeth and II, to ensure that Elizabeth II was what was always printed and not Elizabeth at the end of one line and II at the start of the next.

non-dedicated server: on a *network*, a computer that can function as both a client and a server. This would typically be a desktop machine on a *peer-to-peer network*.

non-disclosure agreement: an agreement produced by software and hardware manufacturers that is agreed by programmers, manufactures and journalists. It allows them to have access to software or hardware before its official launch, but forbids them from passing any information on to other people or organisations. Software companies will sign this type of agreement to get access to new hardware allowing them to develop software for the device ready for its launch. Hardware manufacturers will agree to a similar undertaking to get access to operating systems so they can be sure their hardware will support it.

non-equivalence gate: see *XOR gate*.

non-erasable storage: see *read-only memory (ROM)*.

non-impact printer: *inkjet*, *thermal*, and *laser printers*, or any other printer that prints on paper without striking it mechanically.

non-interlaced scan: the image is created on a display unit by scanning, i.e. passing an electron beam over each row of dots on the screen. An interlaced scan is when the electron beam passes over rows 1, 3, 5, … in the first coverage of the screen and 2, 4, 6, … in the second. A non-interlaced scan passes over the rows in order 1, 2, 3, 4, etc.

non-linear video editing: the editing of compressed video data held on hard disk. The editor produces a list of changes that are to be made to the data (an edit decision list – EDL) including cuts, fades, etc. This edit decision list can then be used to create the edited video using the original video clips.

non-maskable interrupt (NMI): an *interrupt* that cannot be masked out. Some low priority interrupts can be set to be ignored by the operating system of the computer and these are described as maskable interrupts. Non-maskable interrupts are ones that cannot be treated in this way and hence are always noticed by the operating system when they occur.

non-printing codes: characters sent to a printer that are not printed but change the appearance of the characters printed. A non-printable 'bold on' character is sent immediately in front of text which is to be printed in bold. The end of the bold text is identified by non-printable 'bold off' character.

non-procedural language: an alternative name for fourth generation languages. These languages are easier to use than conventional languages (C, Pascal, Fortran, etc.) particularly by non specialist programmers. They allow programs to be created quickly using a language that is closer to *natural language.*

non-text file: a file that cannot be loaded into a *text editor* for viewing.

non-volatile memory: see *read-only memory (ROM).*

NOR gate: a logic gate which is a NOT(OR) gate. Its two inputs have to both be zeros to generate a 1. Its symbol is:

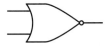

The truth table that represents the actions of the NOR gate is:

Input A	Input B	Output
0	0	1
0	1	0
1	0	0
1	1	0

normalisation of data: a technique which simplifies the structure of data as it is logically seen by the programmer or user. The data requirements for a database are analysed to decide if a particular *attribute* should be an *entity* in its own right or an attribute forming part of another entity. If it is to be a separate entity the link (relationship) with the original entity must be maintained. The main aim of this process is to improve database efficiency. It minimises data duplication and *data redundancy* and also ensures a level of *data independence.* The level of data independence achieved means that new data can subsequently be added to the database without changing the existing logical structure and hence affecting the programs that use the data stored in the database.

Normalisation usually involves dividing a database into tables and defining the relationships between these tables. The main purpose of this process is to ensure that the data is set up so that additions, deletions and modifications of a field can be made in just one table and then made available throughout the rest of the database using the relationships.

Normalisation consists of three stages:

- **First Normal Form (1NF):** each field in a table contains different information. Thus the same field would not appear in two tables.
- **Second Normal Form (2NF):** the information in one field cannot be worked out from another field. All attributes in an entity must be functionally dependent on the primary key.
- **Third Normal Form (3NF):** no duplicate information is permitted.

normalisation of numbers: numbers held in floating point format are normalised to increase the accuracy with which they are held. A floating point number is normalised when the bit following the binary point is a one for a positive number. Thus the mantissa for a positive normalised floating point number lies between 0.5 and 1. See *floating-point notation*.

NOT gate: also know as an inverter because it reverses the input signal. A 1 entered produces a 0 and vice-versa. The symbol for a NOT gate is:

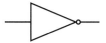

The truth table that represents the actions of the NOT gate is:

Input	Output
0	I
I	0

notebook computer: a small battery-operated portable computer. See *laptop computer*.

Novell Netware: see *Netware*.

null character: a character with the ASCII value 0. A null character is used in the programming language C to mark the end of a string of characters.

null modem: a cable that is used to connect two computers to allow them to transfer data.

null pointer: the *pointer* used to indicate the end of a sequence of data that is connected using pointers. Thus the associated pointer for the last item of data in a linked list would be the null pointer to indicate the end of the list. A leaf on a *tree* structure would have two null pointers.

null string: a string of characters which is, in fact, empty. The term is also used to describe a string of characters where the only character is a *null character*.

num lock key: the (numeric lock) key on the numeric keypad that toggles the status of the keys, determining whether they represent the numbers 0–9 or an alternative function, usually cursor movement and scrolling.

number base: in any number base the column headings are ....b^5, b^4, b^3, b^2, b^1, b^0, e.g. in base two the column headings are ... 2^5, 2^4, 2^3, 2^2, 2^1, 2^0 i.e. ... 32, 16, 8, 4, 2, 1. The number base also known as the radix.

number cruncher: name given to powerful computers capable of handling complex calculations quickly. These computers are used for applications like weather forecasting, where large numbers of complex calculations have to be completed in a limited time scale.

numeric data type: a *data type* that allows only numbers to be stored in any variable identified with the data type. There are many different numeric data types but the two most commonly used are *integer*, which will store only whole numbers, and *real* which allows decimal numbers to be stored.

numeric field: a *field* that has been identified as holding data with a *numeric data type*.

numeric keypad: a block of keys laid out in calculator style on the right side of the keyboard. They can be used to enter numbers. In addition, many of the keys can serve dual purposes, such as cursor movement, scrolling, or editing tasks, depending on the status of the *Num lock* (numeric lock) key.

A numeric keypad includes keys for the digits 0 to 9 and keys for indicating addition, subtraction, multiplication and division. In addition a numeric keypad often includes an Enter key.

numeric overflow: see *overflow error*.

numerical control: the use of digital computer techniques in automating manufacturing processes. Instructions are held on some form of storage and then used by a computer to control equipment used in the manufacturing process. See also *computer-aided manufacturing*.

object: in *object-oriented programming* (OOP), an object is what actually runs in the computer. An object can be regarded as a separate procedure that contains the instructions and data needed to carry out a particular task. A *button* in a Windows program is an object with data that includes the text shown and its position on screen; the code includes the necessary instructions to actually draw the button and place the text in the correct position.

object code: the *machine code* generated when a program is assembled or compiled. See *object program*.

object linking and embedding (OLE): a method of distributing sections of data to the most appropriate type of software for modification. OLE allows a desktop publisher to distribute some text to a word processor for editing and then re-import it, or a word processor to distribute a picture to a graphics package for modification before re-inclusion in the document.

object oriented design (OOD): a design methodology in which a system is modelled as a collection of *objects* which are interrelated. Individual objects are treated as instances of a class within a class hierarchy. The main stages in this methodology are: identify the classes and objects, identify their relationships, specify class and object interfaces. Object-oriented design is normally used whenever *object oriented programming* is to be employed.

object oriented language (OOL): a programming language which allows object oriented programs to be created.

object oriented programming (OOP) attempts to simulate the real world by means of *objects* which have characteristics and functions. An object is a combination of local variables (data) and procedures (called methods) which together form a programming entity. Invoking a method is called passing a message to an object. A programmer does not need to know how an object does something only what it does. New objects can be created that inherit data and methods from one or more previously defined objects – a process known as *inheritance*. A window can be regarded as an object with methods attached to it to open, close and minimise it. Within the window objects could include dialogue boxes, text and buttons. Methods could then be attached to these buttons indicating the actions to be carried out when the user single clicks or double clicks the button. This type of programming is not possible in third generation languages like *Pascal* and Basic.

object program: a program that has been translated from the *source language* in which it was written into machine language. The object program can be executed by the computer without access to a *compiler* or other translation software.

OCCAM: a programming language, developed by Inmos, which deals with the problems of writing programs for an array of *transputers*.

octal notation: (from Latin 'octo' meaning 'eight') A shorthand notation used to represent *binary* numbers using the base eight number system. Octal uses the eight digits: 0, 1, 2, 3, 4, 5, 6, and 7. The number after 7 in the octal counting system is 10 which represents the decimal number 8. The number after 17 is 20 which represents the decimal number 16. In computer programming, the octal equivalent of a *binary* number is sometimes used to represent it, because it is shorter. Conversion from binary to octal is achieved by splitting the binary number into groups of three working from the unit column and converting each group of three bits into its decimal equivalent. For example the binary number

$$0 1 1 0 0 0 1 0 1 0 1 0 1 1 1 1$$

would be split into the following groups of three bits

$$0 \quad 1 1 0 \quad 0 0 1 \quad 0 1 0 \quad 1 0 1 \quad 1 1 1$$

Two extra zeros are added to the most significant positions to make this group into a group of three

$$0 0 0 \quad 1 1 0 \quad 0 0 1 \quad 0 1 0 \quad 1 0 1 \quad 1 1 1$$

These groups of three bits convert to the following decimal digits.

$$0 6 1 2 5 7$$

thus the octal equivalent of the binary number 0 1 1 0 0 0 1 0 1 0 1 0 1 1 1 1 is 061257.

odd parity: see *parity*.

office automation: the use of computer systems to execute a variety of office operations, such as word processing, accounting, database management and e-mail. Office automation is generally achieved by the use of a *network* of computers with a variety of software packages.

Office Suite: the collective name for the group of programs produced by Microsoft that are intended to provide all the software needs of an electronic office.

off-line: not directly connected. The context in which the term is used determines the precise interpretation. A computer that is not connected to a host system or the Internet is said to be off-line. A printer that is off-line will allow the user to perform certain commands like advancing the paper (form feed), but it is not possible to print documents sent from a computer. The opposite of off-line is *on-line*.

off-line browser: a program which allows a user to read *hypertext*. The browser allows *Internet* pages that have been visited during an on-line session to be read at leisure (no telephone costs) and provided the relevant linked pages were visited during the on-line session, navigation between pages is also possible.

off-line storage: external storage on *disks* and *tapes*.

offset: see *relative address*.

off-site storage: files stored in a separate location from the main data library. The location is normally a completely separate building often a considerable distance from the main data library. This type of storage system is set up to provide additional security copies of data and software in case of fire or theft.

on-line: turned on and connected. The context in which the term is used determines the precise interpretation. For example, a printer is said to be on-line when it is ready to receive data from the computer to which it is connected. Users are described as being on-line when the computers they are using are connected and accessing data or software across a network, or they are connected to the Internet. The opposite of on-line is *off-line*.

on-line analytical processing (OLAP): a category of software tools that provides analysis of data stored in a *relational database*. The chief component of OLAP is the OLAP server, which sits between a client and a *database management system*. The OLAP server understands how data is organised in the database and has special functions for analysing the data. Complex OLAP tools enable users to analyse different queries and different levels of multidimensional data. For example, OLAP has the ability to bring together a variety of sources (products, sales, time periods) and find trends in the data that can then be reported in a number of formats.

on-line help: help available to a computer user that is provided by the software. For example, explanations about features of an application which are available within the application or can be accessed via a network, possibly the Internet.

on-line service provider: some *Internet service providers* (ISPs) describe themselves as on-line service providers. In this usage, ISP and OSP mean the same thing.

on-line storage: storage under the control of the central processing unit of a computer system.

on-line transaction processing: handling *transactions* as they occur. This is an application area that is particularly important in banking, airline booking, mail order, supermarkets and insurance. A transaction is processed a very short period of time after it is entered. This allows banks to respond to shops where purchases are being made using credit or debit cards before the goods are removed from the shops. Holidays can be booked and confirmed while the customer is present in the travel agent or on the telephone.

on-line tutorial: a teaching aid, provided with a program package, designed to help people learn to use the application. Such tutorials are frequently interactive and require the user to make responses to certain situations. These are designed to be user-friendly and take the user at their own pace through various stages.

one's complement: a number in the *binary* (base-two) system that is the complement of another number. Because binary is based on only two digits, the one's complement of a number is produced by changing all the 1s to 0s and all the 0s to 1s in the original number. Thus

$$0 0 1 1 1 0 0 0$$

is the one's complement of:

$$1 1 0 0 0 1 1 1$$

one-address instruction: a *machine code* instruction consisting of an *operator* and a single *operand*. See *two-address instruction*.

one-dimensional array: an *array* that is made up of a single row or column, unlike a two-dimensional array which has rows and columns. Each element in a one-dimensional array must hold data of the same type, e.g. integer, string. Where the programming language allows it, an array element can hold a record, which is defined to be of mixed data types.

To access an element a single subscript is used. The elements of the array are held in the computer's memory using consecutive locations. An array *dimensioned* as having 10 elements would be held in memory as:

(0)	(1)	(2)	(3)	(4)	(5)	(6)	(7)	(8)	(9)

The individual elements are accessed using an associated mapping function.

In the above example, the location of element p is: Base address + p

where the first element in the array (subscript 0 in diagram above) is held in the memory location with address Base address.

one-pass assembler: an *assembler* that translates from the *assembly language* to *machine code* by considering each instruction label, etc. only once. As the assembler progresses through the source code, any labels, etc. it meets must already have been established so that the appropriate machine code can be generated.

one-time pad: a system in cryptography in which a randomly generated *private key* is used only once to encrypt a message. Decryption is carried out by the receiver using a matching one-time pad and key. Messages encrypted using this method have the advantage that there is theoretically no way to 'break the code' by analysing a succession of messages. When random keys are used each encryption is unique and not connected to the next or any subsequent encryption. With a one-time pad, however, the decrypting party must have access to the same key used to encrypt the message and this raises the problem of how to get the key to the receiver safely and how to keep both keys secure. The key used in a one-time pad is called a secret key because if it is revealed, the messages encrypted with it can easily be deciphered. This type of encryption is rarely used on the Internet, where public key encryption is more commonly used.

one-to-one relationship: a degree of relationship between two *entities* in a relational database. An example would be a hospital patient and their medical record. Each patient has one medical record and each record refers to one patient.

on site warranty: a guarantee given to the purchaser by a company stating that a product, computer or system is reliable and free from known defects and that the seller will, without charge, repair or replace defective parts within a given time limit and under certain conditions. This will take place at the site of the machine or system.

on the fly: an expression that is used to describe the way an Internet or an HTML page is built up and shown to a user. The pages concerned usually contain information that changes at regular, short intervals. This type of page is sometimes described as a dynamic page, as opposed to a static page, which contains data that rarely changes. Dynamic pages often make use of technologies like Microsoft's Active Server Pages and hence have an extension of ASP.

open loop feedback: see *feedback.*

open systems interconnection (OSI): the umbrella name for a group of *protocols* and specifications that are not owned by any company. Some of the protocols and specifications in the group are: the *open systems interconnection/seven-layer model* (reference model), abstract syntax notation 1 (ASN.1), basic encoding rules (BER), common management information protocol and services (CMIP and CMIS).

open systems interconnection seven-layer model (OSI 7-layer model): also known as the OSI reference model (OSI-RM). A model of *network architecture* and a suite of *protocols* to implement it that was developed by the International Standards Organisation (ISO) as a framework for international standards in network architecture. The OSI architecture is split between seven layers:

- **Physical layer** – the electrical and mechanical connections to the network. Examples of physical layer protocols are CSMA/CD and *token ring.*
- **Data link layer** – this splits data into blocks for sending on the physical layer and receives acknowledgement blocks. It performs error checking and re-transmits frames not received correctly. The data link layer is split into an upper sublayer, logical link control (LLC), and a lower sublayer, *media access control* (MAC).
- **Network layer** – this controls the routing of packets of data from sender to receiver via the data link layer. The most common network layer protocol is *Internet protocol* (IP).
- **Transport layer** – this determines how to use the network layer to provide a virtual error-free, point-to-point connection so that one user can send uncorrupted messages to another in the correct order. It establishes and dissolves connections between users. An example transport layer protocol is *transmission control protocol* (TCP).
- **Session layer** – this uses the transport layer to establish a connection between different user processes. It handles *security* and creation of the session.
- **Presentation layer** – this carries out data compression and format conversion to remove differences between users. It allows incompatible processes in the application layer to communicate via the session layer.
- **Application layer** – this handles issues like network transparency, resource allocation and problem partitioning. The application layer is concerned with the user's view of the network (e.g. formatting electronic mail messages). The presentation layer provides the application layer with a local representation of data that is independent of the format used on the network.

operand: the part of a program instruction that specifies the data (or the location of the data) that is to be used by the instruction.

operating system: the software responsible for providing standard services and supporting standard operations, such as *multitasking* and *file access.* It provides the link between the user and the hardware and, after being initially loaded into the computer by a *boot* program, manages all the other applications software in the computer. Users can interact with the operating system through a command language or *graphical user* *interface* (GUI). The applications software makes use of the operating system by making requests for services through an application program interface.

An operating system can:

- determine the order in which applications in a multitasking system use the processor and the time given to each application
- manage the sharing of internal memory among multiple applications
- handle input and output between the computer and its peripherals, e.g. hard disks and printers
- send messages to the applications or the user about the status of each program and any errors that may have occurred
- on computers that provide parallel processing, manage how to divide the program so that it runs on more than one processor at a time.

Popular operating systems include: *DOS*, MacOS, *Unix, Linux* and *OS/2.*

operational information: is information used mainly on a day-to-day basis for the management of a business. This can be a record of daily transactions, customer orders, invoices, adjustment of stock levels, items sold and organisation of staff. At this level the information is characterised by a high level of detail.

operational mode: the way a computer is used and operated. See *batch processing, transaction processing, interactive processing.*

operator: the part of a computer *instruction* that determines the actions to be carried out by the processor. The assembler instruction 'ADA 100' which when executed would add 100 to the contents of the accumulator, has an operation code 'ADA'.

optical character recognition (OCR): the recognition of printed or written text characters by computer. Each page of text is converted using a scanner to a digital image which is stored in the computer's memory. Special OCR software is then used to convert this image to a text file. The conversion is rarely completely accurate; examples of potential mis-conversions are Q as O, S as 5, etc.

optical fibre: a plastic or glass fibre no thicker than a human hair used to transmit information using infra-red or laser light as the carrier. The light beam is an electromagnetic signal with a frequency in the range of 10^{14} to 10^{15} hertz. Optical fibre is:

- less susceptible to external signals than other transmission media
- cheaper to make than copper wire
- much more difficult to link to connectors than other transmission media
- difficult to tamper with (monitor or inject data in the middle of a cable connection)
- appropriate for secure communications
- more accurate in its data transmissions, since light beams do not escape from the fibre because the material used provides total internal reflection.
- capable of high transmission rates (tests have achieved 420 megabits per second over 161.5 km, and 445.8 megabits per second over a shorter distance; at these rates, the entire text of the ENCYCLOPEDIA BRITANNICA could be transmitted in one second).

optical mark reader (OMR): a special scanning device that can read carefully placed pencil marks on specially designed documents. OMR is frequently used for forms, questionnaires, and multi-choice answer-sheets. Probably the most popular application of OMR in the UK is for the entry forms for the National Lottery.

optical mouse: a computer pointing device that uses a *light-emitting diode* and an optical sensor in place of the traditional mouse ball and rollers. Movement of the optical mouse is detected by interpreting changes in reflected light, whereas an electromechanical mouse detects motion by interpreting the motion of a rolling sphere. An optical mouse does not need cleaning and will last longer, since it has no moving parts to break down. However optical mice will not work on surfaces which are very smooth (e.g. glass), since they depend on irregularities to generate changes in the signal received by the optical sensor. See *mouse*.

optical wand device: see *wand*.

optimising compiler: a compiler that attempts to analyse the code it produces and to produce more efficient code. One way in which code can be optimised is by considering adjacent instructions and looking for combinations that can be replaced with more efficient sequences, for example:

ADD ACC, 1 (add one to register ACC)
ADD ACC, 1 (add one to register ACC)

could be replaced by:

ADD ACC, 2 (add two to register ACC)

OR gate: a logic gate that has an output of 0 if all the inputs are 0; otherwise the output is 1. Its symbol is:

The truth table for an OR gate is:

Input A	Input B	Output O
0	0	0
0	1	1
1	0	1
1	1	1

OR operator: an operator that has an output of FALSE if all the inputs are FALSE; otherwise the output is TRUE. An example of the OR operator is shown in the loop construct below:

While ((Age = 20) OR (Gender = 'M')) Do
Loop instructions

The instructions in the loop will be obeyed if the contents of the variable 'Age' are equal to 20 or the contents of the variable 'Gender' are M. The instructions in the loop will only not be obeyed if the contents of 'Age 'are not equal to 20 and the contents of Gender are not equal to M.

The inputs to the operator must be Booleans (i.e. true or false). In the example above, the result of the condition Age = 20 is either true or false; no other result is possible. The OR operator is written $O = A + B$ in *Boolean algebra* notation.

Input A	Input B	Output O
F	F	F
F	T	T
T	F	T
T	T	T

Oracle: the software company that produces the Oracle family of *relational databases*. Oracle's relational database was the world's first to support the *structured query language* that is now an industry standard. The Oracle relational database is often found on large, commercial computer systems.

ordinal: identifies the position in a sequence of related items. Examples of ordinal numbers are first, third, 17th, and 43rd.

organisational structures are ways in which an organisation is set up. These can be illustrated by charts that indicate the relationships between the people, the functions, the services or the geographical basis for the structure of the organisation. Larger organisations have chains of command that indicate responsibilities and decision-making within the structure. A small business is likely to have a few people all with multiple functions and responsibilities. Large organisations have departments for each function.

The two main types of structure are hierarchical (tall) and flat (horizontal) structures. These are typically illustrated as below.

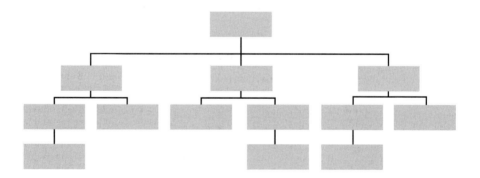

Hierarchical structure

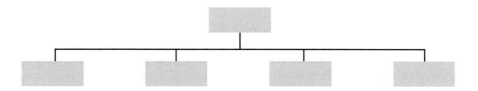

Flat structure

If set out on a functional basis, the structure could look like this:

Chains of command within an organisation are the paths down through the structure, i.e. from the managing director downwards. Staff are responsible **for** the people below them and are responsible **to** the people above them.

There are many levels of staff within an organisation, but these can be categorised into three types that operate at specific levels. Senior management functions at a **strategic** level and is responsible for long-term planning and policy making. Middle management operates at a **functional** or **implementational** level and is responsible for ensuring that the objectives identified at the strategic level are implemented. This can mean making minor decisions to ensure that operations are carried out efficiently. The majority of staff then comprise the workforce and function at an **operational** level, carrying out day-to-day tasks.

The use of ICT in modern organisations has tended to change the way organisations are structured and operate. Due to the growth of word-processing and database management systems, a lot of typing and clerical jobs have disappeared. Robots have replaced many production line workers. At higher levels, *management information systems* have allowed senior management access to large amounts of data in a wide variety of formats to make strategic decisions quicker and more efficiently. These changes have resulted in fewer levels within organisations.

original equipment manufacturer (OEM): a company that makes computers using components from one or more companies, as opposed to one which sells computers made by other companies. These computers normally carry the company name of the OEM and one of their brand names.

orphan: in *word processing*, a term used to describe the effect of the first line of a paragraph being printed at the bottom of a page whereas a *widow* is the last line of a paragraph printed at the top of a new page. Many word processors automatically allow the user to stop this happening as it is regarded as bad style. The 'pages' below show an orphan.

> These computers normally carry the company name of the OEM and one of their brand names.
>
> **orphan:** in word processing, a term used to describe

> the effect of the first line of a paragraph being printed at the bottom of a page, whereas a widow is the last line of a paragraph printed at the top of a new page. Many word processors automatically allow the user to

orphan file: a file stored on a computer that no longer has a purpose. When software is removed (uninstalled) from a computer some of the files originally installed or created by the software while it is in use are left behind. These are orphan files since they serve no purpose without the application. Generally orphan files can be deleted, but some files in Windows are used by several applications, especially those with DLL extensions, and great care should be taken before removing them.

OS/2: IBM and Microsoft's *operating system* that was supposed to replace MS-DOS. Unfortunately the first version had many problems and Windows is now used on most PCs.

outline font: a font defined as a set of lines and curves as opposed to a *bitmap* font. An outline font can be easily modified and scaled to any size to produce high quality results, unlike bitmap fonts. These changes can require a lot of numerical processing.

output bound: see *peripheral bound*.

output device: a *peripheral device* through which information from a computer is communicated to the outside world. Examples of output peripherals include: *display screen, printer, graph plotter* and *speakers*.

outsourcing: paying another company to provide services which a company might otherwise have employed its own staff to perform, e.g. software development.

Overdrive chip: a user-installable microprocessor for the 486 microprocessor series. Many 486-based PCs were built with an Overdrive socket, which allowed the owner to upgrade to a faster microprocessor simply by inserting an Overdrive chip.

overflow error: an error condition that is caused by carrying out a calculation whose result is too large to fit into the destination *register*. Trying to divide any number by zero will produce this error, which sometimes generates an error message of arithmetic overflow.

overflow flag: a *flag* that is set whenever a calculation is carried out that produces a result too great for the result register to hold.

overhead: resources that are used for purposes which are necessary but incidental to the main task. An example would be keeping a program running all the time, which eliminates the overhead of loading and initialising it for each transaction. The term also covers the extra characters and checks that are carried out when data is transmitted over a communications link. These characters and checks take up transmission time; hence the transmission time is greater than if only the data could be sent.

overhead bits: the extra bits added to data when it is transmitted.

overrun: a condition in which data is lost because the receiving device is not able to accept data at the rate it is being transmitted.

overtype: a typing mode in which the characters typed will write over any other characters already on the line. Most PC systems start up in insert mode which creates space for the additional characters. The Insert key acts as a toggle key that allows the user to move between the two modes.

overwrite: to write over data that is already on a disk, for example, when updating a file.

p: see *pico*.

P-code: the intermediate code produced by the Pascal-P compiler.

package: see *software package*.

packed decimal: a method of storing digits in which each byte, except the right-most byte, holds two decimal digits (four bits per digit). The right-most byte uses four bits to hold the sign and the remaining four bits contain one digit. In 'unpacked decimal' each byte holds a single digit or the sign of the number.

packet: a unit of data formatted for transmission on a *network*. Before data is transmitted across a network using packet switching it is split up into packets for sending. Each packet has a header that holds the source and destination workstation identifiers, a packet number, a block of data, and an error-checking code. When packet switching is used, all the data packets related to a message may not take the same route to get to their destination. The message is re-assembled on arrival using the packet numbers to ensure that no packets are missing and they have been put together in the correct order.

packet assembler/disassembler (PAD): a hardware device that allows a work-station not set up for packet switching to use a *packet switched network*. The PAD puts together the packets ready for transmission and disassembles the packets on arrival so they can be used to regenerate the original message. See *packet*.

packet Internet groper (PING): a program used to test whether a particular network destination is online, by sending an Internet control message protocol (ICMP) echo request and timing the response.

packet switched network: a *network* that makes use of packet switching in the transmission of data. See *packet, packet switching system, packet assembler/disassembler*.

packet switching system (PSS): a system that allows messages to be sent over a network as *packets*. The data in the message is broken up into packets for transmission. Each packet has a header that holds the source and destination workstation identifiers, a packet number, a *block* of data, and an error-checking code. When packet switching is used all the data packets related to a message may not take the same route to get to their destination. On arrival the message is re-assembled using the packet numbers to ensure that no packets are missing and they have been put together in the correct order. The international standard for packet switching networks is X.25.

packing density is used in a variety of ways to indicate the number of a particular item stored in a unit of area. For example when referring to electronic components it is used to give the number of such components on a given area of circuit board. When referring to records in a file it is used to indicate the number of records packed into a block.

pad: to fill unused parts of a *data structure* with dummy data such as zeros, blanks, or nulls.

pad character: a dummy character that is used to fill up the unused parts of a *data structure*. For example a *sparse array* holding *integers* might have its many unused locations filled with zero.

paddle: an early type of input device that controlled movement by turning a dial. It was often used for side-to-side or up-and-down movements of an on-screen object such as a 'bat' for hitting a 'ball' in simple early video games. A paddle is less sophisticated than a *joystick* because it permitted the user to specify movement only along a single axis.

page: see *paging*.

page break: in a document, the place where a page ends and a new page begins. A word processor automatically inserts a page break after a specified number of lines of text – a soft page break. The user can enter a command to force a page break at a particular point in a document – a hard page break.

The term is also used to describe the code sent to a printer to tell it to eject the page being currently printed.

page description language (PDL): a language that describes to the printer how to print a page and how to form the type and graphic elements that appear on it. The page description language provides the printer with instructions on how to draw each character from outlines, rather than downloading a font to the printer. An example of a PDL is Adobe *PostScript*.

page footer: an option provided by most word processors that allows the user to insert text that will appear at the bottom of every page in a document. One can use this space to include the name of the document author, page numbers, data printed, date produced, file name, etc. See also *page header*.

page header: an option provided by most word processors that allows the user to insert text that will appear at the top of every page in a document. One can use this space to include the name of the document author, page numbers, date printed, date produced, file name, etc. See also *page footer*.

page printer: a printer that prints a full page at a time; for example, a *laser printer*.

page turn: see *paging*.

paging: the organisation of a computer's main memory into sections of a fixed size. Each of these sections of memory is known as a page and is used to hold the programs and data currently being used by the processor (CPU). This method of organising memory allows the more frequently used parts of a program to be held in main memory, while the parts that are rarely used are held on *backing store*. The process of bringing in a page from backing store is known as page turning. Reducing the number of page turns by modifying the pages installed in main memory initially will result in the program running faster.

painting package: a program that allows a user to draw pictures on the computer screen using a *mouse* or other pointer. The user selects from various drawing and painting tools, such as brushes, spray cans, etc. and a full palette of colours in the production of a picture. Most paint packages use *bitmap* graphics that allow the user to control the colour of each *pixel* but the resulting pictures can occupy large amounts of memory.

palette: the range of colours available for use within *paint, drawing,* photo editing, or page layout programs.

The term is sometimes used to describe the collection of tools available for use within these 'art' programs, e.g. paintbrush, pencil, area fill, airbrush, etc.

palmtop computer: a computer small enough to be held in the hand.

pan: shortened form of panorama. Moving the user's view horizontally across an area in one continuous movement. This is normally achieved on a computer by passing a picture a little at a time in front of the user's eyes.

Pantone Matching System (PMS): a set of standard colours, with each colour designated by a number. In the printing trade, PMS sample books are used to pick colours and inks are mixed to the exact specifications. Many graphics programs allow the user to pick colours by PMS number and display the chosen colours on the screen.

paper feed mechanism: see *friction feed, tractor feed.*

paper tape: see *punched paper tape.*

paper tape punch: a *peripheral device* for producing punched paper tape.

paper tape reader: a *peripheral device* for reading punched paper tape into a computer.

paper-white monitor: a display monitor that resembles the appearance of a printed page on which text and graphics characters are displayed in black against a white background.

paradigm: a paradigm (pronounced PARA-dime, from ancient Greek paradeigma – a pattern) is a pattern or an example of something. The word also connects the ideas of a mental picture and pattern of thought.

parallel adder: the circuitry within the *arithmetic logic unit* (ALU) of a computer that allows the contents of two *registers* to be added together, effectively adding each bit position in the registers at the same time. The circuit shown below is capable of adding two four-bit registers 'a' and 'b' together to produce a sum 's'. The bit positions within each register are (a_0, a_1, a_2, a_3), (b_0, b_1, b_2, b_3) and (s_0, s_1, s_2, s_3).

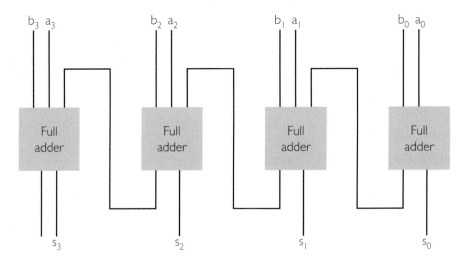

parallel changeover or conversion: see *parallel running*.

parallel computer: a computer that has more than one central processing unit. This type of computer allows several processes to be running at the same time. Such a computer is known in America as a concurrent computer; 'parallel computer' is the European term.

parallel data transmission: the transmission of several bits of data simultaneously down several different wires. Contrast this with *serial data transmission* where the bits are sent one after the other down a single wire. Parallel transmission is often regarded as faster than serial transmission but this applies only when the same transmission medium is being used. Serial transmission along *fibre-optic cables* is faster than parallel transmission along copper wires. Parallel transmission is normally used in the transmission of data to a printer and serial transmission when data is transferred along telephone lines using a modem.

parallel port: a port on a computer through which parallel transmission of data is possible.

parallel printer: a printer that accepts data that has been transmitted in parallel.

parallel processing: the use of more than one computer at the same time, or more than one processor working simultaneously within the same computer, to solve a problem. Parallel processing divides the program instructions between the various processors so that the program completes its operation faster than if one processor was used. This form of processing is a significant advance on the *multiprogramming* possible on larger computers.

parallel running occurs when a new system is implemented and both the old and the new system are run together for a certain period of time. The intention is to ensure that the new system is running correctly before the old system is replaced completely. Errors can be corrected and users learn the new system with the minimum of consequences if mistakes are made. It is, however, costly, takes extra time and can be stressful and confusing with two systems running concurrently.

parameter: information about an item of data, e.g. a name, a number, or a chosen option, that is transferred to a *procedure* or *function* when it is called.

parameter passing: the act of passing *parameters* to a *procedure* or *function*. Parameters can either be passed by value or by reference. When they are passed by value, a local copy of the data passed is used within the procedure or function, and on exit this copy is discarded. When parameters are passed by reference, the address in memory of the data is used and hence changes to the data are effective after exit from the procedure or function. Large *arrays* are rarely passed by value because of the memory demands this method of transfer would make on the computer (two copies of the data would exist while the procedure or function were being executed).

parent directory: the *directory* above another directory. The *root directory* is the only directory that does not have a parent directory. The directories below the parent directory are known as subdirectories. Directories are also known as *folders*.

parent node: the *node* above another node in a *tree* data structure. The *root node* is the only node that does not have a parent node. The nodes immediately below the parent node are known as the children of the parent node.

parentheses: the two characters (and), also known as round brackets. These two characters have ASCII values 40 and 41 and are used for various purposes within text and to ensure the correct sequence of operations is carried out in mathematical calculations.

parity: a self checking code that contains enough information within the coded form of a data item to determine whether the data item has been coded or transmitted correctly. It is used to carry out checks during input, reception and processing. A parity bit is an additional bit which is set to a 0 or a 1 so that the total number of 1s in the data item is even, for even parity, or odd, for odd parity. Using even parity and the most significant bit, for example, the parity bit:

$$0\ 1\ 0\ 1\ 1\ 0\ 1 \quad \text{is correct, with four 1s,}$$
$$\text{but} \quad 1\ 0\ 0\ 0\ 1\ 1\ 0 \quad \text{is incorrect, with three 1s.}$$

parity check: parity checks are used to determine whether the parity of a data item is correct. Parity checks will detect single bit errors, but not necessarily errors in more than one bit.

parse: to analyse a statement in a human or programming language so that it can be used by a computer. Parsing is an important part of many computing disciplines and involves dividing the language statements into small components that can be analysed. For example, parsing of computer statements (instructions) by a compiler must be carried out before they can be translated from the high-level programming language into the machine's language. Parsing is often split into lexical analysis and semantic analysis. During *lexical analysis* the string of characters representing the program instruction is divided into components called tokens, based on the punctuation used and other keys. Semantic analysis then attempts to determine the meaning of the string of characters. See *semantics*.

parser: a software routine that analyses a statement in a human or programming language and converts it into a form that can be understood by a computer.

parsing: the process of analysing the *syntax* of a high level program to determine the relationship between operators, operands, and other tokens in the program. See also *parse*.

partition: a division of a disk or storage area. On PCs, partitions are created when the hard disk is first formatted and are often used to allow the user to install a different operating system in each partition or to create separate logical areas for different users.

Pascal: a programming language designed by Niklaus Wirth for use in teaching that is based on ALGOL. Pascal is renowned for its simplicity and highly structured programs. Its restrictive nature makes it a safe tool for teaching, as students carry forward highly transferable skills, but it can be too restricting in general-purpose programming.

passing parameters: see *parameter passing*.

passive device: a *sensor* that requires no external electrical power source to operate, whereas an active device is a sensor that does need an external power source.

passive file transfer protocol (passive FTP) allows data to be transferred in a relatively secure way. The flow of data is established by the client rather than the server.

passive matrix display: a type of flat panel display commonly found on portable computers. The display is made up of a series of horizontal and vertical criss-crossed wires with a *liquid crystal display* (LCD) placed where the wires intersect. Each LCD is used to represent a separate *pixel* in the display.

password: a sequence of letters and other symbols which the user keeps secret. The password normally appears as a row of asterisks ('********') when it is entered so other people cannot read it. The password allows the user access to resources not available to all users. When logging on to networks users require a 'user ID' and a password. The user ID is needed to ensure that the user is known to the system and the password to act as security for the network. The following are general guidelines to follow when choosing a password:

- do not use a password that can easily be guessed by your friends, e.g. your first name or a relative's name
- do not use a word that can be found in the dictionary; programs exist that can rapidly try every word in the dictionary!
- do not use topical words, e.g. election, budget
- when you change your password make sure the new one is very different from the one previously used
- use a mixture of letters and numbers.

paste: a function available in most software packages that allows the user to transfer text, images, or both from the *clipboard* to a particular location. The expression is taken from *cut and paste*, which is the way it was originally done manually, in the printing industry.

patch: a quick, temporary change to a program that removes a *bug*. During the testing stages (*beta testing*) in the production of a software package, patches are used to provide quick fixes to any problems identified. Before releasing the software the best solutions to the problems identified will be implemented and the patches removed.

Once a program is released any further problems are overcome using patches that are often available on the software developer's web site.

patch panel: used in *network* wiring, a patch panel contains several *port* locations. The panel acts as a switchboard, allowing the computers in an area to be connected to network ports.

path: the hierarchical description of where a folder or file is located on a disk drive. This description includes the drive letter, any *subdirectories* and the name of the file itself e.g. C:\MYWORK\PROGRAMS\MENU.PAS.

pattern recognition: the identification of visual or audio patterns by computers. For patterns to be recognised, images must be converted into digital values that can be compared with patterns already stored. Pattern recognition is used by *optical character recognition* software and by *voice recognition* systems.

PC-DOS: an operating system developed by Microsoft and supplied with IBM PCs. PC-DOS is very similar to MS-DOS, which was developed by Microsoft for use on non-IBM PCs. Both versions are often abbreviated to *DOS*.

peer-to-peer network: a computer *network* in which any computer connected to the network can act as either a client and/or a *server*. Using this type of network any computer can access the files on any other computer in the network.

Pentium: a 32-bit microprocessor developed by Intel. The Pentium processor has seen many modifications since its appearance in 1993 and each new version has had Pentium as part of its name.

peripheral bound: a program is regarded as peripheral bound when it will require extensive use of the available peripherals while it is running and relatively little use of the processor. See *processor bound.*

peripheral component interconnect bus (PCI bus): the bus on a PC that supports the *plug and play* technology. It allows up to seven peripherals to be connected to the bus.

peripheral device: any piece of hardware that is connected to a computer. The term is also used to refer to any component other than the CPU and its working memory. Examples of peripherals include keyboards, mice, monitors, printers, scanners, disk drives, CD drives, DVD drives, microphones, speakers, joysticks, plotters, and digital cameras.

personal computer (PC): the desktop computers originally manufactured by IBM but now produced by many different manufacturers. The PC was created with an 'open architecture' which allowed other manufacturers to legally produce compatible computers capable of running the same operating systems and software. This 'open architecture' approach has led to the PC being the most popular home computer.

personal computer memory card international association card (PCMCIA card): a small device, about the same size as a credit card, which can be inserted into *portable computers* to give them additional features, such as extra memory or a modem.

personal digital assistant (PDA): a personal computer that is so small it will fit into the user's pocket. PDAs can be used to store personal data, e.g. telephone numbers or appointments. The input method is either by use of a small keyboard or a pointing device, like a pen.

personal identification device (PID): a device that is used as part of the *security* for a computer system. The device has to be inserted along with a *password* before access is allowed to the computer system. The most common example of a PID is a cash card used with *automatic teller machines* (ATMs).

personal identification number (PIN): a number normally used with cash cards that acts as a *password*, allowing access to the cardholder's account.

PERT chart: a method of pictorially representing the tasks needed to complete a large project. This type of *project management* tool allows the user to schedule and co-ordinate the many tasks that need to be carried out in the completion of a large project. As such they are often used in large computer projects which can involve several people working on a wide variety of tasks.

petabyte: A quadrillion bytes (10^{15} bytes or 2^{50} bytes).

phase alternation by line (PAL): the standard used for colour television broadcast throughout much of Europe. The picture is made up using 625 lines, with 25 interlaced frames being transmitted every second as an analogue signal.

phase modulation is a method of incorporating a data signal onto an alternating-current waveform by varying the instantaneous phase of the wave.

phased conversion or implementation: a method of changing from one system to another, where parts of the old system are replaced in turn until the whole changeover has happened. With this method of changeover re-training of staff needs to be carried out only on the next part of the system to be changed. This allows staff to become familiar with the parts rather than attempting to understand the detail of the whole new system. The term is also used to cover a changeover which involves changing the whole system but in only part of a company. This type of changeover is used by banks, supermarkets, etc. who introduce new systems at branches as they are refurbished.

phonemes: the individual speech components that are put together to make words.

Photo-CD: an imaging system from Kodak which allows 35 mm slides or negatives to be stored on a *CD-ROM*. Using this technology it is possible to store 100 photographs on a single CD-ROM.

phreaking: a term used to describe the process of hacking into telecommunications systems, generally with the intention of making free telephone calls.

physical layer: in the *open systems interconnection* (OSI) communications model, the physical layer supports the electrical or mechanical interface to the physical medium. For example, this layer determines how to put a stream of bits from the data link layer on to the physical pins for a parallel printer interface.

pico (p): (pronounced pee-ko) the SI prefix meaning one trillionth or 10^{-12}.

pie chart: a method of presenting numerical information graphically. A pie chart shows the proportional size of items that go to make up a series of data. This can make comparisons of figures easier for an audience. For example:

Amount spent in school tuck shop during a typical week

Item	Amount in pounds	% of total spent
Crisps	£12.50	17%
Chocolate	£18.80	26%
Soft drinks	£24.80	34%
Other sweets	£16.50	23%
Total	£72.60	100%

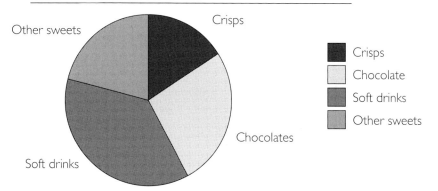

pilot conversion or running: a method of changing from one computer system to an improved system that involves using the two systems alongside each other, but using only a limited amount of data in the new system.

pipeline burst cache: *cache memory* that is designed to be read from, or written to, in a succession of four data transfers. The *buses* in most PCs allow 64 bits (8 bytes) to be transferred at the same time down 64 'wires'. Each line of storage in a cache memory holds 32 bytes and hence four data transfers (sometimes called bursts) are required to fill each line of cache memory. With a pipeline burst cache, the first transfer takes three of the processor's clock speed cycles, and the remaining three transfers take only one cycle each. The last three transfers do not need to locate their storage positions and hence take less time. The adjectives 'pipelining' and 'burst' are used to describe the idea that once the storage location has been addressed and accessed and the first read or write transfer is started, subsequent transfers come rapidly in discrete bursts down (or up) the pipe or data path.

pipeline processing: a method of processing in which a task is performed in stages; the output of one stage is input to the next. This speeds up processing by allowing several parts of different tasks to be run at the same time.

pipelining: overlapping the execution of two or more *instructions*. Without a pipeline, a computer processor fetches the first instruction from memory, executes the instruction and then retrieves the next instruction from memory, and so on. While the instruction is being fetched, the arithmetic part of the processor is idle as it must wait until it gets the next instruction. With pipelining, the computer architecture allows the next instructions to be fetched while the processor is performing arithmetic operations, holding instructions in a *buffer* close to the processor until each operation can be performed. The result is an increase in the number of instructions that can be performed during a given time period.

piracy: software piracy is the illegal copying, distribution, or use of software.

Software piracy causes significant lost revenue for publishers, which in turn results in higher prices for the honest consumer. As part of the installation routine, software users accept a *licensing agreement* which is intended to protect the software program from copyright infringement. Normally the licence allows the user to install the software purchased on one computer and make a single backup copy in case the original is lost or damaged. When companies purchase software packages they install the package on different machines subject to the conditions of the licence purchased. All companies should have a policy that ensures that staff are aware of their obligations when using company computers and software. Part of this policy should include keeping track of what software is installed on which computer.

Types of software piracy include:

- **Softlifting** – involves sharing a program with a friend or associate and is the most common form of piracy. The use of multi-user licenses is intended to stop this type of piracy in companies. Individuals should purchase software only from authorised dealers.
- **Hard-disk loading** – this is committed by computer dealers who install unauthorised copies of software on computers that they sell. This can be

stopped by purchasers insisting on being given the CDs used to install the software when purchasing the computer.

- **Counterfeiting** – making and selling copies of the CDs that contain the software. The ease of access to CD writers on PCs has made this type of piracy more common. Purchasers of software need to look carefully at the quality of the labelling of the CDs if this type of piracy is to be stopped. The use of *dongles* stops this type of piracy but causes problems for legitimate purchasers.
- **Online piracy** – the copying of software from sites on the Internet. Large companies like Microsoft regularly patrol the Internet looking for sites with pirated software.

pitch: the number of characters per inch when using a given typeface. All characters have the same width in fixed-pitch typefaces. In proportional-pitch type, some characters are wider than others, so the pitch is measured as an average character width.

pivot: a particular element of an *array* used by an *algorithm* to rearrange data.

pixel: short for picture element. A pixel is the smallest logical unit of visual information that can be used to build an image. The more pixels in an image, the better its *resolution*.

pixel graphics: graphic images composed of an arrangement of little squares called *pixels*. Such images are also called bitmapped graphics. See *bitmap*.

PKZIP: a file compression utility that is available as *shareware*. The decompression utility is called PKUNZIP. PKZIP was originally written for PC microcomputers using MS-DOS but there are versions available for other computers and operating systems.

plain text: text that is not encrypted, as opposed to ciphertext. See *encryption*.

plasma display: each pixel in a plasma display is a tiny bit of charged gas (plasma). By changing the charge on the gas in each pixel and hence the way in which the gas reacts with the phosphors on the screen it is possible to display over 16 million different colours. Plasma displays are flat and very thin and hence do not have the same distortions at the edges as conventional cathode-ray tube (CRT) displays. Plasma displays are brighter than *liquid-crystal displays*. Plasma displays are sometimes known as 'thin panel' displays.

platform: the type of computer system on which a particular piece of software will run. The *operating system* needed is often included in the definition of the platform. Software will usually be provided with information such as: 'this software runs on a 128 MB PC using the Windows 98 platform'.

plotter: an output device used to draw charts, diagrams, and other line-based graphics on paper or transparencies. Plotters use either pens or electrostatic charges and toner. Pen plotters draw on paper or transparencies with one or more coloured pens. Electrostatic plotters 'draw' a pattern on electrostatically charged dots on the paper and then apply toner and fuse it in place. The most common type of plotter is a flat-bed plotter which holds the paper still while the pen makes all the movements.

plug and play (plug and go): the ability of a computer to automatically detect and configure new hardware components when they are first plugged in, without requiring the user to go through complicated installation procedures. Using this technology it is possible to use a new peripheral almost as soon as it is connected to the computer. A peripheral that is suitable for plug and play technology is said to be 'plug compatible'.

plug in: a small program that adds extra features to a particular application. The term is used extensively to refer to the 'extras' available to make *Internet browsers* more efficient or to give them additional features (sound and video).

point of presence (POP): an access point to the *Internet*. The closest site via which a user can connect to an Internet server. *Internet service providers* (ISPs) have POPs in many locations, allowing most customers to reach the service for the price of a local telephone call. Each POP has a unique *Internet protocol* (IP) address.

point-to-point protocol (PPP): a *protocol* for serial communication between computers using TCP/IP, over standard telephone lines, ISDN, and other high-speed connections. PPP can be used to connect a computer to the Internet and is faster than serial line Internet protocol, with better error correction.

pointer: 1 A symbol displayed on the computer screen that is moved by means of a pointing device such as a mouse, stylus, trackball, etc. The pointer is used to move around documents, select icons, move and copy objects and to select items from menus.

2 In programming, a method of moving from one item of data to the next in a data structure.

point-of-sale terminal (POS terminal): a computer *terminal* used at, for example, supermarket checkouts where goods are paid for. The terminal can have a variety of functions, such as scanning *bar codes* on items, reading the descriptions and prices from the supermarket database and possibly also *electronic funds transfer*. In addition, this assists with stock control as the number of items sold can be subtracted from amounts in stock.

polling: the continuous checking of other programs or devices by one program or device to see what state they are in. Polling is used by operating systems to allow *multiprogramming* to take place. The purpose of the polling is to see if the programs and devices are still connected or want to communicate. Polling is an alternative to using *interrupts*.

pop-up menu: a menu that expands as a long list when selected with a mouse. The list of options remains visible whilst the mouse button is held down. The user selects options by moving the mouse pointer down the menu and releasing the mouse button when the desired option is highlighted.

port: a socket at the back of a computer that is used to connect peripherals to the computer. As well as mouse and keyboard ports most PCs have additional *serial* and *parallel ports*.

port address: the number used to identify a particular *port*. Port numbers are from 0 to 65536. Ports 0 to 1024 are reserved for use by certain privileged services.

portability: the ease with which software can be converted to run on a different computer system than that used to create the original software. Porting is the name given to the task of converting the software and the less porting required the more portable the software is said to be.

portable computer: any computer small and light enough to carry, such as a *laptop*, *notebook*, pocket computer, or *palmtop*.

position independent code: program code that can be placed anywhere in a computer and be executed from that position without any changes being made. See *relocatable code*.

post mortem dump: a printout of the contents of all *variables* and *registers* when a program has failed. The information provided can help a programmer ascertain why the program failed and help with identifying a solution.

postfix notation: see r*everse Polish notation*.

postmaster: the name given to the person in charge of administering *e-mail* for a particular site.

PostScript: a page description language produced by Adobe Systems that uses English phrases and program constructs to describe the appearance of a printed page to the printer. PostScript translates the text and graphic images in the document into printer instructions using *outline fonts* and *vector graphics*. The printer used must be capable of receiving PostScript instructions.

power down: to turn off a computer following the normal procedure. This involves stopping any applications programs that are running before turning off the power. Shutting down a computer in this way ensures there will be no loss of data.

power management: the conservation of battery power on *portable* (laptop) computers by switching to a low power consumption mode when not in use.

power on self-test (POST): the diagnostic testing sequence that a computer's *basic input output system* (BIOS) runs to check that the computer's keyboard, memory, disk drives, and other hardware are working correctly when it is first switched on. If the hardware specified in the *config.sys* file is not detected or is found not to be working correctly, the BIOS issues an error message which may be text on the display screen (if it is working correctly) or a series of coded beeps.

power supply unit (PSU): the unit within a PC that provides all the electrical power needed to run the components of the computer. PSUs need to be able to provide the electricity at different voltages since different parts of the computer require different voltages.

power surge: a sudden rise of current or voltage in an electrical circuit that can cause damage to a computer or its files if there is no surge protector.

PowerPC: a family of high-performance, reduced instruction set computers developed by Apple, Motorola, and IBM (the PowerPC Alliance). The PowerPC processors are designed to emulate other CPUs and hence a PowerPC can run DOS and Macintosh software. These chips have the speed of the *Pentium* but use less power.

precompiled code: a sequence of instructions that comes ready compiled to carry out a particular task. The programmer does not need to know what language was used to produce the code, but does need to know the method of presenting data so that the routine can be carried out successfully.

prefix notation: a way of representing arithmetic or logical expressions in a manner which specifies exactly the order in which operations that all have the same precedence are to be performed. With all *operators* having the same order of precedence there is no need for brackets, which has the advantage of providing a relatively simple way of both evaluating an arithmetic expression and of generating code.

Operators come before *operands* in prefix notation. For example, the infix expression A+B*C translates to +A*BC in prefix notation.

pre-printed stationery: paper which has some information already printed on it. Invoices, orders, etc. are often mass printed, sometimes on continuous stationery, and the computer software then prints information in the relevant spaces. This type of stationery allows a company to include company logos without having to incorporate them into the software. The documents can also include colour without the need for a company to have a colour printer.

presence check: see *validation.*

presentation graphics: the images created with computers and used as part of a business or education presentation. The software used to create these presentations allows the producer to combine text, charts and pictures and build each slide up as required for the presentation. This type of presentation has largely replaced the use of overhead transparencies (OHTs) with which it was impossible to build up the slide while the presenter was talking.

presentation layer: the part of the *open systems interconnection seven-layer model* that ensures that the communications passing through are in the appropriate form for the recipient. For example, a *presentation layer* program may format a *file transfer* request in binary code to ensure a successful file transfer.

pressure pad/switch: a *sensor* that detects changes of pressure.

Pretty Good Privacy (PGP): an *encryption* program based on the *Rivest, Shamir, Adleman algorithm* that allows users to securely exchange files and e-mail messages over all kinds of networks. The receiver needs the encryption key to be able to read the data transferred. PGP also allows users to digitally 'sign' a document or message, in order to provide non-forgeable proof of authorship.

primary domain controller (PDC) and backup domain controller (BDC) are roles that can be allocated to network *servers* using the *Windows NT* operating system. Windows NT splits the network into domains when managing access to network resources. The user logs into a domain to gain access to the resources available within that domain. The resources themselves can be located on several different servers. The server responsible for managing the user database for a domain is known as the primary domain controller. Other servers are designated as backup domain controllers and can step in as primary domain controller if the PDC server fails; they can also help balance the workload if the network is busy.

primary key: the *key field* (attribute) that serves as the unique identifier of a specific row in a database table. Primary keys are nearly always numeric as these are less likely to be duplicated and can also be generated automatically. Text fields are far less likely to be unique. For example, a text field such as 'surname' cannot be a primary key, otherwise once a 'Smith' was entered, no other Smiths could be added. As an example, a database of club members could have a table holding the following fields:

Membership number	First name	Family name	Date of birth
134765	John	Frank	18/04/85
137854	Mike	Richards	25/08/83

The primary key would be the membership number as this is unique and identifies the record. See also *composite key, foreign key, secondary key.*

primary store: the computer *memory* that stores the instructions and data for any programs that are currently running. See *RAM.*

print: the act of producing a hard copy of a file or some data.

print buffer: see *printer buffer.*

print (or printer) cartridge: the container for the ink in a printer.

print hammer: the mechanism in a *daisywheel printer* that strikes the character onto the ink ribbon and hence transfers the ink onto the paper.

print head: the mechanism in a printer that deposits the ink onto the paper.

print job: each file of data, waiting to be printed in a *printer queue* is referred to as a print job.

print quality: describes the final appearance of the text when printed. There are several different qualities:

- *Draft quality* – the lowest quality of printout: it is possible to see small gaps between the spots of ink and there are rough edges to each of the characters
- *Near letter quality* – a term only used when referring to printouts produced on dot-matrix printers; the quality is better than draft but the rough edges can still be seen
- *Letter quality* – again used only to describe the quality of printout produced by a dot-matrix printer; the quality is the same as that produced by a typewriter.

Computer printers are sometimes divided into two categories: those that produce letter quality type, such as *laser, ink-jet,* and *daisywheel* printers; and those that do not, including most *dot-matrix* printers. Modern laser printers can produce print that is considerably better than letter quality, i.e. than that produced by a typewriter.

print queue: see *printer queue.*

print server: a *server* on a *network* that controls the printers on that network. Jobs to be printed are spooled onto the queue associated with the appropriate printer and released for printing when they reach the front of the queue. The disk space for the various print queues is provided on the print server along with the spooling software. The software for managing the printers is also held on the print server.

print spooler: the software that organises the *printer queue,* taking print files as they arrive and storing them on hard disk until the printer is ready to process them. The transfer of the print file has to be complete before the print job is placed in the printer queue.

printer: a device that accepts text and graphic output from a computer and transfers the information to standard size sheets of paper. Printers vary in size, speed, sophistication, and cost. When choosing printers users must consider:

- **Colour** – colour is important for users who need to print pages for maps, presentations, graphics, etc. Colour printers are more expensive to operate since they use several ink or toner cartridges and are generally slower than monochrome printers.
- **Resolution** – the sharpness of text and images on paper is usually measured in dots per inch. The higher the resolution the higher the price, generally.
- **Speed** – the speed of the printer becomes important when large documents are printed. The slowest printers are capable of only about three to six sheets per minute.
- **Memory** – most printers come with a small amount of memory that can be expanded by the user. Having more than the minimum amount of memory is helpful and allows faster printing of pages with large images or tables.

printer buffer: is an area of memory in a printer that stores output from the computer until it can be printed. The computer sends data to the printer faster than the printer can print and the printer buffer is used to absorb these differences in speed. The computer sends data until the buffer is full; the computer stops sending data and printing begins; once the contents of the buffer are printed the computer resumes its transmission of data. See *handshaking*.

Printer Control Language (PCL): the control language developed by Hewlett Packard for use with dot-matrix and LaserJet printers, but now also used by many other manufacturers. PCL tells the printer how to print a page using a set of instructions, each of which begins with the Escape key (hence PCL is sometimes known as 'escape code language'), as do *page description languages*. See *printer languages*.

printer driver: a software *routine* that describes the physical characteristics of a particular printer, and converts data for printing into a form that a printer can understand.

printer languages: commands from the computer to the printer that tell the printer how to format the document being printed. These commands manage *font*, font size, graphics, *compression* of data sent to the printer, colour, etc. The two most popular printer languages are *PostScript* and *Printer Control Language*.

printer queue: a list of items (print jobs) waiting to be output to the printer when it becomes available.

printer types: see *dot-matrix printer, inkjet printer, laser printer*.

printout: a printed copy of a file also referred to as hard copy.

privacy: the concept that a user's data is not to be examined by anyone else without that user's permission. Stored files, databases and e-mails can all contain personal and sensitive information that the user may not wish to have disclosed to unauthorised people or companies. The *Data Protection Act* was brought into force to provide rights for individuals and to try to ensure proper practices when handling data. Physical access to computer systems, software controls, *passwords* and network management are all features that systems use to enhance *security* and prevent unauthorised access to data.

private automatic branch exchange (PABX): most organisations have PABXs to provide internal calls as well as allowing calls in and out of the organisation using the public telephone network.

private branch exchange (PBE): a telephone exchange located on an organisation's premises, for use within the organisation.

private (or secret) key: is an *encryption*/decryption *key* known only to the party or parties that exchange secret messages. At its simplest a key is shared by the communicators so that each can encrypt and decrypt messages. This system is vulnerable to being broken if either party loses the key or it is stolen. A more secure alternative is to use a combination of public and private keys. See *public key cryptography*.

private wide area network: a *network* that uses *leased lines* and can only be accessed if you are a subscriber.

procedural language: a computer language which requires the programmer to show explicitly the order in which program statements are to be executed. The language allows programs to be broken down into *subprogram* units which can be tested individually and makes programs more readable.

procedure: a group of programming instructions that together carry out a specific task. The procedure is normally identified by a name, which is used to identify it in the program into which it is incorporated.

process: a sequentially executing piece of code that runs on one processing unit of a system. A process is started whenever a program is first run.

process control: the use of a computer to automatically monitor and control a manufacturing process such as making beer, baking cakes or packing boxes. This can involve the use of *sensors* and *feedback* to respond to different circumstances.

process state: a term used in a *multiprogramming* environment to describe the state of a program that is running on a computer. A program can be:

- waiting to make use of the processor – ready state
- waiting for a peripheral to become available – blocked state
- aborted – stopped state
- finished using the processor, having completed all its instructions – completed state
- stopped from using the processor because its time allocation is complete – suspended state.

processor: a hardware device that executes the commands in a program held in the computer's memory. Also referred to as the processing unit or central processing unit.

processor bound: a program is regarded as processor bound when it will require extensive use of the processor whilst it is running and relatively little use of any peripherals. See *peripheral bound*.

processor cycle time: see *cycle time*.

product code: see *universal product code*.

program: normally understood to mean a set of instructions that tell a computer what to do. The term is also used to describe the process of creating or changing this set of instructions. Normally the program is put into the computer's RAM before being executed. The computer gets one instruction, executes it and then gets the next instruction. The data used by, and generated by, the instructions in the program are held in RAM. Programs are written in computer *programming languages*, which are understandable by humans and need translating into *machine code* before they can be executed. The program written in human understandable form is called the *source program* and the machine code program is called the *object program*.

program algorithm: the sequence of steps required to successfully carry out a particular task on a computer. The *algorithm* can be represented in a variety of different ways: *program flowchart, pseudo-code,* Jackson structure diagram. However the algorithm is represented, a programmer should be able to code a program that can be used to carry out the required task from the representation.

program code: the actual instructions that form the *source code* for the computer program.

program counter: a *register* in the control unit of a computer that holds the address of the next instruction to be executed. It is important to note that it does not hold a copy of the instruction, merely its location in memory.

program documentation is a complete written description of the program intended for users and, more specifically, for maintenance and modifications at a later stage. Depending on the level of complexity of the program, this can be minimal for very simple programs or include some or all of the following for more complex programs.

Identification and statement of purpose:
- author and date written
- language used
- hardware requirements.

General specification:
- operation under normal circumstances
- restrictions and limitations
- specification of any files
- format for input data.

Program specification:
- *algorithms, pseudo-code,* flowcharts, structure charts, annotated listings
- test data and expected results.

User documentation:
- installation guide
- explanation of the operation of the program
- backup procedures
- manuals and tutorials.

The amount of documentation and the level of detail for any program will be dependent on the application, the needs of the particular user and the likelihood of future maintenance. Future maintenance relies heavily on the quality of the documentation provided.

program evaluation and review technique (PERT): see *PERT chart*.

program features: the characteristics of programs and systems which make these successful. The features that programmers strive to include in the programs and systems they produce include:

- user-friendliness, so that with limited training users are able to make full use of a program
- the ability to handle data entry faults during execution without stopping or failing; a program with this feature is said to be robust
- flexibility – the ability to be adapted for use in different situations
- reliability – sufficiently well designed that the program does not fail as a result of design faults
- portability – the ability to be used on different computer hardware
- a design that allows easy maintenance during the software's lifetime.

program flowchart: a pictorial representation of the logic of a program. The flowchart below represents the stages in calculating a bill where a minimum charge of £50 applies.

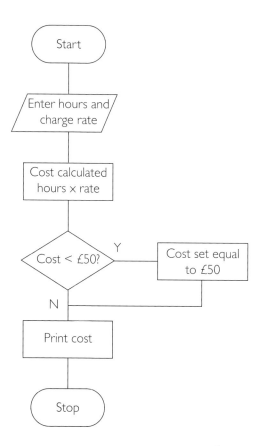

program library: see *software library*.

program listing: a printout of the instructions in a program. This printout is of the *source code*, which is in a form that is easy for humans to read.

program loop: a series of instructions that can be executed several times. The number of times the loop instructions are executed is determined by the type of loop construct used. See *for loop, repeat until loop, while loop.*

program loop time: the time taken by a single repetition of a loop. Programmers can use this information to work on the efficiency of a program.

program maintenance: modification of a computer program after it has been implemented. Maintenance is necessary for three main reasons:

- a fault may occur in the software, which needs attention quickly. This is known as corrective maintenance
- the software is working correctly but needs modification to embrace changes that have occurred. Examples of these changes are: the company has extended the range of products it sells or new legislation has been brought in. This type of maintenance is known as adaptive maintenance
- the software is working correctly but it is possible to make it work more efficiently. This type of maintenance is known as perfective maintenance.

program specification: the detailed documentation that the programmer uses to create a program. This documentation is produced by the systems analyst and reflects the needs of the user.

program statement: a single *instruction* in a program.

program suite: the collection of programs needed to complete all the tasks required within a software system. A company's payroll will normally require several programs to complete all the necessary tasks, e.g. data validation, updating *master files,* producing coin analysis (if cash payments are involved), payslip printing.

program testing: the program must be tested to prove that it fulfils all the *user* requirements and deals with exceptions and errors correctly. To do this the program is tested with three categories of *data*:

- typical – to check that the system performs as expected using normal data
- extreme – to make sure that it is accepted and correctly processed
- erroneous – to prove that illegal or incorrect data is detected, reported and dealt with correctly.

programmable logic array (PLA): see *uncommitted logic array (ULA).*

programmable read-only memory (PROM): a memory *chip* onto which data can be written only once. PROMs are manufactured as blank chips, but data can be written onto them with a PROM programmer or PROM burner. Like *ROMs,* PROMs retain their data when power is removed but the data cannot be changed after it is burnt onto the PROM.

programmer: a person who writes the instructions that allow computers to carry out tasks. These sets of instructions are called *programs.*

programmer analyst: a combination programmer and systems analyst.

programming: designing and writing computer programs. The programmer designs the logic to solve a problem and writes the instructions in a computer programming *language* which can then be translated into *machine code* ready for execution.

programming aids: a term used to describe the various *software* packages used in the production of a program. With some languages, these aids are combined into one package and the programmer provided with a desktop that allows access to the individual aids. A *text editor, interpreter, compiler,* linkage editor and *loader* are the basic aids used in the production of programs.

programming languages: the commands, and *syntax* associated with those commands, that allow programmers to create instructions for a computer. These commands are written in a form that can be understood by humans and need converting into a form the central processing unit can understand. In reality the *software* that allows the instructions to be converted into machine code is the *computer language*. Examples of programming languages are *Pascal, Visual Basic,* Delphi, C and COBOL.

programming tools: see *programming aids*.

project management: the process of planning, monitoring, and controlling the course and development of a particular project. Examples of projects could be: producing a new software system, networking a company's computers or building a new motorway or housing estate. A project needs to be broken down into smaller steps or *tasks*, each of which is then scheduled with an estimate of the time it requires. Consideration has to be given to budgets and overall time scales. On anything but a small scale, project management generally requires a team of people headed by a *project manager*.

project management software: a *software* package designed to assist in the process of *project management*. Features of the package could include:

- breaking down complex tasks into simpler ones
- adding or modifying tasks
- providing start and end dates for tasks
- calculating completion time
- calculating resource requirements
- monitoring resources and allocating resources to tasks
- scheduling tasks and providing critical path analysis to achieve best performance
- printing out information in a variety of formats, e.g. *Gantt charts, PERT charts* and calendars.

project manager: the person in charge of leading a *project management* team. The person must have some or all of the following qualities:

- leadership
- motivation skills
- interpersonal skills
- communication skills
- technical skills
- management skills
- business experience
- ability to delegate
- ability to work under pressure

- ability to co-ordinate various activities
- ability to deal with problems.

PROLOG: a programming language where programming involves entering 'facts' and 'rules' and getting the PROLOG system to deduce conclusions from them.

prompt: a message from a computer that asks the *user* to do something, such as enter a command, enter a *password* or enter *data*. An example is the *DOS* prompt, C:.

proportional spacing: a form of character spacing in which the horizontal space each character occupies is proportional to the width of the character. The letter *i*, for example, takes up less space than the letter *m*.

protocol: properly called *communications protocol*, it is the set of *rules* that regulate the way data is transmitted between computers to ensure the minimum number of errors. Examples are *transmission control protocol, Internet protocol, point of prescence* and SLIP.

prototype: a simple *system* that 'looks' and 'feels' like the final system but does not have any of the detail and *functionality*. This allows the system to be assessed by the user, which can be done at the *analysis* or *design* stage. Prototyping is often done as part of a *feasibility study* to avoid large sums of money, time and effort being spent on an impractical project.

proxy server: a server that provides access to files from other servers by retrieving them either from its local *cache* or from the remote *server*. This type of server is commonly used when linking education networks to the *Internet*. *Web sites* that have recently been downloaded are cached and consequently available to later users much faster than if they had to be downloaded again. As users access more sites, those visited earlier get removed from the cache.

pseudo-code: a method of demonstrating the logic of a program using *statements* which are close to ordinary speech but which can be taken by a programmer and converted into a program using a programming language. The pseudo-code below could be used as the basis of a program to update the *records* held in a *direct access* file using the *transactions* in a transaction file.

```
Open files
While more transactions
        Enter transaction
        If transaction is an insertion
                Set up new record
                Write to file
        If transaction is amendment
                Read record from file
                Update record
                Write record back to file
        If transaction is deletion
                Write blank record to file in location indicated
Close files
```

pseudo random-number generator: see *random number generator*.

public domain software: software that has no *copyright* protection and can be used or copied by anyone free of charge. Much of this software has been donated for the good of the general public by its programmers.

public key cryptography: a form of *message encryption* where each user has a public key and a *private key*. The messages are encrypted with the receiver's public key before being transmitted. On receipt the message is decrypted using the private key which is never disclosed, hence ensuring the security of the system. See *encryption*.

public switched telephone network (PSTN): the world's collection of inter-connected public telephone networks, both commercial and government-owned. The PSTN provides the main infrastructure for the *Internet*.

puck: a small disk-shaped device used for drawing on a *graphics tablet*. It has buttons and a window through which cross-hairs can be viewed. It is used mainly with CAD applications.

pull-down menu: a menu that appears as a long list when selected with a *mouse*. The list of options remains visible while the mouse button is held down. The user selects options by moving the *mouse pointer* down the menu and releasing the mouse button when the desired option is highlighted.

pull technology: the user on the *Internet* decides which *sites* to visit, which *web pages* to look at or which software to *download* rather than signing up to a service that automatically brings it to the user's desktop. This is the opposite of *push technology*.

pulse code modulation (PCM): a method of transmitting analogue data using a digital transmission system. The data being transmitted after pulse code modulation is in binary. These binary values are arrived at by sampling the analogue waveform at regular intervals (several times per second). The frequency of the signal at the sample point is rounded to the nearest predetermined level. The predetermined levels are powers of two that can be represented by three, four, five, or six binary digits (bits). Hence the output of a pulse code modulator is a series of binary numbers, each represented by some 'power of 2' bits.

At the receiving end, a pulse code demodulator converts the binary numbers back into pulses with the same levels as those in the modulator, which can then be further processed to restore the original analogue waveform. See *analogue signal*.

punched paper tape: paper tape with holes punched in it to represent data. This storage medium is now little used.

purge: to delete both a set of data and all references to that data.

push: an expression used when putting data onto a *stack*, e.g. 'the return address is pushed onto the stack'. The term is also used to describe the delivery of data using *push technology*.

push down list: see *stack*.

push up list: see *stack*.

push technology: the process on the *Internet* whereby information can be delivered or 'pushed' directly to a user who has previously requested it. This saves the user having to search for the information on an Internet site. For example, Yahoo will provide news to users who have entered information in a database about subjects they wish to see, e.g. sport, stock exchange, political.

Q

?: a *wildcard* character. A special symbol that can be inserted in a search string that stands for one or more characters. Most *operating systems* and many software packages allow the use of wildcards to identify files and directories. This allows the user to select multiple files with a single specification.

In DOS and Windows, the asterisk (*) is used as the wildcard. The file specification s* therefore, refers to all files that begin with s. Similarly, the specification s*.xls refers to all files that start with s and end with .xls.

Many word processors also support wildcards for performing text searches.

qualitative information: information that cannot be readily measured in numerical terms, e.g. judgements and opinions. Computer systems do not deal well with qualitative information, as it is not easy to represent. See *quantitative information, value judgements.*

quality assurance: a system of procedures undertaken to guarantee that a product or a system adheres or conforms to established standards.

quantitative information: information that can be measured in numerical terms, e.g. the number of books in stock, the price of an item, the scaling factor for feet to metres. Computer systems deal very well with quantitative information, as these are easy to represent and can be used in formulae and mathematical models. See *qualitative information.*

query: a request for information from a database. There are three main methods for generating queries:

- **Selecting options from a drop-down menu** – using this method, the database system provides a list of options from which the user selects the most appropriate. This method of generating queries is perhaps the easiest because the drop-down menus guide the user, but it is also the least flexible.
- **Using the** *query by example* **(QBE) method** – the database provides a blank record and the user enters the values that define the query into the available fields.
- **Using a** *query language* – with this method the user enters the request for information in the form of a short program written in a special query language. This is the most powerful but the most complex method because the user must be able to program in the query language.

query by example (QBE): in *database management systems,* query by example refers to a method of generating *queries* in which the database program displays a blank *record* with a space for each *field.* The user enters the conditions for each field that are required in the query. For example, to find all the records in a database holding information about students and their examination marks where the MARK field is greater than 55, the user would enter >55 in the blank MARK field. QBE is considered easier to learn than using a *query language.*

query language: a specialised programming language used with databases to select information that satisfies specified criteria. For example, the query:

SELECT ALL WHERE thismark > 55 *AND* previousgrade = 'D' would select all records in which the previousgrade field is 'D' and the thismark field has a value greater than 55. Structured query language (SQL) is the de facto standard for query languages. SQL was first introduced as a commercial database system in 1979 by Oracle Corporation and is now the favourite query language for *database management systems*. SQL also works on *distributed databases* (databases that are spread out over several computer systems), which allows several users on a network to access the same database simultaneously.

questionnaire: a paper-based or on-line method of gathering information. Questionnaires need to be designed carefully in order to produce quantitative responses where possible, and also to avoid bias.

queue: a *data structure* in which elements are removed in the same order they were entered. A queue is often referred to as a FIFO (first in, first out) data structure. Queues are used to line up jobs for a computer or device. A print spooler makes use of a queue when the users of a computer system or network try to print several documents at the same time. The documents are placed on the print queue associated with the particular printer. The printer then pulls the documents off the queue one at a time.

A queue requires two *pointers*: one that indicates the front and one for the back of the queue. Diagrammatically, a queue is represented as shown below.

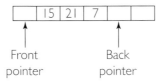

Front pointer

Back pointer

Using the diagram above the following are algorithms for managing the queue.

Adding   If BP < Queue Size Then
                   Move BP up 1 location
                   Add data item at BP
              Else
                   Output 'Queue Full'

Removing If FP <> BP Then
                   Remove item at FP
                   Move FP up 1 location
              Else
                   Output 'Queue Empty'

See *circular queue*.

quick format: removes all *files* from the disk but does not look for bad *sectors*. The quick format option will work only on a disk that has previously been fully formatted. See *format*.

quick key: see *hot key*.

quicksort: a particularly efficient method of sorting data. Quicksort uses *recursion* to sort a list into ascending (or descending) order. A *procedure* in the program accepts a list and uses the first number in the list (the reference number) to split the list into two sublists. The *algorithm* places the reference number in its correct position, with all numbers in the left sublist having values less than the reference number, while numbers in the right sublist are greater than the reference number. This procedure is called recursively using the sublists until all sublists hold only one number.

QuickTime: software components developed by Apple for creating, editing, publishing, and viewing *multimedia* content. QuickTime supports video, animation, graphics, 3D, MIDI, music, sound, and text. It is used in many Macintosh applications. Windows applications can also run QuickTime files, but require the installation of special player software. QuickTime is often used on the World Wide Web to provide web pages with video and animation.

quit: to exit from a program in an orderly way. See *abort, system crash.*

qwerty keyboard: pronounced 'kwer-tee', this is the normal *keyboard* used on UK computers. Its name comes from the arrangement of letters on the keyboard . The first six letters on the first line of alphabetic keys are Q W E R T Y. This arrangement of letters was created at the end of the nineteenth century by Christopher Sholes, the inventor of the typewriter. Apparently he arranged the keys to prevent jamming on mechanical typewriters by separating commonly used letter combinations.

With the emergence of more sophisticated typewriters and computer keyboards, on which jamming is not an issue, new keyboards designed for speed typing have been developed. The best-known is called a Dvorak keyboard. Despite their more rational designs, these new keyboards have not received wide acceptance.

radio button: in *graphical user interfaces,* groups of buttons, of which only one can be on at a time. When you select one button, all the others are automatically deselected. See *check box.*

RAM card: an add-in circuit board containing *random access memory.* It contains the necessary interface logic to decode memory *addresses.*

RAM disk: an area of the computer's main *memory* that is accessible as if it were a disk. It allows much faster access to the data than if it was stored on disk but the software that accesses the data is written as though the data was stored on disk.

random access refers to the ability to access data directly. With random access, the time taken to access any item of data is roughly the same regardless of its position on the storage medium. The opposite of random access is *sequential access.* When random access is provided to the data stored it means the system is able to jump directly to any item of data. Disks are random access media, whereas tapes are sequential access media.

The terms random access and sequential access are often used to describe data files. A random-access data file enables the user to read or write data anywhere in the file. In a sequential-access file, the user can only read and write information sequentially, starting from the beginning of the file.

If the data within the file is always going to be accessed in the same order, a sequential-access file is faster. Payroll is an example of a system that normally uses sequential access for its main file of data. If the system requires access to information in no particular order then any data must be held in a file that allows random access.

Random access is sometimes called *direct access.*

random access memory (RAM): a type of computer *memory* where any byte of memory can be accessed without looking at the preceding bytes. RAM is the most common type of memory found in computers and other devices, such as printers. Within the computer it is often referred to as main memory and allows data to be written to it as well as read from it. RAM is volatile, which means that it loses its contents when power is removed.

There are two basic types of RAM:

- *dynamic RAM (DRAM)*
- *static RAM (SRAM).*

random file: a file normally held on disk that allows very fast *direct access* to the data stored. The records held in the file are normally accessed using a *hashing algorithm.* The *key field* for the record concerned is put through the hashing algorithm to create a disk address, which identifies the sector on disk where the record is held. See *random access.*

random number generation: the process of generating what appear to be random numbers. Most *programming languages* provide a *function* that allows the programmer to generate 'random' numbers that can be used as part of a simulation to create random occurrences of events. The function normally requires a *seed*, i.e. a number, to ensure that the same sequence of random numbers is not generated each time the program is used. This seed can however be fixed to allow the programmer to test the program using the same sequence of random numbers each time.

range check: see *validation*.

raster: the name given to the rectangular area of a display screen that is actually being used to display images. The raster is slightly smaller than the physical dimensions of the display screen to ensure that everything that needs to be seen is visible. The raster varies for different resolutions, e.g. a VGA resolution of 640×480 on a 15-inch monitor produces one raster, whereas a SVGA resolution of $1{,}024 \times 768$ produces a slightly different raster. Most monitors use autosizing, which means that they automatically use the optimal raster depending on the monitor's size and the video adapter's resolution. In addition, most monitors have controls that allow you move and resize the raster.

raster graphics: see *scanning*.

raw data: data that is passed along to an *input/output* device without being interpreted. In contrast, 'cooked' refers to data that is processed before being passed to the input/output device. The term comes from *Unix*, which supports cooked and raw modes for data output to a terminal. In cooked mode, special characters, such as erase and kill are processed by the *device driver* before being sent to the output device.

read: to copy data to a place where it can be used by a program. The term is generally used to describe the copying of data from a storage medium, such as a disk, to a computer's main memory. The data is copied and not moved – it remains in its original position as well as in the new location.

read head: the circuitry that moves over each sector of disk or block of tape and transfers the data held to the computer. Normally these circuits are capable of reading and writing data. See *read/write head*.

read-only access: when a disk, file, *record* or *field* is set up so that the data held can only be displayed and not modified or deleted it is said to be set up with read-only access privileges. All *operating systems* allow the user to protect objects (disks, files, directories, etc.) with a read-only attribute that prevents other users from modifying the object.

read-only memory (ROM): computer *memory* on which the pre-recorded data can only be read and not modified or deleted. ROM is non-volatile, i.e. it retains its contents when the power is removed, unlike main memory (RAM).

The ROM in most personal computers holds the *bootstrap* loader, i.e. the program that *boots* the computer. ROMs are also used in *laser printers* to store their *fonts*.

read/write: an object that is capable of being displayed (read) and modified (written to). Most objects (disks, files, directories) are initially created with read/write status but operating systems allow the user to change an object's read-only attribute to prevent other users from modifying the object.

read/write head: the mechanism and circuitry in a *disk* or *tape drive* that is used to transfer data between the computer's memory and magnetic storage media. Changes in the magnetic field of the material on the disk or tape surface are converted to changing electrical signals and vice versa. Disk drives usually contain one head for each surface that can be read from and written to. There is a separate read/write head for each track on a tape.

read/write memory: see *random access memory*.

readme file: a small text file that comes with many *software packages* and contains information not included in the official documentation. Information that was not available when the original documentation was written is often placed in a readme file.

ready: a program is described as being ready when it is in a position to make use of the processor. See *process state*.

real data type: a data type within programming languages that allows variables to be set up to store *real numbers*.

real number: a number that contains a fractional part. Examples of real numbers are 3.65 and –0.543.

real time: used to describe an event that happens immediately. The term is used to describe a number of different computer features. Real-time operating systems allow programs to respond to input immediately. They are used in many robotic applications when the program must react to a steady flow of new information.

Many simulations make use of the features of real-time programming as events are simulated by a computer to happen at the same speed that they would occur in real life.

real-time clock: the *clock* inside a computer that keeps track of the time even when the computer is turned off. This clock is different from the CPU clock, which is used to control the execution of program instructions. The real-time clock uses a special rechargeable battery.

real-time system: a system making use of the features provided by a real-time *operating system*. See *real time*.

real-time transport protocol (RTP): an *Internet* protocol for transmitting real-time data such as audio and video. RTP provides the mechanisms that allow software applications to send and receive streams of data, but does not guarantee the delivery of data in real time. Generally RTP works alongside the UDP protocol, but it will support other transport protocols.

recalculation: a mode in a *spreadsheet* in which all cells are recalculated whenever a value changes. Automatic recalculation ensures that the spreadsheet data is always up-to-date but the spreadsheet may work more slowly. The alternative to automatic recalculation is to use manual recalculation where the user must explicitly instruct the application to carry out the recalculation.

record: the complete set of information that is stored for an item. Records are made up of *fields*, each of which holds one piece of information. A collection of related records is called a *file*. For example, a student file would hold several records where each record contains all the relevant information about one student. Examples of the fields for the student record might be a surname field, a forename field, an address field and a phone number field.

In *relational database* management systems, records are sometimes known as tuples.

recovery: the process of salvaging *data* stored on damaged media, such as magnetic disks and tapes. It is not always possible to recover all the original data, but data recovery specialists can often restore a surprisingly high percentage of the data on damaged media. The most common causes of data loss are due to disks becoming corrupted or because of viruses. There are a number of software products that can be used help recover data damaged in these ways.

recovery procedures: part of a *contingency plan* to ensure that a rapid recovery can be made from major system disasters caused by floods, fire, sabotage or power disruption. This can mean having an alternative system available, access to alternative communications links or a service agreement that provides replacement equipment. Together with all of the necessary *backups* and storage arrangements, this should ensure that the system will be functional again in the shortest possible time.

recursion: a programming method in which a *routine* calls itself. Recursion is an extremely powerful concept, but it can put heavy demands on a computer's memory resources. LISP and Prolog are programming languages that have been designed to use recursive methods.

A recursive *algorithm* is given below:

```
Global Integer n
n:=5
PRINT factorial(n)
STOP
FUNCTION factorial(n:LOCAL INTEGER)
    IF n = 1 THEN
            factorial := 1
    ELSE
            factorial := factorial(n-1)*n
    ENDIF
ENDFUN
```

The algorithm works out the mathematical concept factorial of a number (in this case 5), i.e. $5 * 4 * 3 * 2 * 1$. To carry out this calculation the function 'factorial' calls itself unless its output value is 1.

recursive subprogram: a *subprogram* that has been written in such a way that it is used recursively. See *recursion*.

red green blue (RGB) monitor: a colour *monitor* that accepts three separate signals, red, green and blue, that are used to create anything from 16 to over 1 million different colours.

reduced instruction set computer (RISC): pronounced 'risk', it is a type of *microprocessor* that recognises a relatively limited number of *instructions*. Until the mid-1980s, most computer manufacturers were building increasingly complex CPUs that had ever-larger sets of instructions. A number of computer manufacturers then started to build CPUs which only used a very limited set of instructions. One advantage of reduced instruction set computers is that they can execute their instructions very fast because the instructions are so simple. Another advantage is that RISC *chips* require fewer transistors, which makes them cheaper to design and produce. A disadvantage is that the software programs produced for these processors are more complex.

Since the emergence of RISC computers, conventional computers have been referred to as complex instruction set computers (CISCs).

redundancy of data occurs when *data* is duplicated unnecessarily. In a file-based system, it is possible for the same data to be held in several different places. This can cause errors and make updating very difficult. A *relational database* approach should ensure that there is no data redundancy.

redundant array of independent disks (RAID): a category of *disk drives* that actually combines two or more drives to provide better performance and a more fault-tolerant unit. RAID disk drives are used frequently on *servers* but are rarely used in personal computers.

There are several different RAID levels. The three most common are 0, 3, and 5:

Level 0 provides data striping (spreading out blocks of each file across multiple disks) but no redundancy. This improves performance but does not deliver fault tolerance.

Level 1 provides disk mirroring.

Level 3 is the same as Level 0, but one dedicated disk is reserved for error correction data. It provides good performance and some level of fault tolerance.

Level 5 provides data striping at the byte level and also stripe error correction information. This results in excellent performance and good fault tolerance.

The I in RAID is sometimes understood to stand for 'inexpensive'.

redundant code: code within a *program* which is never accessed and consequently serves no useful purpose. As changes are made to programs (as a result of software maintenance) it is possible to create sections of code that are no longer used. Examples of circumstances that generate redundant code are:

- the programmer may have written a completely new section of code to replace an existing routine but forgotten to remove the old routine
- the condition for one of the options on a branch instruction might never be met as a result of changes in practice within an organisation.

reference file: see *static file*.

referential integrity: a system of *rules* used by a *relational database* management system (RDBMS) to ensure that relationships between records in related tables are valid, and that related data is not accidentally deleted or changed. It prevents users or applications from entering inconsistent data. Most RDBMSs have various referential *integrity* rules that you can apply when you create a relationship between two tables.

A referential integrity rule could be set up so that when changes are made to the data in a linked field in one table all the records in another table that are linked to it will also be changed.

Referential integrity could also be set up to ensure that when a record is deleted from a table any linked records in another table are also deleted.

If two tables are linked, referential integrity could ensure that it was not possible to add a record to the second table if it cannot be linked to the first table.

refresh rate: refers to the refreshing of the image on a display screen. The lines on a raster display are scanned regularly to re-draw the image before it fades. The frequency with which the lines are scanned is called the refresh rate and is usually several times per second. The old standard for monitor refresh rates was 60 Hz, but a new VESA standard sets the refresh rate at 75 Hz for monitors using resolutions of 640×480 or greater. This means that the monitor redraws the display 75 times per second. The faster the refresh rate, the less the monitor flickers.

If the lines on the display are scanned alternately, i.e. lines 1, 3, 5, etc. on the first scan and lines 2, 4, 6, etc. on the second scan, then the scan is described as an *interlaced scan*.

Refresh rate is also known as vertical frequency, vertical scan rate, frame rate or vertical refresh rate.

See *vector graphics, bit mapped graphics*.

register: a high-speed *memory* location within the CPU that is normally used for a special purpose. All data must be held in a register before it can be processed, although the movement of data in and out of registers is normally completely invisible to users and even to most programmers. Only when programming in *assembly language* does a programmer need to be aware of what data is in a particular register at a particular point in the program.

The size and number of registers built into a processor help to determine its power and speed.

registration: the process of notifying a manufacturer that you have purchased one of its products (hardware or software). Many software companies will check that a person making a request for support has registered the particular product for which support is requested. This helps companies control software piracy.

relational database: a collection of information organised in such a way that required items of data can be retrieved quickly by computer programs. The data in the database is managed and accessed using a collection of programs together known as a *database management system* (DBMS).

The database management system stores information in *tables* and links these tables together by means of *fields* that are common. In a relational database, the rows of a table represent *records* (collections of information about separate items) and the columns represent fields (particular *attributes* of a record). Each table refers to an *entity* (an object or person). As a simple example, here is an entity called PUPIL.

Each column is an attribute
↓

Pupil

Pupil Number	Surname	First name	Date of birth
001	Adams	Sarah	17/06/85
002	Beech	Luke	28/04/85
003	Black	Hannah	04/12/84

← Each row is a record

If we also needed to consider what subjects these pupils were taking and who their teachers were for those subjects, they would not fit comfortably into one table. We need further tables to show entities for SUBJECT, PUPIL_SUBJECTS and TEACHER.

Each of these entities would have their own attributes: for example, TEACHER may need TeacherNumber and TeacherName.

Tables are linked by relationships through common fields. Each row of a table has to be identified by a unique attribute. This is why PUPIL has a PupilNumber as this can be automatically generated to be sequential and different. The PupilNumber attribute is designated as the *primary key* for the PUPIL entity. SUBJECT would have a unique SubjectNumber and then the PUPIL_SUBJECTS entity, which would identify which subjects each pupil is taking, would link these together through the primary keys.

The tables are linked together through relationships. The different forms of relationships are *one-to-one*, one-to-many and *many-to-many*. For example, a one-to-many relationship could be doctors and patients. Each patient has only one doctor but each doctor can have many patients.

Data in the tables has to be normalised to be efficient and avoid duplication. This is achieved by going through processes referred to as *data normalisation* (*first normal form, second normal form* and *third normal form*).

Queries and searches are conducted by using data in specified columns of one table to find additional data in that table or other tables.

Relational database theory is complex and it is only possible here to give an outline of what is involved.

relational operator: an *operator* that allows two items of data to be compared. Hence relational operators are sometimes called comparison operators. An expression involving a relational operator is called a relational expression and always results in a value of either TRUE or FALSE. For example both the expressions:

42 < 57 (42 is less than 57)
'Khalid' > 'Fred' (Khalid is greater than Fred)

produce a TRUE result.

Relational operators		
Symbol	**Mnemonic**	**Meaning**
=	EQ	Equal to
<>	NE	Not equal to
>	GT	Greater than
>=	GE	Greater than or equal to
<	LT	Less than
<=	LE	Less than or equal to

relationship: a term used with relational databases to indicate a link or association between *entities*. These can be *one-to-one*, one-to-many and *many-to-many* relationships. Example of a one-to-many relationship would be a doctor with many patients.

relative address: the location of an item of *data* (its *address*) specified by indicating its distance from another address, called its base address, rather than using its actual address. For example, a relative address might be BA+37, BA being the base address and 37 the distance (called the *offset*). Relative addressing is often used by assembler programmers when implementing an *array*. See *absolute addressing.*

relative path: a *path* that is implied by the current working *directory*. When a user enters a command that refers to a file, if the full pathname is not entered, the current working directory becomes the relative path of the file referred to. A full pathname commences from the root directory, i.e. if the user is currently in network drive M, a file named book.doc can be accessed by M:\library\shelf\book.doc where book.doc is a file in shelf, which is subdirectory contained in a directory named library. If the current working directory is already M:\library\shelf\ then a reference to book.doc would be equivalent.

relative reference: within a *spreadsheet*, references to *cells* or ranges of cells within a formula are usually based upon their position relative to the cell that contains the formula. In the following example, cell B4 contains the formula =A3+2. The spreadsheet finds the value one cell above and one cell to the left of B4. This is known as a relative referencing.

	A	B
1		
2		
3	7	
4		=A3+2

	A	B
1		
2		
3	7	
4		9

When you copy a formula that uses relative references, the references in the pasted formula update and refer to different cells relative to the new position of the formula. In the following example, the formula in cell B4 has been copied to cell B5. The formula in cell B5 changes to =A4+2, which refers to the cell that is one cell above and to the left of the new cell B5.

	A	B
1		
2		
3	7	
4	10	=A3+2
5		=A4+2

	A	B
1		
2		
3	7	
4	10	9
5		12

If you do not want references to change when you copy a formula to a different cell, an *absolute reference* must be used.

release of software: the final part of the life cycle of producing a large-scale piece of software. When the product has gone through the stages of requirements, design, production and testing, then the software can be 'released' or sold to customers.

See also *alpha testing, beta testing.*

reliability: the ability of a program to operate without stopping as a result of design faults. See *robustness.*

relocatable code: *program code* which can be placed anywhere in a computer's memory and still be executed. This is unlike *absolute code*, which must be placed in a specific area of memory for successful execution.

relocation: the process of moving a segment of *program code* to a different area of a computer's memory. See *relocatable code.*

remote access: a workstation which can be connected to a computer by means of a telecommunications link is said to have remote access to the computer. With more people teleworking from home, remote access to their companies' computers becomes an essential part of their daily routine.

remote job entry (RJE): the starting of a *job* from a workstation that is not directly connected to the computer on which the job will be run. The connection from the workstation to the computer is usually by means of a telecommunications link.

remote terminal: a workstation that is not directly connected to a computer but capable of being linked to a computer via a telecommunications link.

rendering: the process of adding realism to a computer *graphic* by adding three-dimensional qualities such as shadows and variations in colour and shade.

repeat until loop: a *loop* structure provided in most programming languages where the condition to determine if the loop is to be executed again is placed at the end of the loop. Since the condition is at the end of the loop the instructions in the loop must be obeyed at least once. This is unlike a *while loop*, where the condition is at the start, so the instructions in the loop might not be executed.

Example: the following loop will continue to be executed until acceptable data has been entered.

```
Display 'Enter data'
Repeat
    Enter data
    Validate data
Until valid data entered
```

repeater: a device which, as well as joining two segments of telecommunications (network) cabling, also amplifies the signal as it passes through.

repetitive strain injury (RSI): an injury produced by repeating the same small movements many times. As more and more people use computers, carpal tunnel syndrome and other forms of RSI have become more prevalent. Amongst suffers a typical symptom is numbness or burning in the fingers or wrist. If RSI is not dealt with when symptoms are first noticed it can cause permanent damage. Adjusting the height and angle of the sufferer's chair and keyboard, and taking frequent breaks from typing can avoid carpal tunnel syndrome developing. Modern office furniture that has been specifically designed for computer use, can also help considerably.

replication: the process of creating and managing duplicate versions of a database. Replication ensures that changes made to one replica are reflected in all the others. Replication allows many users to work with their own local copy of a database but have the database updated as if they were working on a single, centralised database. When database users are geographically widely distributed, replication is often the most efficient method of database management.

The Lotus Notes database system was one of the first to make replication an important component in its design and this has been one of the main reasons for its success.

report generator: part of a *database management system* that allows the user to design a report to extract from one or more files *records* that meet certain conditions and to present selected *fields* in a specified format. Once created, the report can be saved and reused in the future. The report writer is one of the most important components of a database management system because it determines how much flexibility the user has in outputting data.

report program generator (RPG): a *programming language* for developing business applications, especially those that require large numbers of reports to be produced from the data stored.

RPG is also used as an abbreviation for 'role-playing games' i.e. computer games where one or more players adopt a role and act it out in a virtual reality.

reprogrammable read-only memory (RPROM): the name given to *programmable read-only memories* that can under certain conditions can have their contents removed and a new set of data stored.

An *erasable programmable read-only memory* (EPROM) is a PROM that can be erased by exposing it to ultraviolet light. An EEPROM requires only electricity for it to be erased.

requirements specification: within a system's documentation this is the section that gives the customer's requirements. In case of dispute during production of the system this section is referred back to and hence it can act as a legal contact between the customer and the software developer.

reserved word: a special word used by a *programming language* that is not available to the programmer when naming variables or procedures, etc. For example, in Pascal, the word BEGIN is reserved because it is used to identify the beginning of a block of code. Reserved words are sometimes called keywords.

reset: refers to resetting a computer that is already turned on, back to its initial state. Any data or programs in the main memory are erased. See *warm boot, cold boot.*

resident program: a program that is permanently in the computer's *memory.* Normally, a computer does not have enough memory to hold all the programs used. When a user runs a program for which there is insufficient main memory available the operating system frees memory by copying data or programs from main memory to a disk. This process is known as *swapping.* Resident programs are marked as being 'memory resident', which means that the operating system is not permitted to swap them out to disk.

Only programs and data used regularly should be marked as memory resident. This generally includes only the main parts of the operating system.

Another term for memory resident is RAM resident. See *terminate and stay resident.*

resolution: the total number of *pixels* displayed horizontally and vertically by a *monitor.* Resolution is usually given as 640×480, 800×600 or 1024×768, etc. The number of pixels is also determined by the graphics mode and video adapter.

response field: the areas of the screen where users can type data when a *forms dialogue interface* is in use.

return: moving automatically to the beginning of the next line in a text document. Word processors use two types of returns: hard and soft. Both have the effect of adding an additional 'hidden' character to the document while moving the cursor on the screen to the next line in the document. The hard return is used to start a new paragraph and is inserted by pressing the Return (Enter) key. It remains in position until deleted by the user. *Soft returns* are inserted automatically by the word processor as part of its word wrap capability. Whenever too little room remains on the current line for the next word, the word processor inserts a soft return. However the soft return can move if extra text is added or deleted above the soft return character. See *word wrap*.

return to base warranty: a warranty where, if a fault develops on a machine, an engineer does not come out to fix it but the owner has to return the machine to the supplier for repair.

reverse engineer: the process of recreating a design by analysing a final product. Reverse engineering is common in both hardware and software. Several companies have managed to produce Intel-compatible microprocessors through reverse engineering. The legality of reverse engineering has not yet been established by the courts.

reverse Polish notation (RPN): a method of representing arithmetic or logical expressions in a manner which specifies exactly the order in which operations, which all have the same precedence, are to be performed. With all *operators* having the same order of precedence there is no need for brackets, which has the advantage of providing a relatively simple way of both evaluating an arithmetic expression and of generating code.

Operators come after *operands* in RPN. For example, the infix expression A+B*C translates to ABC*+ in RPN, and (A-B)/C+D becomes AB-C/D+. Arithmetic expressions in RPN can be evaluated by a single left-to-right scan utilising a *stack*. The stack is used to hold all of the operands which have been scanned or have been produced as the result of some operation, but which have not yet been used. The algorithm for processing an expression in RPN is as follows:

- If the scanned symbol is a *variable* or constant, push its value to the stack and scan the next symbol.
- If the scanned symbol is a *binary operator*, pop the two topmost values on the stack, apply the operation to them and then push the result to the stack.
- If the scanned symbol is a *unary operator*, pop the top of the stack, apply the operation to this item and then push the result to the stack.

revisable text format file: see *Rich Text Format file*.

Rich Text Format file (RTF file): a document format which allows documents to be transferred between word processors produced by different software manufacturers. The standard was developed by Microsoft Corporation. RTF files are ASCII files with special commands to indicate formatting information, such as fonts and margins. See *hypertext markup language (HTML)* and *Standard Generalised Markup Language (SGML)*.

right alignment: the alignment of text along the right margin.

This paragraph is an example of right-aligned text. Notice that the text goes right up to the right margin and is aligned so that there is no space between the text and the right edge margin.

ring network: a *network topology* where the *workstations* are connected to one another in the shape of a closed loop. Each device is connected directly to two other devices, one on either side of it. Ring topologies are relatively expensive and difficult to install, but they offer high bandwidth and can span large distances.

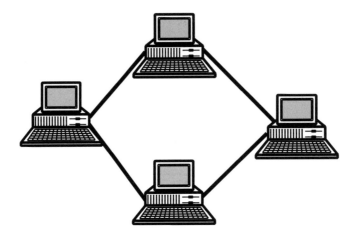

Advantages of a ring network include:

- no dependence on a central computer or *server*
- very high transmission rates are possible
- transmission facilities are shared amongst the users
- transmission of messages is relatively simple, with messages travelling in only one direction.

Disadvantages include:

- the system depends on the reliability of every device in the ring
- it can be difficult to extend the network to add extra workstations.

RISC-OS: an *operating system* written to run on a RISC computer. See *reduced instruction set computer (RISC)*.

risk analysis: the part of a corporate ICT strategy that determines what risks there are to a system and its data, and introduces appropriate measures to stop or reduce their impact. Risks can be of an immediate nature, a likely possibility at some point, or very unlikely but potentially disastrous. Risks can be as likely as power failures, hardware and software failures, *viruses*, theft, and hacking, or as unlikely as floods, fire and earthquakes. The nature of the counter-measure will depend on the cost, the likely time to recover, inconvenience to staff and customers and how often the problem may occur.

Rivest, Shamir, Adleman algorithm (RSA algorithm): a public-key *encryption* technology developed by RSA Data Security, Inc. The RSA *algorithm* is based on the fact that there is no efficient way to work out the factors of very large numbers. Deducing an RSA key, therefore, requires an immense amount of computer processing power and time.

The RSA algorithm has become the de facto standard used for encryption in industry in the USA, especially for data sent over the *Internet*. It is incorporated into many software products, including Netscape Navigator and Microsoft Internet Explorer. The technology is so powerful that the US government has restricted exporting it to foreign countries.

robot: a device that can move and react to sensory input. Robots are now widely used in factories to perform high-precision jobs such as welding and riveting. They are also used in situations that would be dangerous for humans, e.g. cleaning toxic wastes or defusing bombs.

Robots are still not very useful in everyday life, as they are too clumsy to carry out ordinary household chores. See *robotics*.

The word robot was first used by the Czech playwright Karl Capek in his play RUR (Rossum's Universal Robots), which opened in Prague in 1921. Robota is the Czech word for forced labour.

robot arm: see *robot*.

robotics: the field of computer science and engineering concerned with creating devices that can move and react to sensory input. Robotics is one branch of artificial intelligence.

The term robotics was introduced by writer Isaac Asimov. In his science fiction book 'I, Robot', published in 1950, he presented three laws of robotics:

1 A robot may not injure a human being, or, through inaction, allow a human being to come to harm.
2 A robot must obey the orders given it by human beings except where such orders would conflict with the first law.
3 A robot must protect its own existence as long as such protection does not conflict with the first or second law.

See *robot*.

robustness: the ability of a program to deal with errors that occur during execution. The more robust a program the more able it is to deal with errors that occur.

rogue terminator: see *rogue value*.

rogue value: a value used to terminate a sequence of actions. Rogue values are often used in programming to cause an exit from a *loop* structure. They are data values that cannot occur in the context of the loop and hence can be used to cause an exit from the loop. For example, the loop below is exited whenever XXX is entered as a student name and hence XXX is the rogue value for this loop.

```
While Student Name<>'XXX' Do
      Enter Examination Mark
      Enter Student Name
```

root directory: the top *directory* in a hierarchical file system. The root directory is provided by the *operating system* and can hold *files* or *subdirectories*. Similarly subdirectories can hold files and/or other subdirectories. See *hierarchical directory structure*.

root node: the top node in a tree. See *tree*, *binary tree* and *non-binary tree*.

rotation: 1 Where bits shifted out of one end of a register are re-entered at the opposite end.

starting position

I	0	0	I	I	0	0	I

after one shift to the right

I	I	0	0	I	I	0	0

See also *cyclic shift.*

2 Rotation is also the term for the turning text or pictures on a page, e.g.

Rotation

Rotation

The word has been rotated through 90° clockwise.

round-robin: a term used to describe an *operating system* which does not use priorities to determine which process should have access to the CPU, but takes each process in turn and allocates it an equal time slot.

rounding: the process of approximating a number to its nearest equivalent to a given number of significant figures or decimal places. Thus 4.6783 rounded to three decimal places is 4.678, and to one decimal place is 4.7.

rounding error: the error introduced by rounding a number. When 4.6783 is rounded to 1 decimal place the error introduced is 0.0217 (4.7 – 4.6783).

router: a device that is used to connect *local area networks* together. The router uses the information in the *packet* header and a forwarding table to determine the most effective pathway for the data to travel. A router can be used to connect network *segments* together where the different segments use different *protocols* as well as allowing all users on a network to share a single connection to the Internet or a *wide area network* (WAN).

routing: the process of moving a *packet* of *data* from source to destination, which is usually carried out by a *router*. Routing is an important feature of the *Internet* because it enables messages to be passed from one computer to another until they arrive at their destinations. Each of the intermediary computers performs routing by passing along the message to the next computer. The routing process is carried out using information in a forwarding table to determine the best path.

Routing should not be confused with bridging, which is largely hardware based. Routing uses mainly software to determine the best path for the packet. See *bridge.*

routine: one of many terms used to describe a section of a *program* that performs a particular task. Other terms with similar meanings are *procedure, function, subprogram, module* and *subroutine.*

row: in a *spreadsheet,* a horizontal group of *cells* each given a row number 1, 2, 3, etc.

RS-232 interface: short for recommended standard-232C interface, a standard interface approved by the Electronic Industries Association (EIA) for connecting serial devices. There have been various changes to the standard and its name has changed to EIA/TIA-232. However it is generally still referred to as RS-232.

Almost all modems conform to this standard and most personal computers have an RS-232 port for connecting a modem or other device. Many display screens, mice, and serial printers are designed to connect to an RS-232 serial port.

The RS-232 standard supports two types of connectors: a 25-pin D-type connector (DB-25) and a 9-pin D-type connector (DB-9).

RS-432 interface: a standard interface approved by the Electronic Industries Association (EIA) for connecting serial devices. The RS-422 and RS-423 standards are designed to replace the older RS-232 standard because they support higher data rates and greater immunity to electrical interference.

rule-based expert system: a computer application that is capable of carrying out a task that would otherwise be done by a human expert, e.g. diagnosing human illnesses, making financial forecasts or scheduling routes for delivery vehicles. Rule-based expert systems are either designed to take the place of, or to aid, human experts. Rule-based expert systems are one branch of *artificial intelligence.*

A knowledge engineer is the person who studies how human experts make decisions and translates the rules into terms that a computer can understand.

rulebase: see *rules, rule-based expert system.*

rules: the criteria used to make decisions within a *rule-based expert system.*

run time error: an error that occurs while a *program* is executing. For example, a runtime error occurs if an attempt is made to divide by zero, or to access a file that does not exist.

run time system: all the *software* and *data* necessary for a system to be run on a computer.

run time version: a modified version of a software application that allows access to the data provided but does not allow changes to be made to the data. This term is often used to describe *slide shows* or presentations that can be run without having the original software that created the slide show present.

running programs: programs in a *multiprogramming* environment that have started but have not yet finished.

sampling frequency: the rate at which analogue data is sampled for conversion in an *analogue-to-digital* converter. The greater the sampling frequency the more accurate the picture of the external data built up in the computer's memory.

sans serif font: pronounced 'san-serr-if'. This is a *typeface* that does not use small lines known as serifs at the ends of characters. Popular sans serif fonts include Arial, Helvetica and Avant Garde. *Serif fonts* include Times Roman and Courier. Sans serif fonts are generally regarded as more difficult to read and hence are used most often for short pieces of text, e.g. headlines or captions.

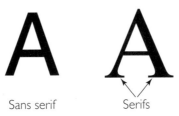

Sans serif   Serifs

satellite communication: satellites are used for international communications and use highly directional, narrow beam, two-way transmission. Each communication channel is capable of carrying a large number of separate transmissions at the same time.

scalable font: a *font* that is defined by its shape not its size. Once defined, a scalable font can be produced accurately in any font size. Examples of scalable fonts are those produced in object-oriented graphics languages such as *PostScript* or *TrueType*. Scalable fonts make the most of an output device's resolution. The greater resolution a printer or monitor has, the better a scalable font will appear.

Scalable fonts are often called *outline fonts* because they are generally represented by defining the outline of each character. Scalable fonts are also called object-oriented fonts or vector fonts.

scalar processor: a computer in the traditional Von Neumann sense in that it is capable of operating only on scalar data. Scalar data types include *integers, characters,* user-defined enumerated *data types,* and (in most implementations) Boolean values.

scanner: a hand-held or desktop peripheral that is used to scan images and text into a computer. The scanner examines a spatial pattern one part after another and generates analogue or digital signals corresponding to the pattern. Scanners are often used in mark sensing, *pattern recognition,* or *character recognition.*

scanning: a term used to describe the process of transferring a document to a computer using a *scanner.*

It also refers to the refreshing of the image on a display screen. The lines on a *raster* display are scanned regularly to re-draw the image before it fades. The frequency with which the lines are scanned is called the scan frequency or refresh rate and is usually several times per second. If the lines on the display are scanned alternately (i.e. lines 1, 3, 5, etc. on the first scan and lines 2, 4, 6, etc. on the second scan) then the scan is described as an *interlaced scan*.

SCART (Syndicat des Constructeurs d'Appareils de Radio et de Télévision): a means of connecting computers, video recorders, etc. to televisions and monitors using standard connections.

scheduler: the part of the *operating system* software that determines which programs (*tasks*) will have access to the *processor*. The scheduler is responsible for *task management*, which involves scheduling, initiation and termination of *jobs*. Scheduling of tasks is done by two different schedulers within the operating system in a *multi-tasking, multi-programming* or *multi-access* environment to allocate processor time.

The high-level scheduler is responsible for selecting the tasks from backing store to be loaded into the computer's memory and this selection is done on a basis of priority (*processor bound, peripheral bound*) and availability of resources. Each task is looked at in priority order, but only if all the resources it needs can be allocated is it actually loaded.

Once tasks are loaded, the low-level scheduler is responsible for selecting the program to get access to the processor and actually 'run'. This selection is done purely on priority (the necessary resources must be available – high-level scheduler) and the highest priority program that is available to 'run' is given access to the processor until an *interrupt* occurs.

schema: the logical definition of a database. The schema or sub-schema is a set of statements, expressed in a *data definition language*, which completely describes the structure of a database.

scope: the sections of a program for which a particular *variable* is valid. A *global variable* is valid throughout the program and hence has a scope which includes the whole program. *Local variables* are only valid within the *procedure* (*subprogram*) that they are declared and hence have a scope restricted to that procedure. Where a procedure has other procedures embedded within it, variables declared within the main procedure are valid in the embedded procedures.

scrambling: the process of making data unintelligible, so that a device or software are needed to decode it and make it understandable. The digital video format used for displaying full-length digital movies (using a DVD video player connected to a television) includes a content scrambling system (CSS) to prevent users from copying disks.

scratch file: a file created during the run of a program that is destroyed when the program terminates. This type of file is also known as a scrap file or scratch tape/disk.

scratch pad: a section of a computer's memory used as a temporary working area. The data within the scratch pad is lost when a program terminates.

screen: see *visual display unit (VDU)*.

screen button: an area of the screen used to select an action. It can be a graphic element in a *dialogue box* that, when activated, performs a specified function. The user activates a button by clicking on it with a *mouse* or, if the button is highlighted, by hitting the Return or Enter key.

screen capture: the act of copying what is currently displayed on a screen to a *file* or *printer*. If the computer is using the *Windows operating system* screen capture is normally carried out by pressing the Print Screen key on the standard keyboard. Pressing the Print Screen key will capture the contents of the whole screen whereas pressing Ctrl and Print Screen will capture only the active window. The screen capture will result in a graphics file containing a bitmap of the image. Screen capture is sometimes referred to as doing a 'screen dump'.

screen editing: the changing of data or images on screen. Screen editors allow the data or image to be loaded into memory and displayed on the screen. Once changed the data or image can be stored under the original or a new name.

screen grabber: a software package that allows detailed selection of the areas of screen to be captured. See *screen capture*.

screen refresh: the process of re-energising a computer display. The surface of a cathode ray tube (screen) needs continuously re-energising to keep the display visible. The process of re-energising the screen is called *scanning* and the number of times a second the screen is refreshed is called the scan frequency.

screen resolution: different quality screens are able to display differing numbers of *pixels* – the higher the number of pixels the better the quality. The screen resolution is the number of pixels that a particular screen is capable of displaying. It is usually quoted as the number of pixels in a row × the number of rows.

screen saver: a program that suspends the display on a screen and replaces it with a continuously moving image. The program is activated if there has been no keyboard/mouse activity within a period of time specified by the user. If a screen is left with one image continuously displayed the image can become permanently fixed on the screen and appear as a shadow whenever the screen is used. The screen saver stops this happening.

scrolling: moving a display image vertically or horizontally so that data that otherwise cannot be seen within the boundaries of the display screen is made visible. In a windows environment, a bar with slider is found at the side of the window and indicates to the user that more information is available in a particular direction and can be scrolled into view. Scroll bars can be either horizontal or vertical

search: looking for a specific item of data from a collection of data. There are various search techniques available of which the most common are *binary search* and *linear search*.

search engine: generally used to describe the programs which search the *World Wide Web* (WWW) for items of interest, although the term can also refer to a program which searches a document for a piece of text. Examples of search engines are:

Alta Vista	http://www.altavista.com
Google	http://www.google.com
Lycos	http://www.lycos.com
Yahoo	http://www.yahoo.com

Search engines are used by entering key words, phrases or subject matter. The search engine then looks for sites containing the key words. This can lead to a list of thousands of sites and it can be quite difficult to narrow down the search to provide a limited, accessible number of sites to check. Various forms of advanced search criteria are provided to assist. A good site for information concerning search engines is www.searchenginewatch.com.

search time (disk): the time taken to find a particular item of data on a disk. The search time is made up of two components: the first is known as the *seek time*, the time taken to move the *read/write* (R/W) heads over the correct *track*; and the second is known as latency and represents the time for the disk to rotate until the R/W head is over the required data item.

search time (searching): the average time taken to find an item of data in a collection of data. Rather than giving a specific time the speed of a particular search method is often described in terms of the number of items of data that must be looked at to find a particular item.

When an (un)ordered list of n items is being searched using a linear search the average number of items of data looked at is $n/2$.

When an ordered list of n items is being searched using a binary search the maximum number of items of data looked at is $\log_2(n)$. (For practical purposes, if the data list contains 4000 items of data the maximum number of items of data that need to be considered is 12, since 2^{12} is greater than 4000.)

second normal form: see *normalisation of data.*

secondary key: as well as having a *primary key* which determines the order of the data in a *relational database*, secondary keys can be specified. Each secondary key has an index associated with it that allows faster access to the data using that field. Secondary keys are created when the user wants fast access to data using a field that is not the primary key.

secondary storage: storage used when maximum speed of access is not required, e.g. *magnetic disk, magnetic tape, CD-ROM* and DVD are forms of secondary storage. Secondary storage is much larger than primary storage, that is the *random access memory* (RAM) and *read only memory* (ROM) of the computer.

sector: *hard* and *floppy disk* surfaces are split into concentric *tracks* and each of these tracks is split into sub-sections called *sectors*. Each sector has a unique number associated with it and is generally the unit of transfer when moving data to and from the disk.

secure data transaction: an electronic data transaction in which encrypted data is sent. It is used for on-line banking and for on-line transactions when using the *Internet* and *World Wide Web*.

secure electronic transaction (SET): a standard/specification for securing payment card transactions over open networks such as the *Internet*. SET was developed by Visa, MasterCard, IBM, and other technology companies. SET has been approved by almost all the major companies involved in electronic commerce, including Microsoft, Netscape, Visa, and MasterCard. SET uses digital signatures, which allow e-commerce companies to verify that buyers are who they claim to be. It protects buyers by providing a mechanism for their credit card numbers to be transferred directly to the credit card issuer for verification and billing without the merchant being able to see the number.

secure HTTP: an extension to the *hypertext transfer protocol* (HTTP) which supports sending data securely over the World Wide Web (WWW). S-HTTP was developed by Enterprise Integration Technologies (EIT), which was acquired by Verifone, Inc. in 1995. Not all Web *browsers* and servers support S-HTTP. An alternative security protocol is *secure socket layer.*

secure socket layer (SSL): a *protocol* developed by Netscape for transmitting private documents via the *Internet.* SSL works by using a private key to encrypt data that is transferred over the SSL connection. Both Netscape Navigator and Internet Explorer support SSL, and many web sites use the protocol to obtain confidential user information, such as credit card numbers. Generally, Web pages that require an SSL connection start with https: instead of http:. An alternative security protocol is *Secure HTTP.*

SSL is designed to establish a onnection between a client and a server, over which any amount of data can be sent securely. S-HTTP is designed to transmit individual messages securely. Therefore SSL and S-HTTP can be seen as complementary rather than competing systems. Both protocols have been approved by the Internet Engineering Task Force (IETF) as standards.

security: the techniques used to ensure that data stored in a computer cannot be read or compromised. Most computer systems' security measures involve *data encryption* and *passwords.* Data encryption involves the conversion of data into a form that is unintelligible without a deciphering mechanism. A password is a secret group of characters, which gives a user access to a particular program or system.

The other aspect of security revolves around the physical aspects of keeping computer systems and data secure. Companies rely on their data as a vital aspect of the success of their business. Wider security measures can involve the use of security staff, alarm systems, door locks, security passes to secure areas and contingency plans for floods, fires and theft, as well as the backup and secure storage of data files.

seed: the number used to start off a pseudo-random number sequence.

seek time: the time taken for the *read/write head* on a disk unit to move to the right *track* on a surface of the disk.

segment: 1 This can refer to a subset of *nodes* in a *network* that are connected by a common physical medium or to a section of a network that is bounded by *bridges, routers, hubs,* or *switches.* Dividing an *Ethernet* network into multiple segments is one of the most common ways of improving the efficiency of the network. If *segmentation* is carried out correctly, most network traffic will remain within a single segment. Hubs and switches are used to connect each segment to the rest of the network.

2 Occasionally the term is used to refer to a section of cable between different components or devices. A segment may consist of a single patch cable or several patch cables that are connected.

3 In Internet communications, the unit of transfer between transmission control protocol functions in different machines is referred to as a segment. Each segment contains control and data fields along with a *checksum* to validate the received data.

4 In *virtual memory* systems a segment is a variable-sized portion of data that is swapped in and out of main memory whereas a *page* is a fixed-sized portion of data.

segmentation: the splitting up of a *network* into separate sections called *segments*. *Hubs* that contain multiple *ports* are often used to connect segments of a *Local Area Network* (LAN). When a *packet* of data arrives at one port, it is copied to the other ports so that all segments of the LAN can see all packets.

A passive *hub* simply allows the packet to go from one segment to another.

Intelligent hubs include extra features that permit an administrator to monitor the number of packets passing through the hub and to configure each port in the hub. Intelligent hubs are also called manageable hubs.

A switching hub reads the destination address of each packet and then forwards the packet to the correct port.

self-documented program: a term sometimes used to describe a software package that includes an *on-line help* system. On-line help systems allow the user to display information on how to use the software. Advanced on-line help systems can be context-sensitive and hence display different information depending on the user's position (context) in the application. This type of documentation is starting to replace the traditional paper *software documentation*.

semantics: the meaning of any statement in a *programming language*. As well as having to be syntactically correct, statements written as part of a program also have to make sense.

An example of a semantic error is

       Pay := Surname + Overtime;

The three variables Pay, Surname and Overtime are all valid variables, the statement is put together correctly (i.e. it obeys the syntax of the language) but it does not make sense semantically if Surname is a string and Overtime and Pay are integers.

semiconductor memory: *memory* made from semiconductors. A semiconductor is a material that has an electrical conductivity half way between that of an insulator and a conductor. Specially treated semiconductors are used to manufacture silicon chips.

sensor: an electronic component that converts energy from one form to another, which can be passed to a computer. Examples of sensors are pressure, humidity, magnetic and tilt sensors.

sequence control register (SCR): see *program counter*.

sequence number: in data communications a sequence number is assigned to a particular *packet* to control the transmission flow and receipt of data. The packets do not necessarily arrive at the destination in the correct sequence, especially when they have been transmitted over large distances on public telecommunications systems. The sequence numbers allow the packets to be re-sequenced into the correct order.

sequential access: a complete list of data is accessed by looking at each item in turn until the required item is found. The data in the list must be in some predetermined order (the sequence) if sequential access is to be used. When using this access method it is possible to ascertain that the required record is not present when the item being considered in the list is sequentially greater than the required item. This type of access is the main method of accessing data held on magnetic tapes. Other methods of accessing data held on file include *serial access* and *direct access*.

sequential file: a *file* in which *records* are stored, one after the other in some pre-determined order. Other file organisations include *serial file, index sequential file* and *random file.*

sequential search: a complete list of data is searched by looking at each item in turn until the required item is found. The data in the list must be in some predetermined order (sequence) if a sequential search is to be used. Using this search technique, it is possible to ascertain that the required record is not present when the item being considered in the list is sequentially greater than the required item. Other search methods include *serial search, binary search.*

serial access: a complete list of data is accessed by looking at each item in turn until the required item is found. When using this access method, it is possible to ascertain only that the required record is not present when the end of the data is reached. This type of access is used mainly when accessing data held on magnetic tapes. Other methods of accessing data include *sequential access* and *direct access.*

serial adder: a logic circuit that adds together the *binary digits* from two *registers* by taking the bits in pairs (one from each register). The circuit that is used to carry out the addition is called a *full adder*, which is made up of two *half adders* and an *OR gate.*

serial data transmission: the transmission of data one *bit* at a time along the same communication line. Serial data transmission is used whenever data has to be transmitted over large distances. Often, a serial connection consists of an *RS-232* connection to a *modem* with the data then transmitted over a telephone line. When shorter distances are involved in the data transmission, *parallel data transmission* is possible.

serial file: a *file* in which *records* are stored one after the other with no regard to order. It is also known as a serial access file.

serial line Internet protocol (SLIP): a protocol used to run the *Internet protocol* (IP) between two systems over serial lines such as telephone lines. This protocol is commonly used by the dial-up *Internet service providers* to connect a user's *modem* to the *Internet.* Using this protocol, *packets* are transmitted down a serial line by adding a simple header. However, more complex protocols, such as *point-to-point protocol* (PPP) are gaining popularity, since they allow better data throughput.

serial port: an access point through which a computer transmits or receives data, one bit at a time. See also *parallel port, serial data transmission.*

serial search: a complete list of data is searched by looking at each item in turn until the required item is found. Using this search technique, it is possible only to ascertain that the required *record* is not present when the end of the list is reached. Alternative methods of searching data include *sequential search* and *binary search.*

serif font: see *sans serif font.*

server: a large powerful computer that provides the central store for software and data on a *network.* On many networks the server is responsible for providing services to one or more clients. Examples include a *file server*, a *print server*, and a *mail server.*

service engineer: a computer specialist, normally employed by a computer maintenance company, who can be called in to find and repair faults on a computer.

service provider: see *Internet service provider.*

session layer: in the *open systems interconnection seven-layer model*, the layer that provides the means necessary for two users to organise and synchronise their dialogue and to manage their data exchange.

shared files: *files* that are accessible to several users over a *network.*

shareware: software for which the user of the *program* is supposed to pay a small fee to the author of the software after trying it out, if they intend to carry on using it. By sending the small fee the user registers with the producer so that service assistance and updates can be provided. The user can copy shareware and pass it on to friends but they are also expected to pay the fee if they use the product. Shareware is inexpensive because advertising and packaging costs are low. Shareware is copyright and hence different from *public domain software.*

sheet feeder: a mechanism that holds a stack of paper and feeds sheets into a printer one at a time. Sheet feeders are built into *laser printers* and modern fax machines. They are also called cut-sheet feeders.

shell: the software interface between a *user* and the *operating system* of a computer. The shell interprets commands and user responses from *peripherals* such as *keyboards,* mice, *touch screens,* etc. and communicates them to the operating system.

shift key: a key on computer *keyboards* that gives the other keys an additional meaning. Holding the Shift key down whilst tapping an alphabetic key causes the system to output a capital letter. Many other keys on the keyboard indicate the effect of using the Shift key by showing two characters on the key. The lower character will be produced if the Shift key is not used while the upper character is produced if the Shift is used.

shutdown: the process of stopping a computer system by following a pre-defined procedure. If a computer is not correctly shut down it will go through several self-checks the next time it is started.

sign and magnitude: a method of representing positive and negative binary numbers. The *most significant bit* (MSB) represents the sign of the number; a 1 indicates the number is negative whilst a 0 means the number is positive. This method of representing binary numbers is also known as 'sign and modulus', since the MSB represents the sign and the remainder of the register holds the modulus of the number. Alternative ways of representing negative numbers in a computer include *two's complement* and *one's complement.*

Using sign and magnitude the contents of the *register* below represents + 5

0	0	0	0	0	I	0	I

Whereas the contents of the register below represents –5

I	0	0	0	0	I	0	I

sign bit: the *binary digit* at the beginning of a binary number, which indicates if the number is positive or negative. The sign bit is not used in any way to indicate the magnitude of the number but exclusively for the allocation of positive or negative. Usually a 0 is positive and a 1 is negative. Methods of representing negative numbers for storage in a computer include *two's complement, sign and magnitude* and *one's complement*.

signal: in computer software, a message that is sent to a *process* to change its behaviour, based on the value sent to it. A signal is an electric current used to convey *data* from one place to another. The simplest form of signal is a direct current (DC) that is switched on and off.

signal amplifier: a device built into communication *networks* to increase the strength of the signal, which will have faded over distance. Signal amplifiers are needed at regular intervals to ensure signals are within tolerance limits at all points on the network.

signal concentrator: any device that allows a single communication channel to carry several communications. See *multiplexer*.

signal-to-noise ratio: a comparison of the strength of the *signal* to the strength of the noise on the *communications link*. All communications links have a background signal that is nothing to do with the main signal. This background signal is known as noise and the stronger it gets the more it interferes with the main signal. When the noise level is too high it is impossible to transmit data communication signals.

signature: data that is used solely for the purposes of identification. It is often used with e-mail communications and on-line transactions.

simple mail transport protocol (SMTP): a *protocol* for passing *e-mail* messages from one machine to another. It is part of the *Internet* suite of protocols. SMTP specifies the mail exchange sequences and the format of the message. It assumes that the *transmission control protocol* (TCP) is the underlying protocol. See also *point of presence (POP)*.

simplex: data transmission that is possible only in one direction. A mouse uses simplex data transmission to pass movement information to the computer. See also *duplex* and *half duplex*.

simulation: where a computer system is used to act as though it is something else. Normally the simulation will be based on a mathematical model. Many of the games machines in amusement arcades are examples of computer simulations, e.g. motor cycle racing, skiing, etc. Other examples include the simulation of a country's economy to help predict the future consequences of changes and simulations used for weather forecasting.

single-address instruction: a *machine code* instruction consisting of an *operator* and a single *operand*. See *two-address instruction*.

single buffering is when only one *buffer* is used between the computer and the *peripheral device*. A buffer is an area of computer memory used between two devices that are working at different speeds. The buffer is filled by one device and, when full, is emptied by the second device. The sequencing of the various transfers is carried out by *handshaking* routines. The use of a second buffer (*double buffering*) allows a faster rate of data transfer.

single in-line memory module (SIMM): an industry standard plug-in *memory* card. There are two standard sizes: 30-pin and 72-pin.

single precision: a term used to describe the method of storing a *real number*. Single precision numbers are held with a restricted range and accuracy. See *double precision*.

single stepping: the execution of a *program*, instruction by instruction. Single stepping can be used by a programmer to find a *bug* which has proved particularly elusive in a program.

single tasking: an *operating system* that allows only one program to be running at any time is said to be a single task operating system. Operating systems capable of apparently running more than one program at a time are either *multi-tasking* or *multiprogramming* operating systems.

site: for a large organisation, a single building or group of buildings in close proximity that contain part of its computer *network*. The term is also used as a shortened form of *web site*.

site licence: software that has been purchased with the agreement that it can be used on any computer system on a single site is said to have a site licence.

slide show: slides produced on a computer screen or projected onto a screen from a computer using a presentation graphics package such as PowerPoint. A slide show can also contain animation and sound. There are various options allowing interesting transitions from one slide to the next and different ways of building each slide up.

small computer systems interface (SCSI): an internationally agreed standard for communicating data between computers and *peripherals*. SCSI cards are normally used to link a computer to *hard drives*, *CD-ROMs* and *scanners*, but they can also be used to link computers together. The data is transmitted along parallel data *paths*.

small scale integration (SSI): *chips* with up to 20 logic circuits are said to use small scale integration.

smalltalk: a library-oriented *programming language* that uses a large library and an interactive environment to produce *window*-based *graphical user interfaces*.

smart card: a credit card that contains a simple *microchip*.

smart key: a device that comes in a variety of different forms but they all carry a *microchip*. They can be used to provide security in buildings or to restrict access to particular computer systems.

snail mail: a derogatory term used to describe the conventional mail system when comparing it to the speed of *e-mail*.

sniffer: a program that monitors the data travelling over a *network*. Sniffers can be used both for legitimate network management functions and for stealing information off a network. Unauthorised sniffers can be extremely dangerous to a network's security because they are almost impossible to detect and can be inserted almost anywhere.

On *TCP/IP* networks sniffers are used to monitor the packets of data as they move round the network and are often known as *packet* sniffers.

soft error: an error that occurs occasionally and hence is very difficult to detect and subsequently solve. The term is also used to refer to an intermittent error on a *network* that requires retransmission of the packet of data. If the number of soft errors on a network is too great the errors could affect the overall reliability of the network.

soft keys: the function keys or user-defined keys on a *keyboard*. Soft keys are given different uses within different *software packages* which reduces the number of key strokes or *mouse* clicks needed to carry out particular operations.

soft return: a return character inserted automatically by a *word processor* to provide *word wrap*. The term 'return' refers to moving automatically to the beginning of the next line in a text document. Word processors utilise two types of returns: hard and soft. Both have the effect of adding an additional 'hidden' character to the document while moving the cursor on the screen to the next line in the document. The hard return is used to start a new paragraph and is inserted by pressing the Return (Enter) key. It remains in position until deleted by the user. Soft returns are inserted automatically by the word processor as part of its word wrap capability. Whenever too little room remains on the current line for the next word, the word processor inserts a soft return. However the soft return can move if extra text is added or deleted above the soft return character.

soft space: a space that is added by the software to even out the text when full *justification* is required. The soft space can move or be deleted if extra text is added or deleted in the text preceding the soft space. See *hard space*.

soft-sectored disk: a *floppy disk* that has been formatted using software. The formatting software determines the size and positions of the sectors on each track of the disk's surface, unlike hard-sectored disks where the format for the disk is specified at the point of manufacture. Using different formatting software will mean the disk can be used on a different type of computer. The format of the disk determines the type of computer that is able to read the disk.

software normally refers to a set of computer instructions that have been written to carry out a particular task, but it can also be used to include *data* held in electronic form. The storage devices and display devices are called *hardware*. The distinction between software and hardware is sometimes confusing; when buying a program a user is purchasing software but the software is held on a disk, i.e. on hardware.

Software is often divided into two categories:

- systems software which includes the operating system and all the utilities that enable the computer to function
- applications software which includes programs that do real work for users, e.g. *word processors, spreadsheets*, and *database management systems*.

software copyright: software is covered by similar laws to those that protect books and other publications. For software, this is the *Copyright, Designs & Patents Act (1988)*. It makes illegal the use of any commercial software that has not been purchased with an appropriate software licence. An organisation called FAST (the *Federation Against Software Theft*) has been set up on behalf of major software manufacturers to guard against theft and, where it can be proven that software is being used illegally (usually by a company) FAST takes action through the courts to sue for damages.

software documentation: instructions for using a computer device or *program*. Documentation comes in a variety of forms, the most common being manuals. When you buy a computer product (hardware or software), it includes documentation that describes how to install and operate the product.

Modern software packages (*self-documented programs*) provide only an online version of the documentation that the user can display on screen or print out on a printer. Any instructions needed to install the software are either printed on the disk or on the software packaging.

Documentation is often divided into the following categories:

Installation – describes how to install a program or device but not how to use it.

Reference – detailed descriptions of particular items presented in alphabetical order. Reference documentation is produced for experienced users of the package or device but may need reminders or help with little-used features.

Tutorial – helps a new user of the package or device to make use of the main features of the product. Tutorials move at a slower pace than reference manuals and generally contain less detail.

software engineering: the production of *software* in a structured way including *programs* and documentation. There is a variety of methodologies adopted by software engineers in the development of software but they all include the production of documentation at all stages, ensuring that the finished software is easily maintainable, rigorously tested and carefully debugged. Software engineers make use of a variety of computer-aided software engineering tools.

software houses: the companies that develop *software*.

software library: in large companies, the disks and tapes holding the company's data and software are held in a software library. However, in programming, a library (sometimes called a subprogram library) is a collection of prewritten, precompiled, fully documented *routines* that a programmer can use when producing software. Libraries are particularly useful for storing frequently used routines because you do not need to link them explicitly to every program that uses them. The linkage editor or *linker* automatically looks in the libraries for routines that it does not find elsewhere. In Microsoft Windows environments, library files have a .dll extension.

software licence: the rules that govern the way an item of software can be used. All software comes with a licensing agreement permitting the person to use the software subject to the rules laid down by its producer/copyright owner. Companies will purchase different types of licence depending on how they intend to make use of the software:

- single user licence – to be used only on one computer system
- *site licence* – used on any computer system on a single site
- network licence – to be used only by computer systems linked to a network
- multi-user licence – to be installed only on the number of computer systems specified or restricted availability on a network.

software life cycle: the stages that *software* goes through from its conception until it is deleted. There are many different views on the specific stages, but the following are always included:

- system requirements
- software requirements
- software design

- software production
- software testing
- production of documentation for release
- acceptance testing
- software release
- maintenance
- obsolescence.

Compare this life cycle with the *system life cycle* that covers hardware as well as software.

software package: a *program* or suite of programs written for a computer. Examples are *word processors, spreadsheets, relational databases*, and *desktop publishing, as* well as general and more specialist software such as that used for drawing up family trees and developing garden designs. Software packages are also called applications.

software requirements: taking the specifications laid down by the customer and producing the requirements for programmers to work to. This is one of the stages in the *software life cycle* and is carried out before the design of the program is considered.

software support staff: the specialist staff employed by *software* companies to answer questions on their software. Software support staff are often said to work at the help desk and provide support for customers using a company's software. This support is often provided by telephone, although at an additional cost support staff will provide on-site support.

software theft: the copying of software by people who have not paid for it.

solid state drive (SSD): a memory *chip* used like a *disk drive* in Pocket Book/ Psion 3.

sort key: the *field* within a *file* record that is used to specify the order in which the file is held. It is also known as the *key field*.

sorting: the process of changing the order in which a *file* is held. A file can be sorted into order on any field within the *record* layout.

sound data: the values stored on a computer that can be used by a sound generator to create audible sounds. The sound generator consists of all the electronic circuits needed for generating audible sounds. The process of generating the sound from stored binary values is called sound synthesis.

sound envelope is a shape that is drawn to describe the volume, pitch and timbre of a note as they change with time. See ASDR.

sound sampler: a device that can take audible sounds and convert them into data that can be stored on computer. The stored data can then be edited to modify the sounds when they are reproduced.

source code: see *source program*.

source language: the *programming language* used by a programmer to produce a program. There are hundreds of different computer programming languages, all written to satisfy particular needs. These languages are known as source languages since they allow programmers to produce code for a computer, ready for translation by an *assembler* or a compiler.

source program: a *program* in a form that a human can read but a computer cannot. The source program has to be compiled or assembled using a compiler or an *assembler* before the computer can understand the instructions.

spamming: advertising on the *Internet* by broadcasting to multiple users and many or all newsgroups, regardless of relevance.

sparse array: an *array* with the majority of its elements equal to zero.

spawn: to create a process from another process.

special interest group (SIG): a *newsgroup* set up on the *Internet* to cover one specific topic. These groups are often health related.

special purpose language: a computer *programming language* developed for a particular purpose and often little used outside that area. Examples include ADA – which is mainly used for military purposes, Forth – which is used in control and graphics applications and LISP – which is used in artificial intelligence applications.

speech recognition: the process whereby data is entered by means of the human voice and is converted into a form a computer can store.

speech synthesis: a computer's ability to produce sound that resembles human speech. Although speech synthesis software cannot produce the full spectrum of human cadences and intonations, it can read text files and output them in an intelligible form. Speech synthesis systems are particularly valuable for visually impaired individuals. Many organisations are now making use of such systems, e.g. directory enquiries.

spell checker: a program that checks the spelling of words in a text document. Spell checkers are normally included as part of any software package that can produce text files. Spell checkers cannot help when the user enters a valid, though incorrect, word, e.g. entering 'there' instead of 'their'; these mistakes can sometimes be detected by a grammar checker.

split screen: the division of the display screen into separate parts, each of which displays a different document/spreadsheet, or different parts of the same document/spreadsheet.

spooler: a program that intercepts *data* going to a *device driver* and writes it to a disk. The data is later printed or plotted when the required device is available. Spoolers are normally associated with *printers*, particularly on networks, although spooling does allow a user on a stand-alone system to print several documents one after the other without having to wait for the preceding printout to be completed. A spooler prevents output from different sources from being intermixed, i.e. it ensures that the pages from one printout are not mixed in with those from another. Spool is an acronym for simultaneous peripheral operations on-line.

spreadsheet: a computer program (*software package*) that allows the user to create and manipulate *worksheets* electronically. The term is often used to describe a worksheet, i.e. a table made up of *cells* arranged in *rows* and *columns* where each cell can contain a number, text or formula. In a spreadsheet application, the user can define what type of data is in each cell, the format to be used when displaying the content of each cell, the name to be associated with a particular cell or group of cells and how different cells are related to each other using formulae.

Having used the spreadsheet application to design the worksheet by defining the cells and the formulae linking them together, the user can enter the data and, by changing the contents of some cells, look at several 'what-if' scenarios.

The more powerful spreadsheet applications include graphics features that enable the user to produce charts and graphs from the data. It is also possible to link one worksheet to another within the spreadsheet application so that a change made in one worksheet automatically affects the other worksheet.

stack: a *data structure* where the last item added is the first to be removed and hence it is known as a *last in first out* (LIFO) structure. A *stack* is held in memory and used to hold temporary data. A stack *pointer* is used to maintain the data structure and identifies the top of the stack either by pointing at the top item or by pointing at the first available location. The number of locations available for use by the stack is determined by the software and is known as the stack size. Other ways of structuring data in memory include *queue, linked list* and *tree* (*binary* and *non-binary*).

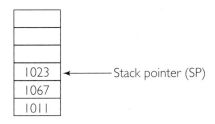

Using the diagram above the following are *algorithms* for managing the stack.

Adding	If SP < Stack Size Then	Removing	If SP <> 0 Then
	Move SP up 1 location		Remove item at SP
	Add data item at SP		Move SP down 1 location
	Else		Else
	Output 'Stack Full'		Output 'Stack Empty'

stack overflow occurs when an attempt is made to add an item of data to a *stack* in which all the allocated locations have been occupied.

stack underflow occurs when an attempt is made to remove an item of data from a *stack* that is empty.

stand-alone computer: a self-contained computer system that is not connected to any type of *network*. This type of computer can be used in isolation from any other device, having a *hard drive* that holds an *operating system,* the software for use on the system and space to store any data generated.

standard function: a *function* that is so common it is provided as part of the programming language and does not need to be generated by the *programmer*. Examples of standard functions include sine and cosine in all mathematical programming languages, and circle and block fill in graphic programming languages. See *function, procedure, subprogram*.

standby power supply: see *uninterruptible power supply (UPS)*.

star network: a *network* of computers where the *nodes* are arranged in a radial, or star-like, configuration connected to a central computer (*server*) in which each node exchanges data directly with the central node.

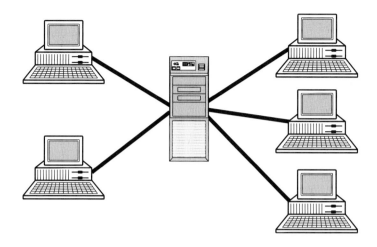

The star can be created by using a *hub* instead of the central server, in which case every signal sent to the hub is sent to every connected computer. However, only the computer the message relates to will respond.

If one of the computer systems in the star fails the others are unaffected but if the hub or central server fails the whole network becomes non-operational.

start bit: an extra *bit* used in asynchronous serial data transmission to indicate the beginning of an item of data (group of bits). See *asynchronous transmission*.

statement: an instruction in a high-level *programming language*.

static file: a *file* that holds reference *data*. The data in the file is available to applications but cannot be changed. This name is sometimes used to describe files that hold data, which change only infrequently, e.g. product description and price.

static IP address: an *Internet protocol (IP) address* permanently assigned to a *user*. Static IP addressing is usually used by organisations with the IP address allocated to a particular computer or person. This allows greater tracking of sites accessed on the *Internet* and actions carried out by a user. Dynamic IP addressing is normally used by most *Internet service providers* (ISPs).

static partition: a *partition* allocated and specified when the system is started. Unlike a dynamic partition, the size of a static partition cannot be changed without restarting the system.

static RAM: *memory* which stores data in such a way that it requires no *memory refresh* cycle and hence has a low power consumption. Generally this type of *random access memory* (RAM) is faster but more expensive than *dynamic random access memory* (DRAM).

station: any *workstation* connected to a network.

station number: a number allocated to each *workstation* on a *network* by the software. This number is in addition to the number given to each network interface card (NIC), which is permanently stored in ROM on the NIC. These unique numbers are used to allow communication on the network and to provide *audit trails*.

status bar: a line displayed either at the top or bottom of the *window* in *Windows* software that contains information about the current position of the task concerned, e.g. the distance from the top and side of a page in a word processor; this can be a measured distance or a line and character number.

| Page 1 | Sec 1 | | 1/1 | At 2.5cm | Ln 1 | Col 1 | | REC | TRK | EXT | OVR | WPH | | | |

step mode: See *single stepping*.

stepper motor: an electric motor that can be precisely controlled by a computer. Each time the motor receives a signal it turns through an exact angle. By controlling the speed that signals are sent to the motor the speed of the motor can also be controlled.

stepwise refinement: see *top-down programming*.

stop bit: an extra *bit* used in asynchronous serial data transmission to indicate the end of an item of data (group of bits). See *asynchronous transmission*.

stopped: a *program* is sometimes described as stopped when it has been aborted for some reason. This is one of many *process states* a program can be in at any moment.

stopping condition: a term used to describe the reason for exiting a conditional *loop* (while or repeat) or the reason for exiting a *recursive* routine.

store and forward technology: a general term for systems like *e-mail*, which store information received and forward it to a recipient only when that person asks for it. This term is used extensively when the *Internet* is being discussed since this is the basis for most of the information stored on the Internet.

store location: a single location in *memory*. The term is normally used to refer to memory locations in *random access memory* (RAM).

story board: a technique used in film and television to create the basic idea of a programme before it is produced. The section of programme is broken down into key frames and produced in detail to allow others to see the plot behind the programme. This term is also used when putting together a *slide show*, when each of the slides is produced in outline before beginning the time consuming exercise of adding the detail.

streaming: the processing of data in a continuous stream. This is becoming increasingly popular on the *Internet* for processing sound and real-time video images. Streaming requires a dedicated link, unlike normal Internet communications where the *packets* can use a variety of routes from source to receiver and hence arrive out of synchronisation.

string data: a series of characters that is manipulated as a group by the computer. Most *programming languages* provide a wide variety of commands for processing string data. These include being able to select any character or group of characters from the string and combine strings to form composite strings.

string operator: an operator that allows the manipulation of *string data* within *programming languages*. Examples of string operators are ones that allow concatenation (joining two strings together), extracting a single character or group of characters, or replacing a single character or group of characters.

string variable: a variable that can hold a collection of characters (*string data*).

strong encryption: the *encryption* of data using very long keys. This method of encryption makes it almost impossible to guess the codes and hence decode the data. Even with the most powerful supercomputers it would take 'hundreds of years' trying to solve the problem by guessing.

strong search: an algorithm that searches for a given *key*, locks the *node* associated with that key, and returns the node. See also *weak search*.

strongly typed language: a *programming language* that validates data as it is transferred into a variable. This ensures that only sensible data is held but has the disadvantage that the program can fail (if badly programmed) if an attempt is made to enter non-valid data into a particular variable. Examples of strongly typed languages are Pascal and ADA. Compilers for strongly typed languages check each statement to ensure that the operations specified are appropriate for the data types used.

structure diagram: a diagram used to represent the ways in which the various *subprograms* will be linked together to form the whole *program*. This type of diagram is used when *structured programming* is being used in the production of a large program. It allows the programmers to see how the part of the program they are producing fits into the whole program.

structured programming: the production of a computer *program* by producing small parts (*subprograms*) which are combined to create the whole program. Programmers normally use *top-down design* methodology to produce this type of program. This allows several programmers to work on one large program that can be written in a variety of *programming languages*.

structured query language (SQL): a *programming language* that is used to define and manipulate data in a *relational database*.

structured systems analysis and design method (SSADM): a system design methodology used extensively within UK government departments. The steps to be carried out at each stage in the system's development are laid out in great detail.

stylus: a device similar to a pen, used for drawing on a *graphics tablet*. As the pen is moved across the tablet, the drawing comes out on the computer screen.

subdirectory: a *directory* contained within another directory in a file system hierarchy.

subprogram: a collective term used to describe all the different types of *modules* used in programming. These include *subroutine, procedure* and *function*.

subroutine: a sequenced set of instructions that can be used in one or more computer programs and at one or more points in a computer program. It is a self-contained part of a program that usually accomplishes a specific task.

subroutine library: see *software library*.

subschema: see *schema*.

subscript: 1 In programming, a symbol or number used to identify an element in an array. Usually, the subscript is placed in brackets following the array name, e.g. 'NAME[18]' identifies element number 18 in an array called NAME. In multidimensional arrays each dimension has its own subscript, e.g. 'MARK[2,3]' identifies the element in the second row of the third column in a two-dimensional array called MARK.

2 In word processing, a character that appears in a smaller font than the surrounding text, slightly below the line, e.g. the 2 in H_2O. See also *superscript*.

sum bit: the two *bits* produced as a result of adding two bits together are known as the sum bit and the carry bit. Adding 0 and 1 produces a sum bit of 1 and a carry bit of 0. Adding 1 and 1 produces a sum bit of 0 and a carry bit of 1.

supercomputer: the fastest and most powerful computer systems available worldwide. Today's supercomputer will be tomorrow's ordinary computer as further developments are made in computing technology. These computers are normally used to carry out mathematically intensive applications such as forecasting the weather or controlling satellites.

super large scale integration (SLSI): more than 100,000 transistors per *chip*.

super video graphics array (SVGA): an enhanced version of the *video graphics array* (VGA). This colour graphics standard indicates that a display is capable of either 880×600 or 1024×768 screen *resolution*.

SuperJANET: a higher bandwidth and more versatile version of the *Joint Academic NETwork* (JANET).

superscript: in word processing, a character that appears in a smaller font than the surrounding text slightly above the preceding text, e.g. the 2 in x^2. See also *subscript*.

supervisor: the part of a control program that co-ordinates the use of resources and maintains the flow of operations within the central processing unit (CPU).

supervisor program: see *supervisor*.

support staff: see *software support staff, service engineer*.

surfing: a term used to describe the process of exploring the *Internet*.

suspended: a program is described as being suspended when the *operating system* has stopped it from using the processor for some reason. One reason for a program to be suspended is that it has taken up more than its allocated amount of processor time, which can happen when the program is in an *infinite loop*. See *process state*.

swapping: exchanging two items of *data*. The term also refers to swapping the contents of a section of real memory for the contents of a section of *virtual memory*.

switch: a device that enables *network* performance to be enhanced by cutting down on competition for *bandwidth*. When a data *packet* is received, it is transferred to the appropriate *port* for the intended recipient. Switches are often used instead of *hubs* to improve the performance of a network.

switched line: a telecommunication line in which the connection is established by dialling. See *integrated services digital network (ISDN)*.

switched network: any network in which the connections between the *workstations* are established by closing switches, e.g. by dialling.

symbol table: a table used by *compilers* and *assemblers* which stores the relationships between the symbolic addressing used by the programmer and the machine addresses on the actual machine.

symbolic address: the use of symbols (characters) in assembly languages to represent a binary address of a memory location A symbolic address acts as a label.

synchronous dynamic random access memory (SDRAM): a faster form of *dynamic RAM* which can run at higher clock speeds, and thus make the memory perform at a faster rate.

synchronous transmission: the transmission of data where the sending and receiving of data is regulated by the *clock* pulse. When two computers are involved the clock on one of the computers will act as the master clock for the system. When a *network* involves multiple *servers* they normally use synchronised clocks to allow synchronous transmission of data.

syntax: the rules that govern the structure of a *language*.

syntax analysis: the stage during compilation when the code produced by the programmer is checked to ensure that the *syntax* rules for that language have been obeyed.

syntax diagram: a pictorial alternative to *Backus–Naur form* (BNF) and extended BNF for describing the *syntax* of a language. The syntax diagram that follows describes a variable which must start with a letter, but can be followed by as many letters or digits as required.

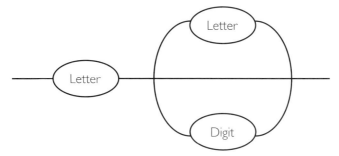

A syntax diagram

syntax error: when an instruction written by a programmer does not obey the rules of the particular language being used. An example of a syntax error is:

B + A := C – D

The left-hand side of any assignment statement indicates the variable to be used to store the result of any operations that have been carried out on the right-hand side. In the above example, no single variable is indicated on the left-hand side and hence the computer would be unable to store the result of the calculation C – D.

synthesiser: a device for creating sounds using a computer. See *sound synthesis*.

sysop: pronounced 'SISS-op', short for system operator, an individual who manages a bulletin board system (BBS), online service, or *special interest group* (SIG).

system: in *data processing*, a collection of people, machines and methods which are used to accomplish a specific task.

system changeover: the process of moving from one *system* to another. This can involve installing new *hardware* as well as new or updated *software*. In large organisations it is important that this is carried out with as little disruption to the staff concerned as possible, with any data files converted to the new format, stationery ordered and adequate training provided before the system is fully operational. There is a variety of methods but all involve compromises of some description.

- **Parallel running** – both the old and the new system are run together for a certain period of time. The intention is to ensure that the new system is running correctly before the old system is replaced completely. Errors can be corrected and users learn the new system with the minimum of consequences if mistakes are made. It is, however, costly, takes extra time and can be stressful and confusing with two systems running concurrently.
- **Pilot conversion or running** – involves using the two systems alongside each other but only in a restricted part of the organisation, e.g. one branch. This type of changeover is used by banks, supermarkets, etc. who introduce new systems at branches as they are refurbished.
- **Direct changeover** – the old system is stopped at the end of one day and the new system is used from the start of the next day. This method is fast, with minimum duplication of work, but there can be problems if faults are found in the new system.
- **Phased conversion** – used with larger systems that can be broken down into self-contained sections. Each section is successfully implemented before starting to change the next section. With this method of changeover, re-training of staff needs to be carried out only on the next part of the system to be changed. This allows staff to become familiar with the parts rather than attempting to understand the detail of the whole new system.

system crash: a serious computer failure. When a system crash occurs, the computer stops working or a *program* aborts unexpectedly. Normally a system crash indicates either a *hardware* malfunction or a very serious software *bug*. 'The computer has hung' or 'the computer has bombed' are expressions used to indicate that a system has crashed.

system development cycle: see *system life cycle*.

system flowchart: a diagrammatic representation of the flow of data through a computer *system*. This type of diagram shows the programs, the source of any data, the destinations of data and the files of data used to store the data in the system.

system implementation: see *system changeover*.

system life cycle: all the activities that are carried out when creating or developing a computer *system*. The activities are cyclical since no system can ever be described as perfect. The activities involved include:

- *system specification*
- *systems analysis*
- *systems design*
- production of the system

- system testing
- *system implementation*
- production of *documentation*.

system operator: full title for a *sysop*.

system requirements: the minimum requirements needed to be able to run a particular application or software package, or support a particular peripheral.

system software: the software used to manage and control the computer and all its peripherals, i.e. the *operating system* and housekeeping utilities.

system specification: the human, organisational, hardware and software requirements of a *system*.

systems analysis: the process of investigating a particular task within an organisation to see if it can be computerised or to see if it can be made more efficient. The systems analyst has to watch what happens as well as talk to all the staff concerned to ensure that an accurate picture of existing practices is gathered.

systems design: production of the necessary information to allow a group of programmers to write the programs for a full *system*. The design will include:

- the *hardware* to be used
- the production software e.g. database, *spreadsheet*, or programming language
- any documents to be used by the system
- the *user interface*
- the screen layouts
- the layout for printed outputs
- the *validation* to be adopted for each piece of data entered
- the file layouts
- the testing strategy
- the method of *system changeover* to be used.

systems documentation: all the documentation associated with a particular *system*. This includes:

- any paperwork collected during the system's analysis
- the analysis documentation itself
- the system design
- the user's guide
- the maintenance guide.

systems network architecture (SNA): a set of communications *protocols* developed by IBM. See *transport control protocol/internet protocol* (TCP/IP) and *open systems interconnection* (OSI).

systems program: see *system software*.

systems programmer: the person who writes code for *system software*.

systems support: see *software support staff, service engineer*.

T-connector: one type of *BNC connector*. They are used with the 10 Base-2 *Ethernet* system to connect two *coaxial cables* to the *network interface* card inside a computer.

tab separated variable files: files in which the data *fields* are separated by the tab character. This type of file is often used when data is moved from one *table* to another or from one *database* to another.

table: in *relational databases* the data is organised into tables which are connected together by *relationships*. The diagram below shows three tables Author, Book and Supplier linked by two one-to-many relationships. One Author can write many books and one Supplier can supply many books.

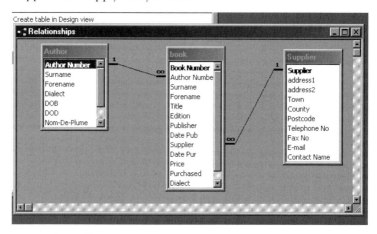

tablet: see *graphics tablet*.

tagged image file format (TIFF): a method of storing *bitmap* graphics that was originally developed to handle scanned images.

tailor made software: software that has been specifically written for a task is often described as being 'tailor made for the task'. Software produced like this is also called *bespoke software*.

tape cartridge: a small cassette used to store large quantities of data. Tape cartridge systems are often used to back up microcomputer systems or network *servers*. This type of storage media provides only *serial access* to the data stored, but can store large quantities of data in a relatively small space.

tape drive: the hardware unit used to read tapes. On micros the tapes are normally small cartridges similar to domestic cassettes, but on mainframe computers they are normally much larger single spools.

tape reader: see *tape drive*.

tape streamer: a tape system used for backing up *hard disks*, usually on a microcomputer or a network *server*. Tape streamers use *tape cartridges* as their storage medium.

task: when a computer is using a *multiprogramming* or multiprocessing *operating system* the jobs to be completed are started by the operator as soon as they are available. These jobs, or sequences of instructions, are treated by the operating system as an element of work to be accomplished by the computer and are often referred to as tasks.

task management: to ensure an efficient use of all the resources available the *operating system* has to manage the flow of *tasks* (i.e. the starting and stopping of programs) to ensure that one process does not hog the system.

Under task management in a *multiprogramming* environment, the highest priority task that is ready for processing is started next. Priorities are allocated on the type of resources needed by the task and *not* its urgency. High priority is given to tasks that require extensive use of peripherals (*peripheral bound*) whilst tasks that require extensive use of the processor (*processor bound*) and little use of the peripherals are given low priorities.

The high-level *scheduler* is responsible for selecting the tasks from backing store to be loaded into the computer's memory and this selection is done on a basis of priority and availability of resources. Each task is looked at in priority order but it is loaded only if all the resources it needs can be allocated. Once tasks are loaded the low-level scheduler is responsible for selecting the program to get access to the processor and actually 'run'.

This selection is done purely on priority (the necessary resources must be available – high-level scheduler) and the highest priority program that is available to 'run' is given access to the processor until an interrupt occurs.

task queue: in a multiprocessing environment (also known as a round robin environment) information about the *tasks* available is held in a task *queue*. When a new task is started it joins the task queue (at the back) and eventually makes its way to the front. Once the program currently using the processor finishes its use of the processor the program at the front of the task queue takes control of the processor. At the end of its time slice the program is placed at the back of the task queue.

task swapping: the process of switching from one application to another. The data for the application presently running in the *foreground* is saved to a storage device. The data for the next application is then loaded.

technical documentation: the detailed documentation of a *system*, including the *programs*, *hardware* and processing procedures. It enables other *programmers* to make modifications to the system. Technical documentation is also known as maintenance or system documentation.

technical support staff: the staff who are responsible for providing support for the *hardware* and *software* in a system. This support is often initially provided by telephone, with staff only visiting the site if the problem cannot be resolved over the telephone. Large organisations will have their own technical support staff who will have access to the technical support provided by their suppliers when they are unable to resolve a problem; smaller organisations are usually dependent on outside support. When software packages are purchased support is often provided free for a limited period, although it often requires long periods waiting in a telephone queue to get through, and the phone calls are sometimes charged at premium rates. Continued technical support is generally available, but can be expensive.

telecommunications: a general term used to describe the transfer of *information* over large distances either using cables or electromagnetic waves.

telecommuting: using technology to work from home yet remaining in close contact with work colleagues. Telecommuting involves the use of the telephone, *e-mail* and *fax*. As technology improves it will also include *video conferencing*. To work from home an employee of a company, as well as having adequate technology (computer, *modem*, *fax machine*, telephone line), needs access to the organisation's main computer systems to allow them to access the data stored there.

teleconferencing: using technology to conduct meetings where the participants can be spread throughout the world. This type of meeting makes extensive use of *video conferencing*.

telematics covers all applications involving the use of computers in conjunction with telecommunications systems. This includes dial-up access to the *Internet* as well as all types of *networks* that use telecommunications to transport data.

telemedicine: the use of *telematics* within and between hospitals to make better use of electronic data and filing systems for records and better use of expensive equipment and resources, such as imaging systems, where pictures can be transferred quickly between sites.

telemetry: using communications systems to control equipment at a distance. Telemetry is used in Formula 1 motor racing to allow the technicians in the pits to make changes to the operation of the car while it is moving, thereby improving the performance of the car.

telephony: the use or operation of systems for the transmission of voice or data communications between separate points.

teleprocessing: using a computer or terminal and communications equipment to access computers and computer files located elsewhere. It is also referred to as remote-access processing. Teleprocessing is a term originated by IBM.

Telnet: in the *Internet* suite of *protocols*, Telnet is the protocol that provides a remote *terminal* connection service. It allows users of one computer to log on to a remote computer and interact as directly attached terminal users of that computer.

template: 1 A thin sheet of plastic or paper placed around the function keys on the keyboard to indicate the meanings allocated to these keys in a particular program.

2 In *spreadsheet* applications, a template is a spreadsheet in which all the cells have been defined, formatted and formulae entered, but no data has yet been inserted.

3 In *word processing* and *desktop publishing* programs, a predesigned document that contains formatting and, in many cases, generic text.

terabyte: $1024 \times 1024 \times 1024 \times 1024$ (1,099,511,627,776) *bytes* of information.

terminal: a device that is usually equipped with a *keyboard* and a display device capable of sending and receiving information.

terminal adapter: a piece of *hardware* for connecting a computer to the *Internet* making use of an *ISDN* link instead of a slower *modem* connection.

terminal emulator: a *program* that allows a device such as a *microcomputer* or personal computer to enter and receive data from a computer system as if it were a particular type of terminal attached to that computer system. When linking a micro-computer to a *mainframe* computer it is often necessary to make the microcomputer emulate a particular type of terminal before the link can be established.

terminal node: the name given to a node on a tree data structure (*binary tree* and *non-binary tree*) that has no descendants. A terminal node is often called a *leaf* to continue the analogy with physical trees.

terminate and stay resident (TSR): a *program* that, when executed, installs part of itself as an extension of the *operating system*. The extension remains in place until the computer is restarted.

test data: the data used to test a system. When test data is being designed the expected results are worked out so that they can be compared with those produced by the system. It is important that considerable care and thought are put into the choice of test data to ensure every eventuality is tested. Test data should include typical, extreme and erroneous data, covering every possible action within the program being tested. When test data is being used the process is described as testing. For large and complex systems, it is impossible to do exhaustive testing.

The test plan gives the complete schedule for testing a system. It ensures that each section of the system is tested at the appropriate point, which allows data produced from one part to be used in another part of the system after the first part has been tested.

There are many different approaches used by organisations to test systems and these include:

- *white-box testing* (structural testing)
- *black-box testing* (functional testing)
- *top-down testing*
- *bottom-up testing*
- *integration testing*.

TeX: Donald Knuth's mathematical typesetting package.

text box: a *box* in which the user may enter text. This can occur in a dialogue box, drawing in Microsoft Word or HTML form, or in a desktop publishing program.

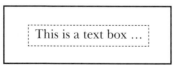

text editor: a simple *word processor* which is used to create files of text with no formatting applied. Text editors are used to construct *source code* for high- or low-level languages, to create the text to be placed in e-mails, to construct batch programs, etc. The files produced by a text editor are called text files and hold data in standard ASCII (*American Standard Code for Information Interchange*) format. Since no formatting is included, these files can be read by most types of software and hence are used to transfer text data from one *software package* to another.

thermal printer: a *printer* that creates the required image on heat-sensitive paper by heating small wires. Each character is made up of a series of dots that are created when a wire is heated.

thesaurus: an accessory which contains synonyms, available in most word processing and desktop publishing packages.

thin client: a computer connected to a *network*, which is unlikely to have a local *hard disk*. A thin client has little or no installed *software* but has access to software that is managed and delivered by the network *servers* it is attached to. Most of the processing is carried out on a very powerful network file server. As almost all of the processing is carried out on the file server, only information needed for screen updates is sent to the thin client machine. A thin client is an alternative to a full-function client such as a PC.

third normal form: see *normalisation of data*.

third party: a supplier, other that the original manufacturer of a system, who supplies *software* or *hardware* for the system

thread: a stream of computer instructions that is in control of a process. A multi-threaded process begins with one stream of instructions (one thread) and may later create other instruction streams to perform tasks.

threshing: the situation in a *virtual memory* system where data is continually being transferred between *memory* and *hard disk*.

throughput: the amount of work being done by a system.

tiling: where the screen has multiple *windows*, to rearrange and resize all open windows, so that they appear on the screen without any overlap.

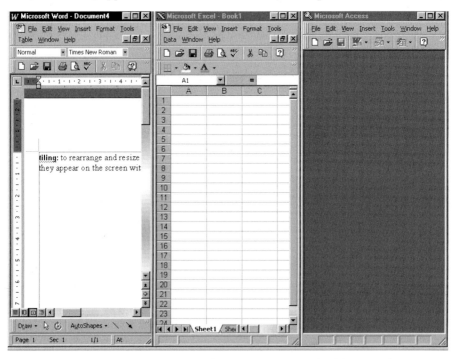

An example of tiling

tilt and swivel: a *monitor* is described as a tilt and swivel monitor when its screen can be turned left or right (swivel) and up or down (tilt) to allow the user to achieve a comfortable working position.

time division multiplexing (TDM): a technique which sends more than one *signal* down a communication line by allocating time slots to each signal. The *multiplexer* is responsible for determining which device connected to it should use the single communications link if more than one packet of data is ready for transmission at a particular moment in time.

time out: an event that occurs at the end of a predetermined period of time. If no response has been received from the *task* concerned within a certain period, the event is stopped and is said to have 'timed out'.

time sharing system: an *operating system* used in a *multiprocessing* environment where each *task, job* or user is allocated a fixed amount of time (time slice) on a rotating basis. In this type of system all tasks are of equal priority. The time slice is the maximum period of time that a task can make use of the processor before it must relinquish it for the next task.

time stamp: attaching the date and time to a *file* or report for *auditing* purposes. In a *database query* the date stamp when a query report was created is used to ensure that the latest report is being used. The query uses the system time and date to place this information on each page of the report.

timer interrupt: an *interrupt* that occurs when a job has run out of allocated processor time, usually by getting stuck in an *infinite loop.*

title bar: the area at the top of each *window* that contains a window title, and the *maximise, minimise* and close buttons.

`W Microsoft Word - Complete T-Z.doc`

toggle: to switch sequentially from one optional state to another.

token: in a token ring *local area network*, the bit pattern that is passed round the network. Data is attached to the token if it has no data already attached and passed on. Subsequent *workstations* each inspect the data and remove it if it is intended for that workstation, leaving the token free to move another block of data.

token ring network: a *network* that uses a ring topology, in which a *token* is passed in a circuit from *workstation* to workstation. A workstation that is ready to send can capture the token and insert data for transmission. As the token passes through a workstation it is checked to see if the data attached is for that workstation and if appropriate the data is removed before passing the empty token onwards. In the IBM token ring network all the workstations are connected to a hub or multiple access unit (MAU). The movement of data is in a logical ring with all signals between workstations passed through the MAU.

The diagram on the next page shows a token ring network.

The major advantage of this topology over the conventional *ring network* is that if one workstation fails the network continues to function.

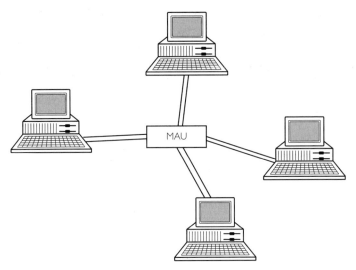

Token ring network

tokenising: as part of the translation of a *program* written in a *high-level language*, part of the *source code* is replaced by *tokens*. The reserved words (commands i.e. IF, WHILE, REPEAT, etc.) in the source code are replaced by tokens to reduce the size of the program, and for interpreted programs to speed up the program execution. During execution when a token is recognised it is used as an offset to the start address of a table of *pointers* to reserve word handling routines.

toolbar: the various actions or processes, represented by screen *buttons*, that can be carried out within an *applications package*. Given below is the toolbar from Drawing in Microsoft Word. Clicking on the button selects the appropriate tool, *menu* or action.

Drop down menu for shapes   Insert WordArt tool   Paintbrush tool

toolbox: a collection of *routines* usually prewritten and compiled, which a *programmer* can use to speed up the writing of *programs*.

top-down programming: a method of designing a solution to a problem by splitting it up into sub-problems (sometimes known as stepwise refinement). The process continues until all the sub-problems are solvable. Putting the solutions together will provide a solution to the original problem. Jackson structure diagrams are often used in the design of *programs* when this methodology is used. The advantages of this methodology are:

- *modules* can be used in various programs with confidence that they will work, since they will already have been tested in the earlier program
- each module is small enough that its logic can be represented on one page using a Jackson structure diagram

- modules are small and hence easier to understand than trying to grapple with the whole problem
- modules can be allocated to different programmers, with more experienced programmers given the most difficult modules
- modules can be written in the most appropriate *programming language* and then linked to the main program using a *linkage editor*
- large programs are easier to monitor and control
- future maintenance of the program is easier because the module requiring maintenance can be easily identified and the necessary changes made before testing and replacing in the original program.

See also: *Jackson structured programming*.

top-down testing: testing of the skeleton of a system with *modules* added as they become available. The main structure of the system is written probably with display messages indicating that a particular module has been called even though that module might not exist. As each module is produced and tested with its own *test data* it is incorporated and the system re-tested. Eventually the whole system will be complete and have been tested.

topology: the physical or logical arrangement of *workstations* in a *network*.

touch screen: a *monitor* with a series of horizontal and vertical infra red beams across its surface. These beams can be broken by pointing a finger at the screen. The combination of beams broken determines which area of the screen is being pointed at. This type of screen is often used for easy selection of on-screen menus.

touchpad: a small, touch-sensitive pad used to control the pointer on some portable computers. The pointer is moved on the screen by moving a finger or other object across the pad. *Icons*, etc. are selected by tapping the pad.

trace table: used to find *bugs* in *programs*, a trace table is a record of the contents of the *variables* in a program as the program is executed. It also shows the *path* taken through the program by indicating the sequence in which the instructions were executed.

track: circular areas on a *floppy disk* or a *hard disk*, used for data storage. Tracks are composed of *sectors* and are recorded on a disk by an operating system during a disk *format* operation.

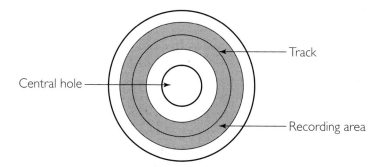

On other storage media, such as tape, data is stored on tracks that run parallel to the edge of the medium. Older systems used ½ inch tape with seven or nine parallel tracks.

trackball: a device for controlling the pointer on the screen. A trackball is a *mouse* lying on its back. The pointer is moved by rotating the ball with thumb, fingers, or the palm of the hand. Next to the ball there are *buttons*, which work like mouse buttons.

Trackballs are useful where space is limited and mouse movements would be difficult. Also, a trackball can be used on any surface unlike a mouse which requires a relatively smooth surface. Trackballs are popular devices to control the screen pointer on portable computers.

tractor feed: a method of feeding paper through *dot-matrix printers*. Tractor feed printers require special paper, which has a row of holes along each side of the paper. These holes are used by two sprocketed wheels on either side of the printer to pull the paper through the printer.

traffic: a term used to describe the amount of activity over a *communications link*.

transaction is used to denote new information ready to be input to a *system*. Transactions can include new *records* to be added to the *master file*, changes to be made to existing records and records which need removing from the master file. In batch systems the transactions are stored together over a period of time in a transaction file and then used to update the master file.

transaction log file: a *file* that records each *transaction* as it is entered. This transaction file can be used as part of an *audit trail* to provide evidence of the date, time and nature of changes made to a *master file*.

The transaction log file can also be used to re-create the master file in the event of a system failure. At the start of processing a *backup* of the master file and a new transaction file are created. If during processing the system fails and the master file is corrupted the log file, together with a copy of the backup of the master file, can be used to re-create the master file at the point of system failure.

transaction processing: as each set of data (*transaction*) is entered it is processed before the next set is entered. An example of an application that uses transaction processing is holiday bookings where all the data associated with a booking is entered and processed before the next booking can be entered.

transducer: a device that converts energy from one form into another. An input transducer converts a physical quantity into an electrical signal, whereas an output transducer takes an electrical signal generated by a computer and converts it into a physical quantity.

translator: translators are software packages that convert one *computer language* into another. Examples of translators are *compilers, interpreters* and *assemblers*.

transmission control protocol/Internet protocol (TCP/IP): a set of protocols used when transferring data on a *network*. The protocol was developed by the US government when the *Internet* was set up. Its use allows the successful transfer across the wide variety of networks linked together to form the Internet.

transmission media: the media used to form the link between computers. The transmission media for a *local area network* (LAN) are the cables used to link the computers, which can be *fibre optic, coaxial, unshielded twisted pair*, etc.

transparent: see *user transparent*.

transposition error: an error that occurs when data is keyed in or written down and characters are swapped around, i.e. entering 1243 instead of 1234.

transputer: a special *processor*, or an arrangement of processors, that allows parallel processing to be carried out.

traversal: the name used to describe the process of moving around a *data structure*.

tree: an abstract *data structure* that represents entities in *nodes*, with at most one parent node for each node, and with only one root node. There are two different categories of tree, *binary tree* and *non-binary tree*, though both can be held in memory using two *arrays*. The data at the node is held in one array and the pointers that maintain the tree structure are held in a two-dimensional array with two columns.

Trojan horse: an apparently harmless program that can be very destructive when executed. Trojan horses are not like *viruses*, which replicate themselves, but they can be just as destructive. The name comes from Greek mythology when the Greeks gave a giant wooden horse to their enemy the Trojans as a bogus peace offering. Greek soldiers were hidden in the horse, and came out at night and opened the city gates to allow the rest of the Greek army to capture the city.

troubleshooting: the act of identifying the source of a problem in a program, computer system, or network and correcting it.

true: see *truth value*.

TrueType font: an *outline font* technology developed by Microsoft and Apple. TrueType support is built into all Windows and Macintosh *operating systems*. Anyone using these operating systems can create documents using TrueType fonts. TrueType is a WYSIWYG font technology, which means that the printed output of TrueType fonts is identical to what appears on the screen.

truncation occurs when all the digits or bits after a specified point are discarded. The truncation of the number 17.456789453 to two decimal places is 17.45. Compare with *rounding*.

truncation error: the error introduced as a result of truncating a number is referred to as the truncation error. The outcome is 17.45 when 17.456789453 is truncated to two decimal places and the error introduced as a result of truncation is 0.006789453. If the number had been *rounded* to two decimal places the result would have been 17.46 with a *rounding error* of 0.003210547.

truth table: a grid used to show the relationship between the outputs and inputs of a logic circuit made up of the various *logic gates* (*AND, OR, NOT, XOR, NAND, NOR, XNOR*). Each row in the grid represents a single input combination and output produced for that input combination. A circuit with n inputs has $2n$ rows to ensure that all possible input combinations are covered.

truth value: a *Boolean variable* has two truth values, True and False.

tuple is the correct term for a row or *record* from a table in a *relational database*. The word 'tuple' is used in relational calculus and relational algebra, which provide the mathematics on which relational databases are based.

turnaround document: a document, output from a computer *system*, which is intended to be fed back into the system at a later stage. Multiple choice exams make use of this type of document. The answer sheet for each candidate is produced by computer with all the necessary information to identify the candidate printed on the document. During the examination, the candidates mark boxes to select their chosen answers. The completed answer sheets are then returned to the examination board where they are fed into an *optical mark reader* (OMR) for subsequent processing. This form of *data capture* involves no data entry by humans other than that needed to enter the candidates details originally.

turnkey system: a computer system that has been built for one specific application. Turnkey systems include all the *hardware* and *software* necessary for the particular application.

turtle: a small *robot* that is often used in primary education to turn programs written in LOGO into physical movements. When a pen is attached to the turtle these movements can produce pictures.

tutorial: a teaching aid, book or manual, or interactive disk-based lessons, designed to help a user learn to find out how a product or application works. This is now frequently provided with the application and can contain a guided tour through the software.

TWAIN: the TWAIN interface is the de facto interface standard for *scanners*, i.e. nearly all scanners come with a TWAIN driver. Such scanners can be used by any TWAIN-supporting software. However, some scanner *software packages* are not TWAIN-compatible.

tweening: the process of generating the necessary frames between two images to create the appearance that the first image changes smoothly into the second image. Tweening is important in all forms of *computer animation*.

twisted pair (TP): a type of *cable* that consists of pairs of insulated wires twisted around one another. One wire carries the signal while the other wire is connected to earth and absorbs any interference to the signal. Normally the cable will be made up of several of these pairs inside an outer sheath.

two-address instruction: an *instruction* that uses two *addresses* to access the data as well as the *operator*. For example

    MLA Add1, Add2

would multiply the contents of the location specified by Add1, by the content of the location specified by Add2, placing the result in the *accumulator*. MLA is the *operator* and Add1 and Add2 are the two addresses.

Using *one-address instructions* the above command could have been achieved by the following program segment:

    LDA Add1
    MUL Add2

where the first instruction would transfer the contents of the location specified by Add1 into the accumulator and the second instruction would multiply the contents of the accumulator by the contents of the location specified by Add2, placing the result in the accumulator.

two-dimensional array: an *array* that is made up of rows and columns, unlike a *one-dimensional array* which only has one row. Each element in an array must hold data of the same type (e.g. *integer, string*). To access an element two *subscripts* are used:

- one subscript represents the row
- the other subscript represents the column of the array.

It is important to be consistent within a system on whether the first subscript represents the row or the column (normal convention is for the first subscript to represent the row). Although two-dimensional arrays are represented as grids they are held in the computer's memory using consecutive locations: row following row or column following column.

An array dimensioned as having four columns and three rows would be represented as shown in the diagram below, with the subscripts for each element indicated.

0.0	0.1	0.2	0.3
1.0	1.1	1.2	1.3
2.0	2.1	2.2	2.3

By rows, this array would be held in memory when stored as:

0,0	0,1	0,2	0,3	1,0	1,1	1,2	1,3	2,0	2,1	2,2	2,3

with an associated mapping function:

The location of element (p,q) is Base address + p*(length of row) + q where element (0,0) is stored in location Base address.

By columns, it would be stored as:

0,0	1,0	2,0	0,1	1,1	2,1	0,2	1,2	2,2	0,3	1,3	2,3

with an associated mapping function:

the location of element (p,q) is Base address + q*(length of column) + p where element (0,0) is stored in location Base address.

Where the programming language allows it, an array element can hold a record, which is defined to be of mixed data types.

two-pass assembler: a program that translates source programs written in *assembly language* into *machine language* by going through the source program twice. During the first pass the symbol table is built up and this is used in the second pass to create the code for the final object program.

two's complement: a method of representing positive and negative numbers in *binary*. The most significant bit (MSB) is the sign bit, with a 1 representing a negative number and a 0 a positive number. Using this representation, complementation changes the sign of the number held in a *register*. One method of complementing the contents of a register is by reversing each bit in the register and adding one to the register.

The register below holds the positive number 18:

0	0	0	1	0	0	1	0

Reversing each bit gives:

I	I	I	0	I	I	I	0	I

Adding one to the register gives:

I	I	I	0	I	I	I	I	0

The contents of this register represents negative 18 using two's complement representation.

To work out the decimal equivalent of the contents of a register:

- check the sign bit (MSB)
- if the sign bit is a 1, two's complement the register, otherwise do nothing
- convert the register from binary to decimal
- if the sign bit in the original register was a 1 then the sign of the number is negative, otherwise it is positive.

Example

Convert the contents of the register below.

I	0	0	I	0	0	I	0

The sign bit is 1, so two's complement the register:

0	I	I	0	I	I	I	0	I

after reversing

0	I	I	0	I	I	I	I	0

after adding 1

Converting the contents of this register to decimal gives 110.

Thus the contents of the original register represent –110 in decimal, using two's complement notation.

Two's complement representation has only one representation for 0, unlike other representations, such as *one's complement,* where sign and magnitude both have two representations +0 and –0.

two-way linked list: a *list* that has both forward and backward *pointers,* which allows movement in both directions through the list.

typeface: the design of the characters making up the text in documents, e.g. Times, Arial, etc. A typeface is not the same as a *font,* which is a specific size of a specific typeface, such as **10 pt Courier bold**.

ultraviolet erasable PROM: a type of erasable *programmable read-only memory* (PROM) *chip* which is erased by exposing the chip to ultraviolet light. Once a chip is erased, other programs or data can be stored on the chip using a PROM programmer device.

unary operator: an *operator* that can act only on a single item of data, e.g. the *NOT* operator. Operators that act on two items of data (+ , − , * , / , *AND* , *OR* , etc.) are known as *binary operators*.

unbundling: the selling of *hardware* and *software* products as separate items rather than together. *Keyboards, monitors* and *operating system* are normally bundled as part of a package, but some suppliers will allow the purchaser to buy these separately.

uncommitted logic array (ULA): a *chip* on which the *logic gates* have not been connected together. The manufacturer of the final chip will add the layer that provides the connections to form the required final circuit. The use of ULAs allows the production of customised chips without the high cost of having the chip specially made.

unconditional jump/branch: an *instruction* within a *program* that changes the sequence in which instructions are executed by making the next instruction to be obeyed the one indicated in the jump instruction. This is a forced jump to another section of a program, with no preconditions. This type of jump can be used to create a *loop* structure, with a conditional jump providing the exit from the loop. The following example uses a conditional jump and an unconditional jump to produce a *while loop*.

```
Label_1:   IF condition THEN Label_2
                program instruction
                program instruction
                ......
                ......
                GOTO Label_1
Label_2:    program instruction
                program instruction
                ......
```

In the above example the GOTO is an unconditional jump, whereas the IF is a conditional jump, the jump being executed only if the condition is true.

UnCover: a service that allows the user to search a database of periodicals and have a copy of any article faxed back at a cost. UnCover can be accessed on the *Internet* at http://www.carl.org/uncover.

undelete: to restore a *file, record* or item of data that has previously been deleted.

underflow: underflow occurs when a number too small to be represented by a particular computer system is generated by a calculation. The opposite effect, of producing a value too large to be stored, is known as overflow.

In general terms underflow occurs if:

- a small number (less than 1) is divided by a large number
- two small numbers (less than 1) are multiplied together,

whereas overflow occurs if:

- a large number is divided by a small number (less than 1)
- two large numbers are multiplied together.

underline: a word processing function to *format* a selection of text so that it is printed with a line slightly below it, as this is.

underscore: an *underline* character (_) often used to emphasise a letter or a word. It is also used as a link in file names where a space is not allowed or inappropriate, e.g. customer_record.

undo: a command provided in many software packages (e.g. *word processors*) which allows the user to return to a previous state. If a block of characters was unintentionally erased, the Undo command would replace them without the user having to type them all back in again.

unformatted:

1. A disk without a basic structure set onto it. A disk cannot be written to until it is formatted for the particular type of computer on which it is going to be used.
2. Text in its simplest form without any attributes such as bold, italic, etc.

ungroup: the action of separating out a *group* of objects into its component parts. It is used in drawing packages with the *group* command to aid selection and editing of a set of objects. Individual objects cannot usually be edited until the objects are ungrouped but the group can be re-sized, with each component increasing in size proportionally.

Unicode: a character encoding system for all the world's characters. It is designed to allow all the world's computer systems to exchange text information unambiguously because each character is encoded as a single code point. Unicode is intended to be backwards compatible with the *American Standard Code for Information Interchange* (ASCII).

uniform resource locator (URL): the *path* that contains the *address* at which a particular resource is located on the *Internet*.

For example, http://www.madaboutbooks.co.uk/index_atoz.asp is the URL used by *web browsers* to locate the web site of the publisher of this book: Hodder & Stoughton. The URL has three components:

- HOW – http which gives the protocol to be used in transferring the page
- WHERE – www.madaboutbooks.co.uk, which identifies the *web site* for the required resource
- WHAT – index_atoz.asp, which gives the file name of the required item.

uninstall: to remove an application from a computer. When a software application is first installed normally several files are added to the computer's hard disk, sometimes in different folders than the main one allocated for the application. Uninstalling removes all these files. In addition, it might also remove files that were subsequently generated by the application. Frequently, however, uninstalling is not entirely effective, and a few *orphan files* remain.

uninterruptable power supply (UPS): a large, rechargeable battery that is used to prevent *volatile store* losing its contents in the event of a power failure. The UPS also ensures that the disk drives are not damaged by *head crashes* as a result of sudden loss of power. Some UPSs last only a few seconds and will not therefore allow the user to keep on computing. Other UPSs provide power for longer periods of time (perhaps 20 min), allowing the user to keep going. They often come with *software* that will automatically use the power available from the UPS to provide an orderly close down, thus avoiding damage to data and *hardware*. UPSs are particularly important on *network servers* where considerable amounts of data can have been changed since the last backup was taken, so loss of a hard drive could have serious consequences.

unique identifier: an *attribute/field* within a *record*, which identifies the record so that it can be distinguished from all other records stored by that system. A unique identifier for one system may not be unique in another, e.g. the *bar code* printed on a book uniquely identifies the book as far as a bookseller is concerned but does not do so when used in a library. Hence libraries have to insert their own bar codes so that they can distinguish between two different copies of the same book.

unit testing involves testing each section of a program as it is produced rather than waiting until the complete program has been produced.

universal asynchronous receiver/transmitter (UART): an *integrated circuit* that converts computer data into *asynchronous* signals that can be transmitted via a telephone line and also carries out the reverse operation. UARTs provide the link between the parallel data moving round inside a computer and the serial data moving down communication links.

universal product code (UPC): the American equivalent of the EAN *bar code* system. It is a standardised bar code layout that has been agreed by the retail trade for use with *point-of-sale terminals*.

universal serial bus (USB): a *serial* bus system used to connect external devices to *microcomputers*. The USB is intended to replace the COM and parallel printer ports that have been provided on microcomputer systems since the early 1980s. A single USB port allows 127 external devices to be connected in a daisy chain and provides improved data transfer speeds and improved *plug and play* facilities.

Unix: a popular and long-lasting multi-user *operating system* used in the professional world for microcomputers, minicomputers and mainframes. This operating system is commonly used on the Internet by many ISPs. A commonly available derivative of Unix is *Linux*.

Unix to Unix copy program (UUCP): the *protocol* that allows *Unix* users to share files, read *Usenet* articles and exchange e-mail messages. The protocol is based on the computer systems *polling* each other to swap data.

unlocked: an operation on a file to allow the usual types of manipulative operations to be performed. Files are *locked* for security purposes.

unpack: to restore or convert *packed* data to its original format.

unpopulated: a description of a circuit board whose sockets are empty.

unprotect: to remove the restrictions or *passwords* from a *file, cell* or *worksheet.*

unrecoverable error: an error generated by a computer system from which there is no method of recovery other than to reboot the computer system.

unset: a *flag* can have two states, set or unset, and is usually used in programming to indicate if an event has happened (set) or not happened (unset).

unshielded twisted pair (UTP): data cable where the core wires are twisted in pairs throughout the length of the cable and held together by a plastic outer coating. UTP cable is commonly used to provide the cabling for *networks.*

unsigned integer: a whole number which does not have a sign included (+ or –). Unsigned integers are 0, 1, 2, 3, etc.

unzip: decompressing a file that has been compressed with the *ZIP* format. ZIP files usually end with a ZIP (.zip) extension and are often created using the *WINZIP* software package. A special kind of zipped file is a self-extracting file, which ends with an EXE (.exe) extension. You can unzip a self-extracting file simply by running it.

update: the process of replacing, adding or deleting information (especially in a file) to produce a more up-to-date version of the data stored.

update file: see *transaction file.*

updating in place (in situ): updating in place is carried out when the *record* to be altered is first read into the computer's memory, adjusted and then written back to its original position on the storage medium. This type of updating is only possible when the medium concerned has direct access capabilities, i.e. magnetic disk. The original record is lost at the end of the updating process, so return to the original state is only possible using previously taken backups of the file.

upgrade: to change parts of the hardware or software in a computer system for later, and hopefully better, versions. Upgrades to software are sometimes provided at low cost to registered users.

upload: to transfer files, programs, etc. from a small computer to a larger computer. See *download.*

upper case: made up of capital letters, i.e. CAPITAL LETTERS is in upper case.

upper memory area (UMA): the area of *memory* between the first 640 Kb and 1 Mb in DOS-based systems. It is sometimes referred to as 'high memory'.

upper memory block (UMB): a *block* of *memory* in the *upper memory area* (UMA). UMBs are often used to hold *device drivers* and are normally managed by a special memory manager.

upward-compatible: a computer product, especially software, designed so that it will still be usable on a future system with a more powerful operating system and hardware. It implies the ability to perform adequately with other products that are expected to become available in the future. Upward compatibility has become easier to achieve because of the use of standards and conventions.

usability: usability implies ease of use and a good design that does not involve unnecessarily complicated procedures. It indicates ease of learning and flexibility and can be applied to software that performs a range of tasks for the user in an uncomplicated manner. A software package that is easy to use is sometimes described as being *user friendly*.

Usenet: a *bulletin board* network that is part of the *Internet* and allows a large group of Internet users to communicate using the *Unix to Unix copy program* protocols. The name is a contraction of users' network. Almost every topic of interest is covered within the newsgroups that have been created.

user: anyone who uses a computer system; the term is usually associated with a limited level of technical expertise or computer knowledge.

user acceptance testing: the testing carried out by the person who is going to use the *system* to ensure that it performs the required actions in an acceptable way.

user account: before being able to access the resources on a *network*, a user will need an account to be established. This account includes the information that identifies the resources that a particular user is allowed to access, change and delete.

user definable: *functions*, *identifiers*, *keyboard* keys, etc., that are able to be defined by the user and which are not an inherent part of the normal structure of the set-up. User-defined keys are keys on the keyboard that have been programmed by the user to carry out certain effects, allowing actions which are carried out repeatedly to be executed by the single press of a key.

user documentation: the manuals for the *users* of a system that describe how to use the system. These manuals should be non-technical but many do not meet the needs of the user.

user environment: one of the many terms to describe the method used to allow people to communicate with computer systems. A common user environment (*user interface*) is WIMP, which is an example of a *graphical user interface*. Collectively, user environments are known as *human–computer interfaces*.

user friendly: a phrase that is much overused, but intended to create the impression that a computer system is easy to use. The term should describe hardware or software that has been designed with the user in mind. User friendly software often involves a *mouse, icons* and *menus*.

user group: 1 On a *network*, a group of users who need and are given the same type of access and share the same access permissions. For example, all members of a personnel department could be in their own user group.

2 A group of people drawn together by interest in the same aspects of computing. User groups can provide support for newcomers and a forum where people can exchange information and ideas.

user ID: the name used to identify the *user* of a computer system or *network*. User ID is a contraction of user identification. To access a computer network a user will normally require a User ID and a *password*. The user ID is public (known to many people) but to provide security the password must not be disclosed to anyone. See *user name*.

user interface: one of the many terms used to describe the procedures and methods people use to communicate with computer systems. See *user environment, graphical user interface, human–computer interface*.

user interface management system (UIMS): UIMSs aim to provide the *user* with an *interface* which has the same look and feel in all areas of the *software*. With UIMS the same method of *menu* presentation is always used and the use of mouse clicks should be consistent throughout (e.g. one click highlights, two clicks selects).

user manual: the instructions provided with a computer system or *software package* that provide the *user* with instructions on how to use the system or package. The user manual will sometimes include instructions on how to set up the system or install the software. Any error messages that can be generated by the system or package are explained, with suggestions on any remedial action to be carried out.

user name: a name allocated to a computer *user* as part of the security process. Also known as a *user ID*, this can be the user's actual name or a contraction, e.g. the user name for Bob Penrose could be bpenrose. This, together with a *password*, allows user level security for entry into a computer system or network. It also allows the system manager or *database administrator* to restrict the level of access to various parts of files or the system for the user and to allocate the user to various groups for specific access. It can also track the use made of the system by the user, for monitoring or *auditing* purposes.

user transparent: a term that describes the actions carried out by a computer system that are not apparent to the *user*. Almost all interaction between the various hardware devices in a computer system are user transparent.

utility program: software that makes managing and using the computer much easier, e.g. disk formatters, *virus* killers and parts of the *operating system*. They generally perform common routine tasks and general housekeeping operations, e.g. sorting data, copying/renaming/deleting files.

Uuencode: a *Unix*-based coding system that allows the transmission of any information over systems that make use of the 7-bit ASCII set. The UUENCODE utility program converts a *binary* file (program or graphics) into ASCII text that can then be transmitted. The receiving computer system then UUDECODES the received text file to produce the original binary file.

V series: the CCITT standards used to define *data transmission* methods using a *modem*. Specific examples of V series standards are V.24, V.25, V.25bis, V.28, V.35 and V.36.

vactor: in a film, an animated character that is moved and voiced by a real life actor using a *waldo* and *data glove*.

valence: 1 the number of edges connected to a vertex in a graph.

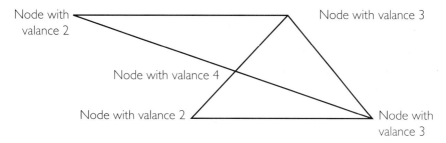

2 Confusingly, valence also means the number of branches below a *tree node*, which is one fewer than the number of edges incident to that node – every node in a *binary tree* has a valence of 2 or less.

validation: the checking of data according to a set of rules, standards and conventions, to see if it is sensible in the context in which it is being used (e.g. a date is not entered as 30022000). Validation checks include the following:

- **Presence check** – a check to ensure a particular item of data is present. For example an application for a driving licence would not be accepted as valid if it did not contain an address.
- **Character count** – a check to ensure that a *field* holds the correct number of characters. For example a date entered DDMMYYYY contains eight characters; any more or less would not be valid.
- **Format check (picture check)** – a check to ensure that the right type and sequence of characters have been entered into a field. For example, a National Insurance number is always made up of two letters, six digits, one letter, e.g. BB123456A.
- **Range check** – a check to ensure that the contents of a *field* lie between two specified limits. For example, the month number must be between one and 12 inclusive.
- *Check digit* – an extra character added to the end of a number to ensure that the likelihood of a transposition error is very low. For example, all ISBNs have a check digit.
- **File lookup** – a check is made to ensure that the contents of the *field* being validated are actually present in the *file* it is going to be used to update. For example a product number could be looked up in a file to check whether that particular code had been used.

value: a specific occurrence of an *attribute*; for example, 'blue' for the attribute 'colour'. It is also used for a quantity assigned to a *constant, variable, parameter,* or symbol.

value added network (VAN): a commercial *network* that offers specific services other than the ability to transfer files, etc. Examples include networks that offer stock prices, weather information, etc.

value added reseller (VAR): a company that buys *hardware* and adds extra features or offers additional services before selling it on.

value judgement: information that is an opinion and not a fact. One person may think that someone's eyes are green while another thinks that they are grey. Depending on who enters the information into the computer and what choices there are available, the outcome could be inaccurate or imprecise.

vapourware: products that exist in name only.

variable: in *programming languages,* an object that can take different values while the program is running. A variable is declared as a different data type (*variable type*) to restrict the data that can be held in different variables. In most programming languages the following data types are available for variable declaration:

- *integer* – only whole numbers allowed
- *real* – decimal numbers are allowed
- *string* – any combination of characters
- *char* – a single character
- *Boolean* – only able to take the values true or false
- *array* – a collection of several variables identified by the same name, with *subscripts* to identify each element of the array.

More complex data types are available in many languages. Each variable can only hold one value at a time but the value can be changed while the *program* is running.

variable length field: a *field,* the size of which is adjusted to take the number of *characters* entered. This type of field is used when the numbers of characters in the field in different records vary considerably. An example would be an address field: one address might contain very few characters while another might be much longer. If the large address is to be held accurately then there will be a considerable amount of wasted space in the field holding the small address if a *fixed length field* is used. In a file which contains thousands of records, this can lead to a significant amount of wasted storage space.

When a variable length field is used in a record, some method must be established of determining the actual size of the field in each record, unlike fixed length fields which have the number of characters pre-determined at the design stage. One method of establishing the size of the field is to introduce an extra small field whose contents is the number of characters in the field. This extra field reduces the saving in space but it is easier to process the record.

An alternative approach is to add an extra, special character at the end of the field. This method saves more storage space but increases processing time since the field has to be read character by character until the special character is reached.

variable length file: the size of the *file* is determined by the amount of data that has been entered and stored in the file. This is unlike files whose maximum size is determined when they are first created.

variable partition: a section of the *memory* of a computer whose size is adjusted by the operating system while the computer is in use. Each program and its associated *data* are held within a *partition*, and a *program* is not allowed to access memory locations outside its partition. Different programs require different amounts of memory and hence to manage the computer's memory efficiently it must be possible to change the sizes of partitions rather than set up the computer's memory with fixed partitions, which would waste large sections of memory. Depending on the order in which programs are loaded into memory they will occupy different sections of memory (partitions), which is why programs are written in *relocatable code*.

variable type: the type of a *variable* indicates the group of data that can be assigned to that variable. A variable with a specified data type of *integer* can hold only whole numbers. Other data types include character, *string, real, Boolean*, etc.

VAX (Virtual Address eXtension): the name given to DEC's range of *mini-computers*.

vector: a *pointer* that is used to hold the start address of a *routine* which is held somewhere else, either on *backing store* or in another area of main memory. The process of transferring control from one part of a *program* to another using a vector is known as vectoring. Altering the vector allows the positions of routines to be held in different parts of the memory on different computers. A computer where vectoring is possible normally uses a vector processor to carry out the vectoring. This is a separate processor that is used to carry out calculations on vectors. Most vector processors rely heavily on *pipelining* to achieve high performance.

vector font: see *outline font*.

vector graphics: a graphics system that uses line length and direction relative to an origin to draw objects. Graphics drawn using this method can be scaled easily without any loss of accuracy or detail, unlike *bitmap graphics* where the greater the scale factor the greater the possible degradation. *Zooming* in on a vector graphic results in no degradation of the image. Vector graphics are used in applications where accuracy of the representations of objects is important, e.g. designs for cars, houses, etc. Vector graphics are also known as object oriented graphics.

vectored interrupt: an *interrupt* routine where the location of the action to be carried out is indicated by the contents of the *vector*. The vector points to the start location of the routine to be carried out as a result of the interrupt.

vendor-independent messaging: a standard that allows electronic messages to be sent between different applications software. This is particularly important when a user has several software applications in use that are produced by different companies and one application needs to send a message, but it is not the currently active application.

verification: a check to see that data has been entered into a computer correctly from a source document, e.g. the name 'Hodder' might have been inaccurately entered as 'Hoder'. Verification ensures that what has been entered on the source document is what has been entered into the computer; no attempt is made to check on the validity of the data, which is done by *validation* routines. Verification might be done visually by checking that the screen matches the document but is more thoroughly done by a double-entry system.

Using the double-entry system, a second operator enters the data from the same document and this entry is compared by the computer with the first data entered for an exact match. Any discrepancies found are reported and the second person is responsible for ensuring the correctness of the data entered.

version: a copy of a *program* that is separately licensed and normally has significant new code or new functions. Each version is given a separate version number to distinguish it from other versions. For example, Microsoft Word 97 and Microsoft Word 2000 are two versions of Microsoft Word.

version control: when several programmers work on a single piece of software this software utility records the changes made by each programmer to the source code and ensures the changes are made in the main source file.

vertex: in a graph, the point at the end of an arc or the intersection of multiple arcs is called a vertex. A vertex is also known as a *node* particularly in *network topologies*.

vertical justification: adjustment of the spaces between lines of text to make it fit onto a page.

vertical redundancy check (VRC): a *parity* check carried out on every character in a block to ensure that there have been no transmission errors.

very high data rate digital subscriber line (VDSL): telephone lines that allow a maximum of 52 Mbit/s to be transmitted. Special equipment is required at the exchange and at the client end for this type of transmission to be possible.

very large scale integration (VLSI): a name given to the technology which allows between 20 000 and 100 000 transistors to be included on a *chip*.

very long instruction word (VLIW): the use of extremely long *instructions* (256 bits or more) in a computer to improve its ability to chain operations together.

video accelerator card: an add-in board for a computer that contains a processor and deals with the display, thus freeing the main processor for other tasks. The use of a video accelerator card significantly speeds up a computer using a *WIMP* environment.

video adapter: an add-in board for a computer that generates all the signals required to display text and graphics on the computer's video display (monitor). The section of memory normally on the video adapter board that holds the bit map of the image being displayed is called the video buffer.

video capture board: an add-in board for a computer that takes an incoming video signal and digitises and stores it in memory so that it can be processed.

video compression: the compressing of *analogue* video signals so that they can be efficiently broadcast by digital TV networks.

video conferencing: the setting up and linking of computers so that they can capture real time video and sound, allowing users in different locations to see and hear the other participants. This allows people in different locations to hold meetings where they can see each other on their computer screens and hear each other through speakers attached to the computers. A video camera is connected to each computer and captures the image before transmitting it to the other computers via telephone lines. A microphone is used to capture the sound, which is transmitted with the image.

video controller: either an add-in board for a computer that controls its display *monitor* or a piece of hardware that allows a computer to control a video recorder.

video digitiser: a video camera and an add-in board for a computer that allows the user to store in memory an image captured from a video camera, so that the image can subsequently be processed.

Video Electronics Standards Association (VESA): a group of PC manufacturers who have come together to specify a standard for *video adapters*.

Video For Windows™ (VFW): a software driver and utilities for Microsoft Windows 3.1 that allows AVI-format video files to be shown in a window.

video game: a computer game with action shown on the monitor.

video graphics array (VGA): one type of graphics standard on a PC that allows 256 colours in low resolution or 16 colours in high resolution.

video lookup table: a table of values stored in memory that represents the different colours.

video monitor: a device capable of displaying data from a computer without sound.

video phone: a telephone which can display real-time vision as well as allowing the user to hear the person at the other end.

video RAM (VRAM): fast *random access memory* (RAM) which is used for storing video information in a adapter on a PC. It is usually accessed by the computer's processor and by the video controller at the same time, allowing the computer to change the screen display and the video controller to continuously generate a signal to the monitor.

videocassette recorder (VCR): a device for recording or playing back analogue video signals held on video cassettes. The most popular method of formatting data on the ½ inch videotapes is vertical helical scan (VHS), although other formats are available. VHS was developed by JVC.

videodisk: a disk on which programs have been recorded for playback on a computer or a television set. The most common format in the United States and Japan is an NTSC signal recorded in the optical reflective format. Videodisks are played back on a special device called a videodisk player.

videotex: an interactive system in which text and low-resolution graphics can be displayed on a *monitor*. This is not the same as teletext (available on domestic televisions), which is not interactive. Videotext is also known as Viewdata.

virtual circuit: in *packet* switching the user 'sees' a link between the two ends of the transmission. This link is known as a virtual circuit because the packets can each use different routes in travelling between the two end points rather than all following the same route. There is no direct dedicated link.

virtual machine: a *data-processing* system that appears to be for the exclusive use of a particular user but this is achieved by sharing the resources of a large computer between many users.

virtual memory: the use of part of a *hard disk* as *memory* to give the illusion that a computer has more RAM than is really available. The use of virtual memory allows more processes to be running than could be held in the computer's actual memory. When it is a process's turn to use the CPU, space is made in the actual memory by transferring the existing process out to disk while the process to be executed is transferred from disk to actual memory (RAM).

virtual peripheral: a peripheral that is shared by many users, e.g. a printer. At the time of using the peripheral the user is under the impression that it is dedicated to them.

virtual point of presence (VPOP): this allows the user to connect to a distant point of presence (POP) for the price of a local phone call.

virtual reality (VR): a computer-simulated world with which the user interacts by the use of *data gloves* and special helmets, etc.

virtual reality modelling language (VRML): a *language* that allows 3D worlds to be created on a *web page*.

virtual shared memory: *memory* that appears to users as a single block but which is actually physically disjointed.

virtual world: the illusion created by *virtual reality*, which is normally achieved using a *virtual reality modelling language* (VRML).

virus: software that is illegally introduced to a computer, which often has annoying or even catastrophic results. It is designed to propagate itself without the user intending it and to infect other computer systems.

There are many types of virus. Two categories that include several well-known viruses are time bombs, which are triggered by a particular date, and logic bombs, which are triggered by a set of conditions. Boot sector viruses on hard disks are activated every time that hard disk is used to start the computer system.

Once loaded into a computer's memory, the virus is subsequently transferred to any floppy disk used on the computer when data is written to that floppy disk. Using that floppy disk in any other computer will infect that computer and so the process of spreading continues.

The increased use of the Internet means that viruses can spread very quickly right round the world whenever a data file is transmitted from one computer to another. Software is available to provide virus protection, but can only detect known viruses and consequently needs regular updating. Virus protection software (sometimes called a 'virus checker') is normally *memory resident*, having been loaded automatically when the computer was switched on and remains in memory until removed by the user or the computer is switched off.

Visual Basic: Microsoft's *graphical-user-interface*-based software developer environment. It uses the BASIC *programming language* and an approach known as *object oriented programming*. It comes with all the tools and programs necessary to create fully *WIMP*-based programs. A modified version called Visual Basic for Applications (VBA) is available for use within applications like Word, Excel and Access, and is based largely on *macros.*

Visual Basic Script (VBScript): a scripting language that was developed by Microsoft for use with the Internet Explorer *browser.* Used to write customised routines as an add-on to many Microsoft applications it also does similar things to JavaScript if you have a suitably equipped web browser.

Visual C++: Microsoft's *graphical-user-interface*-based program developer environment uses C++ and comes with all the tools and programs to create fully *WIMP*-based programs. Programmers using this language use *object oriented programming* in the production of the programs.

visual display unit (VDU): a computer screen or *monitor* that is used to display the output of a computer. It is also referred to as a monitor or CRT (cathode ray tube).

Visual Java++: a visual programming environment for Microsoft's *Java* programming language.

vital product data (VPD): information that uniquely defines the hardware, software, and microcode elements of a processing system.

voice data entry: data or commands spoken into a microphone that are translated by a computer using *voice recognition* technology and displayed on the screen (data) or executed (commands), depending on the context. Text entered into a word processor can then be edited using voice commands. Examples of packages are IBM Voicepad, IBM ViaVoice or Dragon's Naturally Speaking. To achieve any degree of accuracy, the voice recognition system has to be trained by speaking a number of lengthy pieces of text. The more text that is read in and corrected, the more accurate will be the output.

voice mail: audio version of electronic mail (*e-mail*). To the person making the call, voice mail is just like leaving a message on an answering machine. However, the message is actually stored on a computer.

voice modem: a *modem* capable of handling voice as well as data communications.

voice output: synthesised human speech. A speech synthesiser is used to generate sounds that resemble human speech. The sound is produced either by selecting from a collection of stored sounds or by using the noise patterns which represent the basic speech sounds or *phonemes.*

voice print: the stored digital representation of a human voice, often used as a security measure usually to gain access to a secure area.

voice recognition: the human voice used to control a machine. Recognition is achieved by analysing the incoming sounds and comparing them with stored sound patterns. The best match is chosen. Voice recognition systems normally require the user to 'teach' the computer by repeatedly saying the same words until an average pattern for the word is established.

volatile store: memory that loses its contents if the power is removed from the computer. *Random access memory* (RAM) is an example of a volatile store whereas *read only memory* (ROM) is non-volatile.

volatility of a file: the frequency with which updates are performed on a file. A file with a high volatility has a lot of new *records* added, existing records deleted and changes made to existing records in a short space of time.

volume: the name given to identify a *hard disk, CD-ROM*, tape, etc. within a computer.

volume envelope: a shape that is used to describe the changes in volume, pitch and timbre of a sound as it changes with time. One common way of describing a volume envelope is known as ASDR. This is an acronym for *attack, decay, sustain* and *release*. See these terms for individual definitions.

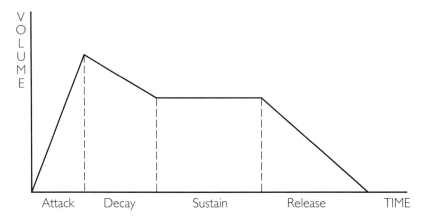

volume table of contents (VTOC): a table on a *hard disk, CD-ROM*, tape, etc. that describes the position, size and other properties of each file on the particular medium. This table is used to display on the screen the contents of a disk, with the user selecting which aspects are to be shown, e.g. file name, file extension, date created, etc.

von Neumann architecture: used to describe any computer that that takes a single *instruction* and obeys it before progressing to the next instruction, i.e. the computer does not employ concurrency or parallelism. The architecture is named after John von Neumann, a mathematician (1903–1957) who is credited with the invention of the basic architecture of current sequential computers. Most digital computer systems use this architecture, since they have only one processor. Using this type of architecture, a single control unit manages program control, following a cycle of fetching, decoding and executing instructions one at a time.

von Neumann bottleneck: the queuing up of instructions waiting to be processed.

VT emulation: the use of software that enables a computer to emulate Digital Equipment Corporation (DEC) terminals such as the VT52, VT100, VT200, and VT220. VT emulation is widely used with *Unix* systems.

wafer: a thin, round slice of a large single crystal of silicon onto which hundreds of individual *integrated circuits* are constructed before being cut into individual *chips*.

wait state: a delay that is introduced to allow a fast central processor to store or retrieve data from slower memory components. A processor is described as being in a wait state when it is not active but waiting for input from *peripherals*.

waldo: a mechanical device that can be connected to a computer and made to follow the movements of a human limb. It was developed for use in the nuclear industry for handling hazardous substances in a safe way.

walkthrough: a technique for finding faults in *software* systems by examining each step carried out by each piece of software.

wallpaper: an image or pattern used as a background in a *window*.

wand: a hand held *peripheral* commonly used in stores to read *bar codes* on products. The peripheral is sometimes called an optical wand-device.

warm boot: a reset operation that will load the *operating system*, but does not clear all of the computer's memory or check the computer's *hardware*.

WAV or WAVE file: the standard way of storing *analogue signals* in digital form under Microsoft *Windows*. A WAV file is commonly used to hold sounds or music.

wave table: the memory in a sound card that contains a recording of a real musical instrument to be played back; this method of producing sounds is different from an FM synthesis sound card that generates the sound using mathematical equations.

waveform digitisation: the conversion and storage of waveforms in numerical form using an *analogue-to-digital converter*.

waveform editor: software that displays a graphical representation of a sound wave which has been stored as a *WAV file* and allows the user to edit, adjust levels and frequencies or add special effects before re-saving.

weak encryption: a weak *encryption* technique is one that can be easily broken in a sensible amount of time using a large and powerful supercomputer. Some governments advocate that weak encryption should be used, so that law-enforcement agencies can crack the codes.

weak search: a search *algorithm* that searches for a key and returns the *node* that contained the key at the time it was examined. Weak searches are not guaranteed to provide an up-to-date result. See also *strong search*.

web: see *World Wide Web* and *Internet*.

web application: software that is available on a *web server* and accessed from a web page. The software uses *hypertext transfer protocol* (HTTP) to deliver information to a user. Examples of web applications are databases of information that can be searched from a *web page* or a method of ordering and paying for a product using a web page.

web authoring tool: software that can be used to create *web pages*. A basic web authoring tool allows the user to make changes to the *hypertext mark up language* (HTML) code for a web page, i.e. the source code that determines how a web page is constructed and how it looks. An example of web authoring software is Microsoft Frontpage.

web browser: the software used to move through *World Wide Web* (WWW) pages on the *Internet*. Users of web browsers are said to be 'surfing the net'. Having requested a page from an Internet server a browser takes the *hypertext mark up language* (HTML) code for the page and displays it on the screen making *hotspots* and *hyperlinks* clear to the user. Common examples of web browsers are Netscape Navigator and Internet Explorer.

web cam: a video camera linked to a *web site* that allows visitors to the site to see live video images of a scene. There are now several sites on the *World Wide Web* (WWW) using web cams for a variety of purposes.

web crawler: a program that explores the *World Wide Web*, following the links and searching for information or building a database. Such programs are often used by *search engines* to build automated indexes for the web, allowing users to do keyword searches for web documents. It is also the name used by one of the most popular publicly available keyword searching engines.

The WebCrawler (http://WebCrawler.com/) is owned by America Online Inc. and operated at their web studio in San Francisco. It regularly reads all the *web pages* it possibly can, and stores a huge database of indexing information.

web master: the system administrator for a *web server*. However, the term is also used as a job title for the person in charge of a *web site*.

web page: a single file stored on a *web server* that contains *hypertext mark up language* (HTML) commands which when viewed using a *web browser* can be displayed as *graphics*, text, *hyperlinks*, etc.

web page design software: software that provides features that make it easier for a user to create *web pages*. Similar to *desktop publishing* (DTP) software, it allows the user to create and edit pages without having a detailed knowledge of *hypertext mark up language* (HTML) commands.

web server: a computer that stores *web sites*. Some large organisations will have dedicated web servers for the collection of *web pages* that make up their web sites.

web site: the collection of *hypertext mark up language* (HTML) *web pages*, that have been produced by a particular company or individual. The pages are connected by *hyperlinks* and can be accessed separately, but normally each site has a single *home page* allowing easy access to it. Each site needs a unique domain name on the *Internet* and these now regularly appear in advertisements.

webzine: a magazine that is published on the *World Wide Web* (WWW) and not available in paper format, e.g. *SLATE*, which is funded by Microsoft.

well-behaved software: *software* is said to be well-behaved if it does not make any non-standard system calls. Thus only the standard BIOS input/output calls are made rather than *peripherals* or memory being addressed directly. To be *portable*, software has to be well-behaved.

what-if analysis: models developed in a *spreadsheet* application that allow the user to see what the effects of changes might be. Certain values in the spreadsheet are changed in order to reveal the effects of those changes. For example, changing prices and different selling quantities can be used to show potential profits.

whetstone: the first major synthetic *benchmark program*, intended to be representative for floating-point intensive programming. It is based on statistics gathered using an Algol 60 compiler, which translated Algol into instructions for the imaginary Whetstone machine.

while loop: a programming *loop* construct that checks a *Boolean* condition is true before executing the loop statements. If the Boolean condition is false when the WHILE instruction is first encountered the loop statements are not executed. A while loop is chosen whenever the number of times the loop must be executed is not known at the start of the loop execution and it is possible that the loop instructions might not need executing at all. Examples of the use of while loops are:

- searching arrays – the number of elements to be checked to find the item, or fail to find it, is not known at the start of each search
- processing files sequentially or serially – the number of records in the file is not known before the processing starts.

Example search *algorithm*:

```
count := 1;
while not((surname=surnam[count]) or (count>number)) do
    count := count + 1;
writeln('Person found in location ',count,' of array');
```

The loop will exit when the contents of 'surname' and 'surnam[count]' match, or the contents of 'count' are greater than the contents of 'number'. If the contents of 'surname' and 'surnam[count]' match when count contains 1 the loop instructions (count := count + 1) will not be executed.

white book: the formal video *CD* standard published by Philips and JVC that defines how digital video can be stored on a *CD-ROM*. The specification provides 72 minutes of full motion video compressed with the moving picture experts group (MPEG) algorithm.

white pages: a database of users and their *e-mail* addresses stored on the *Internet* to help other users find an e-mail address. Normally a user has to add their own e-mail address to the database.

white writer: a *laser printer* that directs its laser beam on the points that are not going to be printed. Using a white printer the black areas are printed evenly but edges and borders are not so sharp.

whiteboard: a system used to transmit doodles over the *Internet* while the user is using a voice or video system.

white-box testing is applied to the software *module* under test by identifying the paths through the project. This is done by creating a directed graph from the sub-modules of the module under test (using the '*loops*' and 'self-contained chunks of linear code', etc. as a guide). Once the directed graph for the module has been created, counting up the number of regions in the graph, and applying some common sense, can establish the paths through the code. Once all of the unique paths through the code have been documented, *black-box testing* methods are applied to each of these paths. The main weakness of white-box testing is that it will not detect missing functions in the software, since it is intended only to test that all aspects of the software produced work.

Whois: a searchable database that holds every registered domain on the *Internet,* together with the name of the domain owner. A special application called Whois is needed to search the database.

wide area information server (WAIS): a system that allows a user to search for and retrieve information from a range of archives stored on the *Internet.*

wide area network (WAN): a group of computers connected together by radio, telephone or microwave connections spanning a large region, or global in proportion. A WAN allows the users to share resources (hardware, software and data) and transmit data between widespread subscribers. When the computer systems involved are all on the same physical *site*, the network is said to be a *local area network* (LAN).

wideband: a transmission method that combines several channels of data onto a carrier signal and can carry the data over long distances.

widow: in word processing, the last line of a paragraph appearing at the top of the next page. If only the first line appears at the bottom of a page it is called an *orphan*. Widows and orphans are not considered to be desirable on printed output. Widows can be avoided by adding a page break earlier in the paragraph or by setting options within the software. The diagram below shows how text could generate a widow.

> **widow:** in word processing, the last line of a paragraph appearing at the top of the next page. These are not considered to be desirable on printed output. Widows can be avoided by adding a page break earlier in the

> paragraph or by setting options within the software.

wildcard: a character that can be used to replace a group of other characters. Wildcards are normally used when searching a *database*, e.g. TEXT* in the search field would find all records which started with the word TEXT.

WIMP (windows, icons, mouse, pointer): the desktop operating environment provided on almost all computer systems purchased for home use. The screen contains graphics or *icons* that are used to control the *software* and make it easier than command line systems for the user to start and use software. System commands do not have to be typed in by the user, who only needs to move the *mouse* pointer over the appropriate icon and click the mouse button. The image here shows a Microsoft Windows™ desktop.

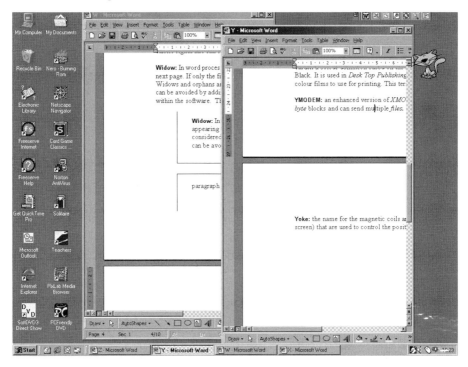

win.ini: the initialisation file, in *Windows* 3.*x*, used to store the initial program configuration information necessary to run the operating environment. The win.ini file has been replaced by the Registry database in Windows 95 and later versions of Windows.

Winchester disk: a *hard disk drive* that makes use of Winchester technology (now just called a hard disk).

WinCode: an *encryption* program that uses *bit* shifting on the data held in files so that they can be transmitted over *on-line* systems and the *Internet* securely. WinCode is copyright but distributed as *freeware*.

window: a part of the screen through which the user can see either a separate application or some other scene such as a directory.

WINDOWS™: a graphical user interface developed by Microsoft Corporation for use on the PC microcomputer. Originally it was just the graphical user interface that worked with the DOS operating system. Later versions can best be regarded as the operating system for the computer. There are many different versions of Windows in use including:

- **Windows CE:** a cut down version of Windows for use on palm tops and personal digital assistant system (PDAS).
- **Windows For Workgroups™:** a version of Windows that includes basic peer-to-peer file sharing functions, and e-mail, fax and scheduler utilities.

- **Windows NT:** Windows New Technology, a 32-bit version of Windows that does not use DOS. It is regarded as being more robust and secure than Windows 95 or 98 and was renamed Windows 2000.
- **Windows 3.1 or 4:** an early version of Windows that has been superseded by Windows 95, Windows 98, Windows 2000 and Windows ME.
- **Windows 98** gives users a more global view of their potential resources and makes Web technology (Internet Explorer) part of the user interface. Windows 98 also provides a 32-bit file allocation table that allows a single-partition disk drive larger than 2 Gbytes. Support is also include for USB, DVD and ACPI.
- **Windows 2000:** a version of Windows built on Windows NT that is designed to appeal to small businesses and professional users, as well as to the more technical and larger business market for which NT was designed.
- **Windows Me** was developed specifically for the home user. Microsoft claims that this update to Windows 98 has a more intuitive interface for the new user with added functionality for the experienced user.
- **Windows XP** (code named Whistler by Microsoft) is expected to bring a new, more personalised look to the desktop that will also make it easier for users to scan or copy in images and to acquire music files on the web and transfer them to portable devices.

Windows API: a set of standard *functions* and commands defined by Microsoft, that allow a programmer to control the *Windows* operating system from a *programming language*.

Windows Explorer: a *utility program* (sometimes called a housekeeping utility) included with *Windows* 95 and later versions that lets the user view the folders and files on a hard disk, floppy disk, *CD-ROM* and any shared network drive of a computer system.

Windows GDI: A set of standard functions defined by Microsoft, that allows a programmer to draw images within the *Windows* operating system.

Windows Metafile format (WMF): a graphics file format used by *Windows* to store *vector graphics*. This format allows graphics information to be exchanged between applications.

Windows RAM (WRAM): an efficient way of utilising *random access memory* (RAM) in a *Windows* environment.

Windows SDK™: a set of software tools and libraries that make it easier for a programmer to write applications that will work under the *Windows* operating systems.

Windows Sockets (WINSOCK): utility software that is required to control a modem when connecting to the *Internet* under MS-DOS or *Windows* 3 and allows the computer to communicate using the *transmission control protocol/Internet protocol* (TCP/IP). This utility is built into Windows 95 and subsequent versions of Windows and is automatically configured when the user installs software provided by an *Internet service provider* (ISP).

WinZip: one of the standard file-*compression* utilities.

wipe: to clean data from a disk.

wire-frame model: a 3D image displayed using just the outline edges. The production of wire-frame models of real or potentially real objects is called wire-frame modelling.

wired gloves: an interface worn on the hands for use in *virtual reality* applications. The gloves detect the movement of the hands, enabling the user to touch and move objects in a virtual world. They are also known as *data gloves*.

wireless application protocol (WAP): a standard designed to provide *Internet* access, *e-mail*, electronic transactions, news, and weather reports, over wireless networks such as digital mobile telephones. The WAP specification is intended to work across different types of wireless network. WAP mobile telephones can use a WAP *browser* to access pages of information. These pages are coded in WML, a language especially designed to take account of the limitations of mobile phones. The WAP specification was introduced in 1998 by a WAP forum consisting of the companies Ericsson, Motorola, Nokia and Unwired Planet.

wireless communication covers a whole range of possible methods of data transmission which can be used for linking computers within *networks*. Methods of transmitting data using wireless technology include: *microwave transmissions, infra-red communication, satellite communication.*

wireless markup language (WML): a *markup language* designed to specify the content and user interfaces on *narrow band* wireless devices such as pagers and cellular phones. The language is based on the extensible markup language (XML) which is a simplified version of Standard Generalised Markup language (SGML). XML was developed by the *World Wide Web Consortium* and allows developers to create customised tags that organise the content of pages efficiently. SGML allows the same information to be presented in different ways and is used as the basis of *hypertext mark up language* (HTML).

wizard: a method of helping the user to achieve a set task without having to get involved in the complexities of the task. A typical wizard will ask the user simple questions and provide default or sensible values to help the user make appropriate choices. Wizards are provided in Microsoft Excel to create pie charts, bar charts, etc. and within Microsoft Access to create queries, reports, etc.

word: a separate item of data on a computer, formed of a group of *bits*, stored in a single location in memory. The number of bits in a word (word length) depends on the particular computer system and is the number of bits that the CPU treats as a single working unit, usually 8, 16, 32, 64 or 128.

word processor (WP): a software *applications package* used for the creation of mainly text-based documents. Word processors have several important features, such as *templates, spell checkers* and grammar checkers, *mail-merge, WYSIWYG* capability and the ability to view the document in different sizes and layouts. Word processing is the production, editing, formatting, storing and outputting of typed documents such as letters, agendas and memos.

word wrap: a system in an editing or word processing application in which the operator does not have to indicate the line endings, but can use the keyboard continuously, leaving the word processor to insert word breaks and to continue the text on the next line. See also *wrap around, soft return*.

words accessed randomly per second (WARPS): a measure of memory access performance. It is equal to the rate of uniformly random accesses across the whole of the address space visible to a process that a machine supports.

work file: a backing store file reserved as a temporary working area for use by an application.

workbook: a *file* containing a number of related *worksheets* in a *spreadsheet* program.

workgroup: a general term that refers to a collection of computers connected by a *network*. The workgroup would normally refer to a group of PCs that are being used to do similar things, for example data entry stations, or which form a section of a company such as a payroll department. Several workgroups can be connected to the same cabling system.

working set: those values from shared memory that a process has copied into its private memory, or those pages of *virtual memory* being used by a process. Other processes do not automatically see changes a process makes to the values in its working set.

working store: a section of *memory* reserved as a temporary working area for use by an application.

worksheet: in a *spreadsheet* application, a page appearing on screen organised into *rows* and *columns*. A *cell* in the worksheet is identified by letter(s) and a number, e.g. B23 (column B row 23), AA34 (column AA row 34), CE5 (column CE row 5). Each cell can contain

- a number (e.g. 36)
- text (e.g. 'Materials cost')
- a formula (e.g. =B4 + C5).

The user can define what type of data is in each cell, the format to be used when displaying the content of each cell (currency, number of decimal places, etc.), the name to be associated with a particular cell or group of cells and how different cells are related to each other using formulae.

Having designed the worksheet by defining the cells and the formulae linking them together, the user can enter the data. By changing the contents of cells the user can look at several 'what-if' scenarios.

The more powerful spreadsheet applications include graphics features that enable the user to produce charts and graphs from the data. It is also possible to link one worksheet to another so that a change made in one worksheet automatically affects the other worksheet.

workstation: the term is now used to refer to any *personal computer*, such as an IBM PC or an Apple Macintosh linked to a network.

Historically the term was used to refer to powerful computer systems, usually with graphics-oriented displays intended for use on *local area networks*. Workstations in this sense usually ran the *Unix* operating system and were often made by Sun or Hewlett Packard.

world: a three-dimensional (3D) scene that is displayed on a *web site* and allows a user to move around the scene exploring the visible objects; the entire scene is created using a special *plug-in* extension to a *web browser*.

World Wide Web (WWW)(W3): a collection of all the resources (HTML documents, images, and other files, as well as CGI interface programs) accessible on the *Internet*, mainly via the *hypertext transfer protocol* (HTTP) but also via older protocols and mechanisms, such as the *file transfer protocol* (FTP) or *Gopher*, which are supported by most *web browsers*. The emergence of web browsers has made access to these resources achievable to a broad base of users beyond the more technically aware traditional users of the Internet, who relied on less user-friendly access tools than currently available browsers.

'Internet' and 'World Wide Web' are becoming interchangable terms through misuse in the media. The Internet is the world wide 'network of networks', whereas the World Wide Web is the name for the resources accessible on the Internet.

World Wide Web Consortium (W3C): this international group includes representatives from industry and academia and is based at Massachusetts Institute of Technology (MIT). The members of the group work together to develop common standards for the *World Wide Web* and the group was responsible for the *hypertext mark up language* (HTML) standard for building *web pages*.

worm: a type of computer *virus* commonly found on *networks* and in particular the *Internet*. A worm replicates itself and hides in a computer's memory, causing the system to crash (*system crash*) or slow down, but does not damage or destroy files. Many worms are created as a research or programming challenge. Successful worms can seriously slow down the Internet.

wormhole routing: a technique for routing messages in which the head of the message establishes a path, which is reserved for the message until the tail has passed through it. Using this method of data transmission the tail proceeds at a rate dictated by the progress of the head, which reduces the demand for intermediate buffering. See also *packet switching*.

wrap around: the flowing or 'wrapping' of text around a text box, shape, picture or object within a document. In the example on page 252 the text is wrapped around the image of two graduates.

To move text to the next line rather than stopping when the cursor reaches the end of the current line (word wrap). It is also applied to text flowing or 'wrapping' around a text box, shape, picture or object within a document.

The term is also sometimes used to indicate the moving of text to the beginning of the next line, rather than stopping when the cursor reaches the end of the current line (*word wrap*).

wrist support: a device placed in front of a *keyboard* to support the wrists, thereby safeguarding the user against *repetitive strain injuries* (RSI).

writable instruction set computer (WISC): a *processor* design that allows a programmer to add extra *machine code* instructions using *microcode* to customise the *instruction set*.

write: a term used when a *record* of *data* in memory is made on some suitable storage medium. The act of writing data will usually destroy (overwrite) any data that used to be stored in the same place.

write-back cache: see *write-in cache*.

write black printer: a laser *printer* where toner sticks to the points hit by the laser beam when the image drum is scanned. This type of printer produces sharp edges and graphics but large areas of black are muddy. See also *white writer*.

write head: the part of the *magnetic disk* or *magnetic tape* unit that writes the data to the magnetic media. See also *read/write head*.

write-in cache: *cache* memory that holds the data until a device is ready for the transfer to take place. This type of temporary cache memory only saves the data to disk or main memory when the central *processor* instructs it to do so. This type of cache is also referred to as write-back cache.

write inhibit ring: a ring on a reel of *magnetic tape* which, if it is present, stops the tape from being overwritten or erased.

On some magnetic tape units the technology is set up in the opposite way so that the ring acts as a *write permit ring*. Computer operators moving to different companies need to be sure of the technology in use at their new organisation.

write once read many (WORM): one type of optical disk that allows the user to write data to it once but read that data back many times. Some WORMs allow data to be overwritten so that it is erased. A multi-session *CD-R* is an example of a WORM.

write permit ring: a ring on a reel of *magnetic tape* which allows the tape to be overwritten or erased when it is present. The ring is placed in a groove on the back of the tape spool and only when it is present can data be transferred to the tape. The ring depresses a small switch that activates the write circuits on the tape unit. The equivalent on magnetic tape cassettes is the tab on the back of the cassette that can be removed to protect the contents of the cassette. However, once removed this tab cannot be replaced.

On some magnetic tape units the technology is set up in the opposite way so that the ring acts as a *write inhibit ring*. Computer operators moving to different companies need to be sure of the technology in use at their new organisation.

write protection: a device on disks and tapes that provides data *security* by allowing data to be read but not deleted, altered or overwritten. An example of write protection is the notch in the top right of a *floppy disk*. Closing the slider on the floppy disk so that the hole is closed means the disk is not write protected whereas opening the hole so that light shines through means that the disk is write protected.

write-through cache: *cache* memory in which writes to memory are performed concurrently in both the cache memory and in the main memory.

WYSIAYG: an acronym for 'what you see is all you get'. The output on screen for software applications with this feature cannot be printed out in any other form, i.e. it cannot contain hidden print or formatting commands.

WYSIWYG: an acronym for 'what you see is what you get', that is the screen contents reflect what would be printed out.

X/Open: a group of organisations that is responsible for promoting open systems. The group merged with the Open Software Foundation to form The Open Group in 1996.

x-axis: the horizontal axis of a graph, chart or grid that has horizontal and vertical dimensions. In mathematics, the x-axis and the *y-axis* are together called Cartesian co-ordinates.

Xerographic printer: a printer that makes use of the photocopying techniques developed by the Xerox company.

XGA: extended graphics array. A standard for colour video graphics adapters used in PCs which allows a resolution of 1024×768 pixels with 256 colours or 25,536 colours with a resolution of 640×480 pixels on an *interlaced* display.

XMODEM: the standard file transfer and error detecting protocol used when transmitting data from computer to computer using a *modem* (asynchronous data transmissions). This *file-transfer protocol* (FTP) was established to make transferring data over telephone lines fast and error free.

XMS: extended memory specification. The rules that define how a *program* should access extended memory fitted in a PC.

XNOR gate: a logic gate that is a NOT(XOR) gate. The two inputs to the logic gate have to be the same to generate a 1 as output. The truth table that represents the actions of the XNOR gate is:

Input A	Input B	Output
0	0	1
0	1	0
1	0	0
1	1	1

In electronic circuit diagrams the symbol for the XNOR gate is:

XNS: the Xerox Networking Standard. It is Xerox's proprietary networking suite of *protocols* and is similar to *transmission control protocol/Internet protocol* (TCP/IP).

XON/XOFF: an *asynchronous transmission protocol* that allows the user at each end to control the data flow by transmitting special codes.

XOR gate: a logic gate that is similar to an *OR gate* but excludes the situation where all inputs are 1, which in this case gives a 0 output. The two inputs to the logic gate have to be different to generate a 1 output. The truth table that represents the actions of the XOR gate is:

Input A	Input B	Output
0	0	0
0	I	I
I	0	I
I	I	0

In electronic circuit diagrams the symbol for the XOR gate is:

x-y plotter: a device for drawing lines on paper between given co-ordinates. The paper is normally laid flat on the *plotter* and the pen moved by a pair of motors connected to the penholder. Changing the colour of the line is achieved by changing the pen, which can be done automatically or by hand, depending on the cost of the plotter.

y-axis: the vertical axis of a graph, chart or grid that has horizontal and vertical dimensions. In mathematics, the *x-axis* and the y-axis are together called Cartesian co-ordinates. 'Money generated' represents the y-axis and 'Course titles' the x-axis in the chart below.

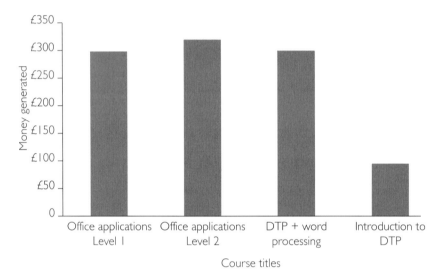

Y2K: an acronym for the year 2000 problem, where programmers wrote *program source code* before 1999 without considering how it would work beyond 1999. This problem arose as a consequence of programmers only allowing two digits for the year when storing dates. One problem that arises as a result of this is that data will not sort into date order correctly. Dates are stored Year, Month, Day to allow sorting to take place, e.g. 18th Mar 1997 is held as 970318. Thus the three dates 18th Mar 1997(970318), 5th April 1999 (990405) and 23rd Nov 2000 (001123) would appear in the order 23rd Nov 2000, 18th Mar 1997, 5th April 1999 when sorted into ascending order (001123 is less than 970318, which is less than 990405). This order is clearly not the order the user would expect (18th Mar 1997, 5th April 1999, 23rd Nov 2000), which is achieved by allowing four digits for the year.

Many old programs used two digits for the year and because they are made up of thousands of lines of code it took many hours to find the lines that need modification.

Yahoo: a *search engine* for the *World Wide Web* (WWW) based on a catalogue of indexed resources. It was created by two students at Stanford University and was for some time the only search engine available for the WWW. It can be found at http://www.yahoo.com.

Yellow Pages: a database that contains a list of *web sites* together with a brief description of each site. This database can be searched by *Internet* users to find relevant sites. A similar database of e-mail addresses is called *White pages*.

YMODEM: an enhanced version of *XMODEM*. A *file-transfer protocol* that uses 1024 byte blocks and can send multiple *files*.

zap: to wipe out or destroy all the data in a workspace.

z-axis: the axis in a three-dimensional graph that normally represents depth.

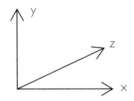

zero fill: to fill a section of memory with zero values. The term is often used when every cell in a block of cells in a spreadsheet has to be filled with the value zero.

zero insertion force socket (ZIF socket) is a socket for a *chip* that has moveable connection terminals. The chip is inserted without using any force, then a small lever is turned to make the connection terminals grip the legs of the chip. Removal of the chip is carried out by first releasing the lever.

zero wait state: the state of a device that is fast enough to run at the same speed as the other components in a computer. A device in this state does not have to be slowed by inserting wait states.

ZIP: an open standard for compression and decompression of files. It is widely used for storing large files on Internet sites, allowing faster download times. It is also used when archiving files or backups, where limited storage space is available. ZIP files are normally generated by WINZIP or a shareware utility program called PKZIP.

Zip disk: a 100 Mbyte or 250 Mbyte removable disk developed by Iomega. Zip disks are normally used to backup part of a hard drive or to transfer data from one computer to another.

Zmodem: an enhanced version of *XMODEM*. It is a file transfer *protocol* that includes error detection and the ability to re-start a data transfer where it left off if the connection is lost.

zoom: enlarging an area of a graphic or section of text to make it easier to work on. Many programs, for example drawing, spreadsheet and word processing programs, have zoom as a function or menu option. It allows the user to select a small part of an image or a document in a window, select zoom, and make changes to the enlarged portion at a finer level of detail.

APPENDIX 1
ACRONYMS

3GL	third generation language
4GL	fourth generation language
A to D	analogue to digital
ACC	accumulator
ACIA	asynchronous communications interface adapter
ADC	analogue to digital converter
ADFS	advanced disk filing system
ADSR	attack, decay, sustain and release
AI	artificial intelligence
ALU	arithmetic logic unit
AM	amplitude modulation
ANSI	American National Standards Institute
AOL	America Online
APT	automatically programmed tools
ARM	advanced RISC machine
ARPAnet	Advanced Research Project Agency network
ARQ	automatic repeat request
ASCII	American Standard Code for Information Interchange
ASR	automatic send receive
ATAPI	advanced technology attachment packet interface
ATM	automatic teller machine
AUP	acceptable use policy
BBS	bulletin board system
BCC	block check character
BCD	binary coded decimal
BIOS	basic input output system
BIT	binary digit
BNF	Bachus–Naur form
BPI	bits per inch
BPP	bits per pixel
BPS	bits per second
BSA	Business Software Alliance
BSI	British Standards Institute
CAD	computer-aided design
CAI	computer-aided instruction
CAL	computer-aided learning
CAM	computer-aided manufacturing
CASE	computer-aided software engineering
CBT	computer-based training
CD	compact disk
CD-R	compact disk–recordable
CD-ROM	compact disk–read-only memory

acronyms

CD-RW	compact disk–rewritable
CGA	colour graphics adapter
CIR	current instruction register
CISC	complex instruction set computer
CML	computer managed learning
CMOS	complementary metal oxide semiconductor
CMYK	cyan, magenta, yellow, key (black)
COM	computer output on microfilm
CPS	characters per second
CPU	central processing unit
CR/LF	carriage return/line feed
CRC	cyclic redundancy check
CRT	cathode ray tube
CSCD	carrier sense collision detect
CSMA-CD	carrier sense multiple access collision detection
CSS	content scrambling system
CUG	closed user group
D to A	digital to analogue
DAC	digital-to-analogue converter
DAT	digital audio tape
DBA	database administrator
DBMS	database management system
DCD	data carrier detect
DDE	direct data entry
DDE	dynamic data exchange
DDL	data description language
DEC	Digital Equipment Corporation
DES	data encryption standard
DFD	data flow diagram
DIL	dual in line
DIN	Deutsche Industrie Norm
DIP	dual in-line package
DMA	direct memory access
DML	data manipulation language
DOS	disk operating system
DPA	Data Protection Act
DRAM	dynamic random access memory
DTE	data terminal equipment
DTP	desktop publishing
DVD	digital versatile disc
DVD	digital video disc
EAN	European article number
EAROM	electrically alterable read-only memory
EBCDIC	extended binary coded decimal interchange code
EDI	electronic data interchange
E-form	electronic form
EFT	electronic funds transfer

EFTPOS	electronic funds transfer at point of sale
EGA	enhanced graphics adapter
EISA	extended industry standard architecture
E-mail	electronic mail
EOF	end of file
EOR	exclusive-OR
EPOS	electronic point of sale
EPROM	erasable programmable read-only memory
Esc	escape key
FAQ	frequently asked question
FAST	Federation Against Software Theft
FAT	file-allocation table
FAX	facsimile
FDDI	fibre-distributed data interface
FDM	frequency division multiplexing
FIFO	first in first out
FM	frequency modulation
FMV	full-motion video
FSM	frequency shift modulation
FTP	file-transfer protocol
Gb	gigabyte
GIGO	garbage in garbage out
GIS	geographical information system
GUI	graphical user interface
Hex	hexadecimal
HTML	hypertext mark up language
HTTP	hypertext transfer protocol
I/O	input/output
IAB	Internet Architecture Board
IAM	immediate access memory
IAP	Internet access provider
IAR	instruction address register
IAS	immediate access store
IBG	inter-block gap
IC	integrated circuit
ICANN	Internet Corporation of Assigned Names and Numbers
IDE	integrated drive electronics
IKBS	intelligent knowledge-based system
InterNIC	Internet Network Information Centre
IP	Internet protocol
IR	instruction register
IRC	Internet relay chat
ISA	industry standard architecture
ISAM	indexed sequential access method
ISBN	international standard book number
ISDN	integrated services digital network
ISM	industry structure model

acronyms

ISO	International Standards Organisation
ISOC	Internet Society
ISP	Internet service provider
ISR	interrupt service routine
ITDM	intelligent time division multiplexing
JANET	joint academic network
JCL	job-control language
JDBC	Java database connectivity
JPEG	joint photographic expert group
JSD	Jackson structured development
JSP	Jackson structured programming
Kb	kilobyte
KBS	knowledge-based system
LAN	local area network
LAWN	local area wireless network
LCD	liquid-crystal display
LED	light emitting diode
LIFO	last in first out
LQ	letter quality
LRC	longitudinal redundancy check
LSB	least significant bit
LSI	large-scale integration
MAC address	media access control address
MAC protocol	medium access control protocol
MAN	metropolitan area network
MAR	memory address register
MAU	multiple access unit
Mb	megabyte
MBONE	multicast backbone
MBR	memory buffer register
MDR	memory data register
MICR	magnetic-ink character recognition
MIDI	musical instrument digital interface
MIME	multipurpose Internet mail extension
MIPS	million instructions per second
MIS	management information systems
MMI	man–machine interface
MMU	memory management unit
MOS	metal oxide semiconductor
MP3	motion picture expert group audio layer 3
MPEG	moving picture experts group
ms	millisecond
MSB	most significant bit
MS-DOS	Microsoft disk operating system
MSI	medium scale integration
MTBF	mean time between failures
MTF	mean time to failure

MUD	multi-user dungeon
NAP	network access points
NBCD	natural binary coded decimal
NETBIOS	network basic input/output system
NIC	network interface card
NLQ	near letter quality
NMI	non-maskable interrupt
NNTP	network news transfer protocol
NOS	network operating system
ns	nanosecond
NTP	network time protocol
OCR	optical character recognition
OEM	original equipment manufacturer
OLAP	on-line analytical processing
OLE	object linking and embedding
OMR	optical mark reader
OOD	object oriented design
OOL	object oriented language
OOP	object oriented programming
OS	operating system
OSI	open systems interconnection
PABX	private automatic branch exchange
PAD	packet assembler/disassembler
PAL	phase alternation by line
passive FTP	passive file transfer protocol
PBE	private branch exchange
PC	program counter
PC	personal computer
PCI bus	peripheral component interconnect bus
PCL	printer control language
PCM	pulse code modulation
PCMCIA card	personal computer memory card international association card
PDA	personal digital assistant
PDL	page description language
PDM	pulse duration modulation
PERT	program evaluation and review technique
PGP	pretty good privacy
PID	personal identification device
PIN	personal identification number
PING	packet Internet groper
PIO	parallel input/output
PLA	programmable logic array
PMS	pantone matching system
POP	point of presence
POS terminal	point-of-sale terminal
POST	power on self-test
PPM	pages per minute

acronyms

PPP	point-to-point protocol
PROM	programmable read-only memory
PRR	pulse repetition rate
PSN	packet switched network
PSS	packet switching system
PSTN	public switched telephone network
PSU	power supply unit
QBE	query by example
R/W	read/write
RAID	redundant array of independent (or inexpensive) disks
RAM	random access memory
RDBMS	relational database management systems
RGB	red green blue
RISC	reduced instruction set computer
RJE	remote job entry
ROM	read-only memory
RPG	report program generator
RPN	reverse polish notation
RPROM	reprogrammable read-only memory
RSA algorithm	Rivest, Shamir, Adleman algorithm
RSI	repetitive strain injury
RTF	rich text format
RTP	real-time transport protocol
SCART	Syndicat des Constructeurs d'Appareils de Radio et de Télévision
SCR	sequence control register
SCSI	small computer systems interface
SDRAM	synchronous dynamic random access memory
SET	secure electronic transaction
SIG	special interest group
SIMM	single in-line memory module
SIO	serial input/output
SLIP	serial line Internet protocol
SLSI	super large scale integration
SMPTE	Society of Motion Picture and Television Engineers (USA)
SMTP	simple mail transport protocol
SNA	systems network architecture
SP	stack pointer
SQL	structured query language
SSADM	structured systems analysis and design method
SSD	solid state drive
SSI	small scale integration
SSL	secure socket layer
SVGA	super video graphics array
SYSOP	system operator
TCP	transmission control protocol
TCP/IP	transmission control protocol/Internet protocol
TDM	time division multiplexing

acronyms

TIFF	tagged image file format
TP	twisted pair
TSR	terminate and stay resident
UART	universal asynchronous receiver/transmitter
UIMS	user interface management system
ULA	uncommitted logic array
UMA	upper memory area
UMB	upper memory block
UPC	universal product code
UPS	uninterruptable power supply
URL	uniform resource locator
USART	universal synchronous/asynchronous receiver/transmitter
USB	universal serial bus
USRT	universal synchronous receiver/transmitter
UTP	unshielded twisted pair
UUCP	Unix to Unix copy program
UV	ultraviolet
VAN	value added network
VANS	value added network service
VAR	value added reseller
VAX	Virtual Address eXtension
VBA	Visual Basic for applications
VBScript	Visual Basic Script
VCR	videocassette recorder
VDSL	very high data rate digital subscriber line
VDU	visual display unit
VESA	Video Electronics Standards Association
VFW	Video For Windows™
VGA	video graphics array
VHF	very high frequency
VHS	vertical helical scan
VLIW	very long instruction word
VLSI	very large scale integration
VM	virtual memory
VPD	vital product data
VPOP	virtual point of presence
VR	virtual reality
VRAM	video random access memory
VRC	vertical redundancy check
VRML	virtual reality modelling language
VRR	vertical refresh rate
VTOC	volume table of contents
W3	World Wide Web
W3C	World Wide Web Consortium
WAIS	wide area information server
WAN	wide area network
WAP	wireless application protocol

acronyms

WARPS	words accessed randomly per second
WIMP	windows, icons, mouse, pointer
WINSOCK	Windows Sockets
WISC	writable instruction set computer
WMF	Windows metafile format
WML	wireless markup language
WORM	write once read many
WP	word processor
WRAM	Windows random access memory
WWW	World Wide Web
WYSIAYG	what you see is all you get
WYSIWYG	what you see is what you get
XGA	extended graphics array
XMS	extended memory specification
XNS	Xerox networking standard
Y2K	year 2000 problem
ZIF	zero insertion force

acronyms

APPENDIX 2
FILE EXTENSIONS

File extension	Type of file
.123	Lotus 123 spreadsheet file
.ad	After Dark screensaver file
.ada	source file in Ada
.ai	Adobe Illustrator vector graphic file
.ani	**1** animation file **2** animated cursor file in Microsoft Windows 9*x* and Windows NT
.aps	Microsoft Visual C++ source file
.arc	archive file compressed with ARC
.arj	archive file compressed with ARJ
.asc	ASCII text file
.asm	assembler source file
.atm	Adobe Type Manager file
.avi	audio visual interleaved data file
.bac	see .bak
.bak	backup file
.bas	Basic source file
.bat	batch program file
.bfc	briefcase file in Microsoft Windows 9*x*.
.bin	**1** binary file **2** archive file compressed with MacBinary
.bk	see .bak
.bmk	bookmarked file
.bmp	raster graphics file stored in bitmap format
.box	Lotus Notes mailbox file
.c	C source file
.c++	C++ source file
.cas	comma-delimited ASCII text file.
.cb	Microsoft Windows clean boot file
.cbl	Cobol source file
.cca	Lotus cc:mail e-mail message
.cda	CD audio track
.cdr	Corel Draw vector graphics file
.cgm	vector graphics file in computer graphics metafile format
.chk	portions of unidentifiable files saved in Windows by the Disk Defragmentor or ScanDisk utilities
.chm	file containing compiled HTML
.clp	temporary file created by the Microsoft Windows clipboard utility
.cmd	command file in Windows NT, OS/2, MS-DOS, and CP/M
.cmf	Corel Metafile file

file extensions

.cob	Cobol source file
.com	command file or program
.cpl	control panel file in Microsoft Windows 9*x*.
.cpp	C++ source file
.csv	comma-delimited text file (comma separated values)
.ct	Paint Shop Pro graphics file
.cur	cursor file in Windows
.cxx	C++ source file
.dat	data file
.dbf	database in DBASE and FoxPro
.dcr	Macromedia Shockwave multimedia file
.dif	data interchange format file
.dll	dynamic-link library file
.doc	**1** Microsoft Word document file
	2 document file formatted for a word processor
.dos	MS-DOS-related files in Microsoft Windows 9*x*
.dot	Microsoft Word document template
.drv	device driver
.dtp	Microsoft Publisher document file
.dv	video file
.emf	file in Enhanced Windows Metafile format.
.eml	Microsoft Outlook Express mail message
.eps	encapsulated PostScript file
.exe	executable program or file.
.F	Fortran source file
.fax	fax file in many fax programs.
.fdf	Adobe Acrobat Forms file
.fla	Macromedia Flash movie file
.flf	device driver in OS/2.
.fm	Adobe FrameMaker document file
.fon	Windows system font file
.for	Fortran source file
.fp	FileMaker Pro file
.fpt	see .fp
.frm	Adobe FrameMaker document file
.gid	index file in Windows 9*x*.
.gif	raster image file in GIF format
.giff	see .gif
.hex	file encoded with Macintosh BinHex utility
.hlp	Microsoft Windows help file
.htm	see .html
.html	HTML file, most commonly used as a web page
.ico	icon file in Microsoft Windows 95 or 98
.image	image file in Macintosh disk image format
.inf	device information file, which contains scripts used to control hardware operations in MS-DOS and Windows 3.*x*

.ini	an initialisation file, which contains user preferences and start up information about an application program
.jav	Java source file
.java	Java source file
.jpeg	see .jpg
.jpg	graphic image file encoded in the JPEG file interchange format
.js	JavaScript source file
.l	LISP source file
.lha	see .lzh
.lib	library file in many programming languages
.lnk	Windows 95, 98 and NT 4 shortcut file
.log	log file
.lsp	LISP source file
.lzh	archive file compressed with LZH
.mac	MacPaint image file
.mak	Microsoft Visual Basic or Visual C++ project file
.mbx	Microsoft Outlook address file
.mcw	Microsoft Word for Macintosh document file
.mdb	Microsoft Access database
.mid	music file in MIDI format
.midi	see .mid
.mime	file encoded in MIME format
.moov	see .mov
.mov	Apple QuickTime video file
.movie	see .mov
.mpe	see .mpg
.mpeg	see .mpg
.mpg	compressed video and audio file in MPEG format
.mpp	1 CAD format graphics file 2 Microsoft Project file
.msg	Microsoft Outlook e-mail message
.net	network configuration file
.nsf	Lotus Notes database
.nws	Microsoft Outlook Express news message file
.obd	Microsoft Office binder file
.ocx	Microsoft OLE control
.ole	Microsoft OLE object
.pas	Pascal source file
.p65	PageMaker 6.5 document file
.pab	Microsoft Outlook address book file
.pcx	PC Paintbrush bitmapped image file
.pdf	document file encoded in Adobe Portable Document Format
.pic	1 PC. Paint format image file 2 see .pict
.pict	Macintosh PICT image file
.pl	Prolog source file

file extensions

.pps	**1** Paint Shop Pro image file
	2 Microsoft PowerPoint slide show file
.ppt	Microsoft PowerPoint presentation file
.ps	PostScript printer file
.psd	Adobe PhotoShop image file
.pst	Microsoft Outlook personal file folder
.pub	document file in Adobe PageMaker, Microsoft Publisher or Ventura Publisher
.pwl	Microsoft Windows 95 or 98 password file
.qic	back-up file in Microsoft Backup
.qif	see .qti
.qt	see .qtm
.qti	Apple QuickTime image file
.qtif	see .qti
.qtm	Apple QuickTime movie file
.qts	see .qti
.qtx	see .qti
.qxd	QuarkXPress document file
.ra	RealAudio sound file
.ras	RealAudio metafile
.rm	RealAudio video file
.rtf	rich text format document file
.sam	Lotus Ami Professional document file
.s	assembler source file
.sav	**1** saved backup file
	2 saved file in many games
.scd	Microsoft Schedule+ file
.scr	Microsoft Windows screensaver file
.shtml	secure file in HTML
.sig	signature file for e-mail or Internet newsgroup
.snd	sound resource file on the Macintosh.
.spl	Macromedia Shockwave Flash file
.sql	SQL query or report file
.swa	Macromedia Shockwave audio file
.swf	Macromedia Shockwave Flash file
.swp	Microsoft Windows swap file
.sys	system configuration file
.tif	bitmap images in TIFF format
.tiff	see .tif
.tmp	Windows temporary file
.tsv	tab separated values file
.ttf	TrueType font file
.txt	ASCII text file
.url	shortcut file on the Internet for a URL
.uu	see .uud.
.uud	binary file that has been translated into ASCII format using uuencode

.uue	file that has been decoded from ASCII format back into binary format using uudecode
.vbx	Microsoft Visual Basic custom control
.vp	Ventura Publisher document file
.vxd	Microsoft Windows virtual device driver
.wab	Microsoft Outlook Express e-mail file
.wav	sound file stored in waveform audio format (WAV)
.wmf	vector image file encoded as Windows Metafile
.wp	Corel WordPerfect document file
.wp6	Corel WordPerfect 6.*x* document file
.wpd	see .wp
.wpg	Corel WordPerfect graphic file
.wps	Microsoft Works document file
.wri	Microsoft Write document file
.xls	Microsoft Excel spreadsheet file
.xlt	Microsoft Excel spreadsheet template
.xlw	Microsoft Excel workbook
.zip	PKZIP or WinZip archive file compressed in ZIP format

APPENDIX 3
USEFUL WEB SITE ADDRESSES

Search engines

AltaVista:	http://www.altavista.com
AOL Search:	http://search.aol.com/
Ask Jeeves:	http://www.ask.co.uk/
Excite:	http://www.excite.com/
Google:	http://www.google.com
HotBot:	http://hotbot.lycos.com/
LookSmart:	http://www.looksmart.com/
Lycos:	http://www.lycos.co.uk/
MSN Search:	http://search.msn.com/
Netscape Search:	http://search.netscape.com/
Yahoo:	http://www.yahoo.com/

Information about search engines

Search Engine Watch:	http://www.searchenginewatch.com/

Sites with information on other important aspects of ICT and Computing

British Computer Society:	http://www.bcs.org.uk
Business Software Alliance:	http://www.bsa.org
Data Protection Act 1998:	http://www.dataprotection.gov.uk/
	http://www.dpr.gov.uk/
	http://www.hmso.gov.uk/acts/acts1998/19980029.htm
Internet Society:	http://www.isoc.org/
UnCover:	http://www.carl.org/uncover

APPENDIX 4
EXAMINERS' TERMS

Introduction

The following entries should help explain what examiners mean by the words they use in exam questions. It is important to remember, though, that the words are only half the story. The other key factor is the mark allocation. This not only gives an indication of the length of answer, but also the depth required.

Most A-level candidates put many hours into revising and go into the examination with a sound knowledge and understanding of a lot of basic computing/ICT. Unfortunately, some fail to do themselves credit when it comes to turning this hard-won knowledge into marks. One of the main reasons for this is that they fail to follow the instructions given in the questions.

Every year, this point is noted by the examiners and such statements as 'many candidates did not appreciate that the words "describe" and "explain" do not have the same meaning' and 'many candidates did not relate their answers to the specific application area given in the question', appear regularly in the examiners' reports produced by the different boards. Use this appendix from the start of your course to make sure that you get into the habit of giving the required answer. The one expression that you will not find in any examination question is 'Write all you know about …' and yet that is what many candidates do! Surprising as it may seem, the examiners are on your side and want to reward you for the work you've done preparing for the examination. They want to see what you know and give you credit. They can help you only if you help yourself by following the instructions that you have been given.

The following list explains the terms that examiners use.

Compare: this requires candidates to point out similarities and differences between given terms or items. Do not put a positive feature for one and then a negative feature for the other: e.g. e-mail is normally a very fast way of communicating; ordinary post is not a quick way of communicating.

Define requires a simple explanation of the technical term in the context of the question as precisely as you can; giving an example or drawing a diagram can help, but is not a substitute for explanation.

Describe usually means give a step-by-step account of what is being asked for. The amount of detail can be determined by looking at the mark allocation.

Discuss means put forward both sides of a case before coming to a conclusion. Discussion would require continuous writing.

Evaluate: this vital term means to weigh up evidence in order to reach a judgement. In the context of an essay, you will have to present that evidence before reaching a conclusion. As the term invites your judgement, do be willing to state your opinion within the conclusion; e.g. 'In my view …'.

Explain: this is asking you why? or to expand upon, in order to show your understanding of the term or theory being tested. It is not a description but is looking for reasons and for you to show more than simple recall. This is probably the term that loses candidates the most marks, as they do not interpret it correctly. The depth of explanation required will be indicated by the mark allocation. Giving a well chosen example will often gain a mark.

Give: this means list, as in, 'Give three current advantages … '. There is no requirement to explain the points you make. Point-form answers are acceptable. Do not write out the question again and do not make the answer into a lengthy sentence. If it says 'Give two examples', then give only two examples and make sure that they are significantly different.

Give two reasons/Give three examples: if a number of reasons or examples is required, these must be different from each other. Care should be taken to give no more than the required number of points.

Identify: to name one or more examples of the topic being examined. Usually this would require no more than a list, with one mark awarded per point made.

Justify your answer: present an argument in favour of the views you are expressing, for example: 'Should the Ambulance Service be computerised? Justify your answer.' Although the question appears to be expecting a yes or no at the outset, it is better to wait until the end to state your opinion, because by then you will have given the matter enough thought to be able to justify your decision.

List: (the same as *give*) briefly state, not necessarily in a full sentence.

Name: the same as *list* or *give*.

Show your working: this phrase is often used with numerical questions, but should never be ignored. In the pressure of the exam room, almost every candidate will slip up somewhere in a complex calculation.

Sketch a diagram: this suggests a quick drawing on the ordinary exam writing paper, paying little attention to precision in the lines being drawn. However, to convey any meaning, the sketch will need to be properly labelled. With sketches, the labelling may carry more marks than the diagram itself.

State: this means the same as *give*.

State and explain: this should be tackled exactly in this way; i.e. give a reason (in perhaps 4–8 words) then explain it (in perhaps 4–8 lines).

Suggest means to put forward an idea. If few marks are allocated, this might require no more than a list of points. The word is used more commonly, though, in the context of identifying appropriate peripherals for an application; e.g. 'Suggest a suitable interface for a partially sighted person.' In this case you would need to give a full explanation and justification for the suggestions made.

What do you understand by (or **What is meant by?**): explain the meaning of the term or phrase given. An example may be helpful, but is not a substitute for explanation.

APPENDIX 5
HINTS FOR EXAM SUCCESS

Examiners see the work of large numbers of candidates over a number of years. It is quite surprising how often the same basic mistakes and errors continue to be made. This section contains a number of basic hints on how to revise and includes a number of the more common errors made by examination candidates.

You will need to work out which method of revision works best for you. Some people work best late at night; others like to get up at some unearthly hour in the morning. Some like silence, others need the radio on. The best advice that can he given is to say: revise in the way that suits you best. However, there are several general points that are worth bearing in mind.

You need to work out your limitations and which areas of the syllabus you have difficulties with.

- You need a **revision plan**. You are probably taking more than one subject, so get the balance right. Build in the things that matter. If you have your 18th birthday coming up, allow time for the celebrations. Have your Friday evenings off. It is important to be realistic rather than idealistic.

- It is **quality** not quantity that counts. There is not very much point in working five or six hours a night if all you end up doing is gently turning pages over with very little going in. It is much better to work in short, manageable sessions during which time you keep your mind firmly on the task in hand. One and a half to two hours is about as much as most people can manage at a time. Then have a break before continuing.

- Set yourself sensible **targets**. Break the subject into bits. It is far more rewarding if, at the end of a two-hour session, you have achieved what you set out to do. So do not try to do the whole of Computing; try instead to master a single topic, e.g. ICT related legislation.

- Vary your revision where possible; read other books, read articles in ICT/computing trade papers, watch any relevant TV programmes, use interactive revision programs, etc.

- Give yourself a **reward**. When you have achieved your target, then is the time to have your cup of coffee, watch something on the television or whatever you want to do. Not before you start.

- There are things to learn and these must be learnt, but there are also skills to practise and these can only be mastered by working through examination questions in past papers. So … build into your revision programme time to learn and time to practise.

- Examiners rarely put unnecessary words in exam questions, so make sure that you read all of the question carefully.

- Make sure that you understand the work that you have done, if you only try to remember it then you will not be able to apply it.

- Make sure that you understand the ICT and computing terms in this book and that you can spell them correctly, e.g. Backus–Naur Form, validation, teleworking, etc.

- ICT is a very 'real' subject and you must understand why people/organisations use ICT – they use it for what it can do for them.

- Think bigger. Most students have a tendency to think in terms of the PC on their desk at home, or the school network. Think of rooms the size of a football pitch full of nothing but processors and disk storage or being able to withdraw money from a bank account in Manchester from Australia!

- Get a good night's sleep or take a decent lunch break before the exam! The most important thing that goes into the exam room is your brain and it does not function well if you have not had enough rest. Think of exam preparation in the same way as preparation for taking part in a sporting event.

- Stay calm! Everyone gets nervous in some way, so work out how best to relax yourself before you start writing.

- Read the whole paper through first. This is not a waste of time. It helps you to collect your thoughts and to get an idea of how long you can spend on each question. It also helps you to sort out which questions are on which topics.

- Read each question through completely before you start to answer it. This helps you to avoid problems like writing the answer needed for part b) in part a) of a question.

- Be very careful about using words like **it** and **them**. Make sure that the examiner knows what you are talking about.

- Longer questions and essays need careful planning. Don't think of this as a waste of time.

- Use an extra piece of paper to jot down ideas as you are working through the paper. You often think of points to include in answers as you go along.

- Use clear English and good handwriting. If the examiner cannot read or understand your answer then you will get no marks!

- Using examples can often help you to explain certain points if you are getting stuck putting your ideas down in writing.

- Do not use correction fluid; cross out neatly any answers that you don't want to include.

- Do not cramp your answers – the better laid out that they are, the easier they are to mark.

- Answer the questions in order; if you cannot answer a specific question or part of a question, leave a big enough space so that you can come back to it later.

- Read through your answers if you have time when you have finished. You just might think of something else to add in that could make the difference of a grade.

- Answer all of the questions. There is no point in leaving blank spaces. You just might get something down that is correct!

- Do you look at the **mark allocations**? They are there to help you. In general terms, each mark requires you to make one valid A-level point. So, three marks give you three points. You should be constantly checking on this. If you produce an answer to a question worth three marks, make sure that you have made three worthwhile points. This is a skill to practise whenever you are answering past questions. Get into the habit early and you will do it automatically in the examination. Do not spend an excessive amount of time on a three mark question.

- Perhaps you are pushed for **time**? One thing that you might bear in mind is that you do not have to write out the question before starting to put down your answer.

- And, finally, write the question numbers in the boxes provided on the front of the paper.

APPENDIX 6
REVISION LISTS FOR INFORMATION AND
COMMUNICATION TECHNOLOGY

ICT is a diverse and continually changing subject. Updates, innovations, improvements and new developments come faster than specifications can keep up. It is vital that students read as widely as possible across all topics to ensure that their knowledge is current. Specifications are written at least two years and examination papers frequently created up to a year before the students take the examinations. Although all of the basic concepts and terminology are found within this book, students should always check with their own specifications to ensure that they know which topics are within the AS and which within the A2 specifications. Frequently, topics will be given in their basic form and developed at a later stage. Different examination specifications may place topics at different levels.

The following lists contain the major topics areas and terms that are essential to an informed understanding of the whole subject and the basis of a revision framework. The lists are in alphabetical order and not comprehensive but if used together with the terms in the body of the book will give you every opportunity for examination success.

1 Knowledge, information and data

Accurate

Characteristics of information

Complete

Context

Data

Data capture

Delivery

Encoding information

Good information

Information

Knowledge

Presentation

Relevant

User confidence

Validation

Value and importance

Value judgements

Verification

2 Capabilities and limitations of ICT

Facility to search and combine data

Limitations

Quality information

Repetitive processing

Vast storage capability

3 Hardware and software

α testing, β testing
Application generators
Applications software
Communications devices
Data portability
Data protocols and standards
Display devices
Evaluation criteria
Generic software
Human/computer interface
Input and output devices
Macro capabilities

Operating system
Package software
Printers and other peripheral drivers
Processing devices
Reliability
Software evaluation
Specific and bespoke software
Storage devices
Systems software
Training
Upgrades
User support

4 Communication systems

E-mail
Fax
Internet
Recent developments
Remote databases

Teleconferencing
Telephone
Viewdata

5 Networks

Access rights
Characteristics
Elements of network environments
Local area network
Network accounting

Network audit
Network security
Passwords
Relative advantages
Wide area network

6 Legal framework

Audit requirements
Audit trails
Computer crime
Computer Misuse Act
Data Protection Act
Detection
Disciplinary procedures
Health and safety
Investigation procedures

Licensing agreements
Malpractice
Prevention of misuse
Obligations on holders of personal data
Security policy within an organisation
Software copyright
Software misuse legislation
Staff responsibilities

7 Social impact

Commerce
Education
Industry
Manufacturing

Medicine
Social, moral and ethical issues
Teleworking
The home

8 Databases

Backup procedures
Client/server database
Data consistency
Data independence
Data integrity
Data normalisation
Data redundancy
Data security
Database administrator

Distributed databases
Entity relationships
Levels of permitted access
Nature and purpose
Passwords
Relational databases
Restoration and recovery procedures
Write protect mechanisms

9 Data processing

Batch
Interactive
Output formats

Real -time
Report generation
Transaction

10 Organisational structures

Backup strategies
Codes of practice
Contingency plans
Decision making
Disaster recovery management
Future proofing
General organisation structure
Information flow
Information systems
IT professional

Legal and audit requirements
Life cycle of an information system
Management information system (MIS)
Management of change
Personnel
Project management
Responsibility for the information
    system within an organisation
Risk analysis
Success or failure of an MIS

APPENDIX 7
REVISION LISTS FOR COMPUTING

This appendix helps you with study and revision. Pick the topic you want to revise, then look up the terms listed in alphabetical order under each heading. Cross-references in the text will help you to build on these starting points. These lists are not intended to provide a comprehensive revision list but are a good starting point.

Computing has a vast number of technical terms that it is important you use confidently in your examination answers. The different syllabuses cover different aspects of what is a wide subject so it is important that you refer to the syllabus you are studying and extract the terms mentioned there to add to the lists below.

1   Applications

Artificial intelligence
Computer-aided design
Computer-aided learning
Computer-aided manufacturing
Computer-based training
Cybershopping
Desktop publishing
E-commerce
E-learning
Electronic data interchange
Electronic funds transfer
Electronic funds transfer at point-of-sale
E-mail
Expert systems
Geographical information system
Handwriting recognition
Image recognition
Informatics
Internet shopping
Knowledge-based systems
Mail merge
Natural-language processing
Neural networks
Simulation
Telecommuting

2   Binary

Adder/half adder
American Standard Code for Information Interchange
Binary coded decimal
Byte
Character code
Exponent
Extended binary coded decimal interchange code
Fixed-point notation
Floating-point notation
Hexadecimal
Least significant bit
Mantissa
Most significant bit
Normalisation of numbers
Octal notation
One's complement
Overflow error
Packed decimal
Parallel adder
Rounding error
Serial adder
Sign and magnitude
Sign bit
Truncation error
Two's complement
Unicode

3 Computer memory

Absolute address
Accumulator
Address
Address generation
Cache memory
Direct addressing
Direct memory access
Disk cache
Immediate addressing
Indexed addressing
Indirect addressing

K (kilo)
Logical address
Machine address
Main store
Mega (M)
Memory cache
Random access memory
Read-only memory
Register
Relative address
Virtual memory

4 Control applications

Actuator
Analogue signal
Analogue-to-digital converter
Automation
Digital signal
Digital-to-analogue converter

Feedback
Mask
Masking rules
Real time
Sensor

5 Databases

Candidate key
Client/server database
Composite key
Data consistency
Data definition or description language
Data dictionary
Data independence
Data-manipulation language
Data model
Data redundancy
Database management system
Database server
Distributed database
Entity

Entity-relationship diagram
Flat file database
Foreign key
Hypertext database
Normalisation of data
Primary key
Query
Query by example
Redundancy of data
Referential integrity
Relational database
Schema
Secondary key

6   Data capture and security

Access controls or levels	Hash total
Access privileges or rights	Integrity
Audit controls	Log file
Automatic data capture	Mirror site
Backup	Password
Contingency plan	Personal identification device
Data capture	Personal identification number
Data integrity	Recovery procedures
Data security	Risk analysis
Disaster avoidance	Security
Encryption	Validation
Hacker	Verification

7   Data communication

Asynchronous transmission	Half duplex
Bandwidth	Handshake
Baud	Packet
Communications link	Packet assembler/disassembler
Communications protocol	Packet switching system
Communications security	Parallel data transmission
Communications technology	Parity
Data transmission	Serial data transmission
Echo	Simplex
Full duplex	Synchronous transmission

8   Data structures

Array	Null pointer
Binary tree	One-dimensional array
Deque	Queue
Dimension	Stack
First in, first out	Subscript
Last in first out	Tree
Linked list	Two-dimensional array
Non-binary tree	Two-way linked list

9 Files

Access time
Archive file
Block
Blocking factor
Disk cylinder
End of file marker
Field
File
Hit
Index file
Index sequential file
Indexed sequential access method
Inter-block gap
Master file

Path
Random access
Random file
Record
Relative path
Sector
Seek time
Sequential access
Sequential file
Serial file
Static file
Transaction log file
Variable length field
Variable length file

10 Internet

Active content
ActiveX
Alias
Applet
ARPAnet
@ (at) sign
Attachment
Browse
Bulletin board
Data compression
Dynamic IP address
File-transfer protocol
Gopher
Home page
Hosting service

Hot spot
Hypertext mark up language
Hypertext transfer protocol
Hyperlink
Hypertext
Hypertext database
Internet
Internet protocol
Internet protocol address
Internet Relay Chat
Internet service provider
Multicast
Packet Internet groper
Web site
World Wide Web

11 Legislation

Abuse – computer
Acceptable-use policy
Codes of conduct
Codes of practice
Computer crime
Computer Misuse Act
Copyright, Designs & Patents Act
  (1988)
Data Protection Act 1998
European Union Health and Safety

  Regulations
Federation Against Software Theft
Freedom of Information Acts
Health & Safety (Display Screen
  Equipment) Regulations 1992
Licence agreement
Non-disclosure agreement
Site licence
Software copyright
Software licence

12 Networks

Account
Authentication
Backbone
Bridge
Client/server architecture
Distributed network
Ethernet
Extranet
Fibre-distributed data interface
Fibre-optic cable
Firewall
Gateway
Heterogeneous network
Homogenous network
Hub
Integrated services digital network
Local area network

Metropolitan area network
Network
Network accounting software
Network accounts
Network directory
Network security
Network topology
Open systems interconnection
Peer-to-peer network
Ring network
Router
Segment
Star network
Token ring network
Topology
Wide area network

13 Operating systems

Autonomous peripheral transfer
Background processing
Batch processing
Bootstrap
Deadlock
Foreground/background processing
Interactive processing
Interrupt
Job-control program
Job scheduling
Kernel
Loader
Memory protection
Multi-access

Multiprogramming
Multi-tasking
On-line transaction processing
Operating system
Parallel processing
Pipelining
Polling
Process state
Real time
Round robin
Scheduler
Single tasking
Task management
Time sharing system

14 Peripherals

Automatic teller machine
Backing store
Bar code reader or scanner
CD-ROM drive
Digital versatile disk
Document reader
Dot-matrix printer
Double buffering
Flatbed plotter
Flatbed scanner
Floppy disk drive
Graph plotter
Graphics pad or tablet

Hand-held scanner
Hard disk drive
Hot swapping
Laser printer
Magnetic-ink character recognition
Magnetic strip card
Mark sense reader
Mouse
Optical character recognition
Optical mark reader
Plotter
Point-of-sale terminal
Scanner

15 Program constructs

Assignment operator
Boolean variable
Branch instruction
Declaration
Dummy variable
Flag
For loop
Function
Global variable
Iteration
Jump
Label
Literal

Local variable
Loop
Nested structure (loops, procedures, etc.)
Numeric data type
Procedure
Recursion
Repeat until loop
Rogue value
Subprogram
Unconditional jump/branch
Variable
While loop

16 Program language types

Assembly language
Bespoke software
Block structured language
Computer languages
Customising software
Declarative language
Functional programming
Generic software
Imperative language

Low-level language
Machine code
Non-procedural language
Object linking and embedding
Object oriented language
Object oriented programming
Procedural language
Source language
Strongly typed language

17 Program production

Algorithm
Bottom-up programming
Decision table
Event-driven program
High-level language
Inheritance
Jackson structured programming
Macro
Modular design
Module
Object
Object program

Parameter passing
Program
Program documentation
Program features
Program maintenance
Scope
Software library
Source program
Structure diagram
Structured programming
Top-down programming

18 Program translation

Absolute code
Application generator
Assembler
Assembler directives
Compiler
Disassembler
Emulation
Interpreter
Lexical analysis
Linker
One-pass assembler

Optimising compiler
Parse
Portability
Precompiled code
Relocatable code
Semantics
Symbol table
Syntax analysis
Syntax error
Tokenising

19 Program testing

Alpha testing
Benchmark or benchmark tests
Beta testing
Black-box testing
Bottom-up testing
Breakpoint
Bug
Debugger
Diagnostic program
Dry run

Execution error
Infinite loop
Logical error
Program testing
Robustness
Run time error
Test data
Top-down testing
Trace table
White-box testing

20 Searching and sorting

Binary search
Bubble sort
Linear search
Quicksort
Search time (disk)

Search time (searching)
Sequential search
Serial access
Serial search

21 Spreadsheets

Absolute reference
Active cell
Cell
Column
Formula
Lookup table

Recalculation
Relative reference
Row
Spreadsheet
Worksheet

22 System design

Acceptance testing
Analysis
Changeover
Data flow diagram
Design
Direct changeover
Feasibility study
Functional specification
Gannt chart
Implementation
Object oriented design
Parallel running

PERT chart
Phased conversion or implementation
Pilot conversion or running
Software documentation
Software life cycle
Structured systems analysis and design
  method
System changeover
System flowchart
System life cycle
Systems analysis
Systems design

23 User interfaces

Forms dialogue
Graphical user interface
Human–computer interface
Immediate mode
Menu selection interface

User interface
User interface management system
WIMP (windows, icons, mouse,
  pointer)

Further *Complete A–Z Handbooks* are available from Hodder & Stoughton. Why not use them to support your other A levels and Advanced GNVQs? All the *A–Zs* are written by experienced authors and Chief Examiners.

0 340 65467 8	*The Complete A–Z Business Studies* Third Edition £9.99
0 340 65489 9	*The Complete A–Z Geography Handbook* Second Edition £9.99
0 340 64789 2	*The Complete A–Z Leisure, Travel and Tourism Handbook* £9.99
0 340 65832 0	*The Complete A–Z Sociology Handbook* Second Edition £9.99
0 340 65490 2	*The Complete A–Z Psychology Handbook* Second Edition £9.99
0 340 66985 3	*The Complete A–Z Economics and Business Studies Handbook* Second Edition £9.99
0 340 66373 1	*The Complete A–Z Biology Handbook* Second Edition £9.99
0 340 68804 1	*The Complete A–Z Physics Handbook* Second Edition £9.99
0 340 68803 3	*The Complete A–Z Mathematics Handbook* Second Edition £9.99
0 340 67996 4	*The Complete A–Z 20th Century European History Handbook* £9.99
0 340 69131 X	*The Complete A–Z Media and Communication Handbook* £9.99
0 340 68847 5	*The Complete A–Z Business Studies CD-ROM* £55.00 + VAT
0 340 69124 7	*The Complete A–Z Accounting Handbook* £9.99
0 340 67378 8	*The Complete A–Z 19th and 20th Century British History Handbook* £9.99
0 340 72513 3	*The Complete A–Z Chemistry Handbook* Second Edition £9.99
0 340 70557 4	*The Complete A–Z Health & Social Care Handbook* £9.99
0 340 71220 0	*The Complete A–Z Law Handbook* £9.99
0 340 77213 1	*The Complete A–Z Physical Education Handbook* £9.99
0 340 80289 8	*The Complete A–Z Business Studies Coursework Handbook* Second Edition £6.99
0 340 80291 X	*The Complete A–Z Sociology Coursework Handbook* Second Edition £6.99
0 340 79063 6	*The Complete A–Z Psychology Coursework Handbook* £6.99
0 340 78954 9	*The Complete A–Z Economics Handbook* £9.99
0 340 78291 9	*The Complete A–Z English Literature Handbook* £9.99

All Hodder & Stoughton *Educational* books are available at your local bookshop, or can be ordered direct from the publisher. Just tick the titles you would like and complete the details below. Prices and availability are subject to change without prior notice.

Buy four books from the selection above and get free postage and packaging. Just send a cheque or postal order made payable to *Bookpoint Limited* to the value of the total cover price of four books. This should be sent to: Hodder & Stoughton Educational, 39 Milton Park, Abingdon, Oxon OX14 4TD, UK. EMail address: orders@bookpoint.co.uk. Alternatively, if you wish to buy fewer than four books, the following postage and packaging costs apply:

UK & BFPO: £4.30 for one book; £6.30 for two books; £8.30 for three books.
Overseas and Eire: £4.80 for one book; £7.10 for 2 or 3 books (surface mail).

If you would like to pay by credit card, our centre team would be delighted to take your order by telephone. Our direct line (44) 01235 827720 (lines open 9.00am - 6.00pm, Monday to Saturday, with a 24 hour answering service). Alternatively you can send a fax to (44) 01235 400454.

Title _____ First name _____ Surname _____

Address _____

Postcode _____ Daytime telephone no. _____

If you would prefer to pay by credit card, please complete:

Please debit my Master Card / Access / Diner's Card / American Express
(delete as applicable)

Card number _____ Expiry date _____ Signature _____

If you would not like to receive further information on our products, please tick the box ☐